2011

SHANGHAI'S
BEST
RESTAURANTS
上海最佳餐厅(英文版)

上海诺施国际出版顾问有限公司 编

世纪出版集团

上海人民出版社出版

图书在版编目（CIP）数据

2011上海最佳餐厅 = 2011 Shanghai's Best
Restaurants：英文／上海诺施国际出版顾问有限公司
编 . —上海：上海人民出版社，2011
ISBN 978 – 7 – 208 – 09825 – 1

I. ①2… II. ①上… III. ①餐厅－简介－上海市－
2011 IV. ① F719.3

中国版本图书馆 CIP 数据核字 (2011)第 024680号

策划编辑	张　剑	王蘅敏		
特约编辑	张志华			
责任编辑	苏贻鸣	张晓玲		
评　委	江礼旸	江礼明	王蘅敏	DUCCIO ALABISO
	陈　蓓	莫　云	赵荣华	钱　堃　詹岑宏
	吕　佳	蒋　琦	张鲁楠	

2011上海最佳餐厅（英文版）

2011 Shanghai's Best Restaurants

上海诺施国际出版顾问有限公司 编

世 纪 出 版 集 团

上 海 人 民 出 版 社 出版

(200001 上海福建中路 193号　www.ewen.cc)

世纪出版集团发行中心发行

常熟市双乐彩印包装有限公司印刷

开本 889 x 1194 1/24 印张 8 字数 200,000

2011年4月第1版　2011年4月第1次印刷

印数 1–3,250

ISBN 978–7–208–09825–1/G·1420

定价 69.00元

最顶端的亚洲菜

尽在3.TOP

Date with friends for tasty
and delicious Asian food @ 3.TOP

3. TOP RESTAURANT & BAR

上海新乐路47号（近襄阳北路）
47 Xinle Road, near Xiangyang (N) Road Shanghai
Tel: 021-54038896 Fax: 021-54038621
www.diningcity.com/shanghai/restaurantthreetop

CONTENT

DINING IN SHANGHAI

INDEX

EDITOR'S NOTE

To Shanghai city, the year 2010 is of great significance. Since then, friends from all over the world has flooded into Shanghai, and Shanghai welcomes them with her warmest and best service. As we all know, gourmet has a significant place in Shanghai. At the same time, there are countless world-renowned Western cuisines such as French, Italian, Spanish and Portuguese cuisines. Therefore, it is no exaggeration to say that Shanghai is a condensed version of the gourmet world.

As in previous years, SHANGHAI TATLER presents to the readers *2011 Shanghai Best Restaurants* exclusively at this time of the year. If you are a regular reader of this book, you must know that it is the best tool for gourmets to pursue delicacies. With its unique reading style, detailed information of restaurants and precise orientation of map, this book has been a model in gourmet industry for years. With such a book in hand, those who have a passion for delicacies can, conveniently and quickly, spot them in any corner of the city.

Compared with previous years, *2011 Shanghai Best Restaurants* does not only add a lot of contents, but also invites about 12 judges who are active in Shanghai, Jiangsu, Zhejiang and other places. It has been the first time to have such a huge cast within similar publications. Their professional, impartial and detailed articles also help the readers feel the charm of delicacies between the lines. Among the 160 restaurants selected this year, 120 are the conventional Shanghai restaurants, and the remaining 40 ones are selected from Nanjing, Hangzhou, Suzhou, Ningbo. It is a great breakthrough both in quantity and quality compared with that in previous years. These restaurants, which are located in major cities of Yangtze River Delta, range from magnificent hotels to inns with unique style. It is indeed a feast for the eyes to see the works of celebrities compete with each other in this field.

What's more, *2011 Shanghai Best Restaurants* makes more changes in the format. Though the book remains a good assistant for you to pursue delicacies, it will bring you more different experiences as you read it.

Eric Zhang
Managing Editor

CONTRIBUTORS

JIANG LIYANG
Foodie and the deputy secretary-general of Shanghai Food Culture Research Association. He has visited and eaten at more than 3000 restaurants across Shanghai because of his love for food and cooking.

JIANG LIMING
Working now at the Information Resource Centre in Medical College of Shanghai Jiaotong University, he loves food and writing and has published many food-review articles. He also tries to cook some of the dishes which he is good at occasionally.

NANNAN-HENGMIN WANG

As the Editor of *Shanghai Tatler* magazine in charge of dining, Nannan is passionate about fine food and wine whether consumed at a banquet or in a more intimate setting. Through her international travels she has enjoyed a diverse range of wines and cuisine and has come to understand how, where and what to eat and drink.

DUCCIO ALABISO

He was born in Parma which is home to good food and thus he has always had a passion for food and cooking. He has worked as a consultant for many gourmet magazines. He likes making chocolate mousse and some other desserts.

CHEN BEI

Senior media person. She loves traveling and all the people and stories during the journey. In addition, she also has a taste for food and enjoys stories related to it.

CRYSTYL MO

American editor and journalist Crystyl Mo has 15 years of experience in China. She is the Food Editor of *Time Out Shanghai* and a contributor to numerous international magazines including *Food&Wine* and *Departures*.

ANTHONY ZHAO

After over a decade working as a chef at high-end restaurants in Shanghai, Anthony Zhao launched his career as a restaurant consultant, helping companies launch new restaurants, develop menus and train chefs. Zhao has also worked on numerous food television programs both in China and abroad, as a host and a producer.

QIAN KUN

He likes to write after he is full. His words are always irrelevant but also with meaning of certainty. He loves food and writing and has bended down to his own worship.

BACON ZHAN

Former editor of a gourmet magazine. He has a strong love for food and cooking. Braised pork and pasta are his favorites.

LU JIA

She is a well-known young Kunqu opera actress, giving performances around the world every year. Therefore, she has tasted all kinds of cuisines worldwide and enjoyed extensive contacts with dishes from both home and abroad.

JIANG QI

She is very fond of traveling and has been to most parts of China and south-east Asia. She has tasted all kinds of cuisines and has been working in several wine companies of premium brands.

ZHANG LUNAN

She is not a gourmet but merely a food lover, and hopes that the food from her articles is like a living thing, dancing in the dishes and blooming among the taste buds.

USING THE GUIDE

Cuisine Category

Restaurant name in English

ITALIAN

GIOVANNI'S ITALIAN RESTAURANT

♀8 � 9 ♀8 ▧ 9

SETTING: The spacious and elegant dining hall is tranquil and filled with gentle and soft Italian country music.

FOOD: From style to taste, Giovanni's authentic Tuscan delicacies are a feast for the senses, from the appetizers right through to the desserts, all being prepared by Italian chefs. The Beef Salad appetizer lusciously melts in the mouth, blending the savory, thinly-cut raw beef with sour cream vanilla syrup. The goose liver Foie Gras with Apple and Cranberry is an absolute must try. The delightfully creamy goose liver accompanied with the sweet flavor of cranberry and apple is a divine combination. As to soups, we ordered the Potato Bread Soup that is rich in natural flavors and very authentic. The waiter divided the soup into two bowls for us, which is quite considerate. There are many other choices of soup beside this, such as seafood soup and Tomato soup. For main courses, Spinosini with Hot Salmon Caviar Sauce is a firm favorite. It's a traditional Tuscan recipe that reveals all the best features of Italian cuisine. This rich fish pasta differs from the usual tomato based pasta dishes as the salmon sauce is a bit spicy. Of the desserts, Tiramisu and chocolate are the stand out choices. You'll find everything you could wish for in an Italian restaurant at Giovanni's.

SIGNATURE DISHES
> Tuna Carpaccio
> Seafood Soup
> Tomato Soup
> Veal Cutlet Milanese Style With Arugula Cherry Tomato
> Lamb Ragout
> Salmon Beet Root Salad

WINE: Giovanni's provides a rich collection of wines ranging from exported wines to various drinks, juices and coffee.

SERVICE: Waiters serve with hospitality and sincerity.

27F, 5 ZUNYI ROAD S., SHANGHAI **TEL:** 021-62758888-4276
地址： 上海遵义南路5号虹桥嘉来登上海太平洋大饭店27楼

RESERVATIONS: Necessary for Dinner	**VEGETARIAN DISHES:** 3-5
DRESS CODE: Smart casual	**NO SMOKING SECTION:** Yes
LUNCH HOURS: 12:00 am-14:00 pm	**CAR VALET:** Yes
DINNER HOURS: 18:00 pm-22:30 pm	**CREDIT CARDS:** AE, D, J, MC, UP, V
LAST ORDER DINNER: 22:15 pm	**YEAR ESTABLISHED:** 1999
WEBSITE: sheraton.com/hongqiao	**PRICE:** RMB 500/Person

More on this restaurant, visit LuxeDining.com   41

Setting
Food
Wine
Service

9-10 Excellent to Exceptional
7-8 Good to Very good
5-6 Average
1-4 Poor

If a restaurant is overly exceptional, it will get three to one BRG Avatars

Signature dishes of the restaurant

Signature Wine

Service

The reasons to go to this restaurant

The details of the dishes in the restaurant

Telephone number, Chinese address

Other information of the restaurant

Sincere Catering

Since its inception in 1998, Sincere Restaurant has thrived steadily and now had four brands and seven branches under it. It enjoys favor from all walks of life. With a professional team consisting of talents in management, cooking, service and publicity from Mainland China, Hong Kong China, Canada and New Zealand, the company adopts a modern management approach to secure product quality, purchase quality food materials and constantly maintain and improve service .

Sticking to its maxim, "sincere attitude, sincere food", Sincere Restaurant, constantly pursuing quality food materials, has set up two farms, one at the National Organic Agriculture Zone in Jiangsu Province and one at Qing'an, Zhengjiang Province, where products supply exclusively to its branches. In the farms, vegetables are planted with no use of pesticides and chemical fertilizers and livestock are raised naturally with no artificialhormone additives, thus ensuring a fresh and healthy dining experience for its customers.

SHANGHAI
HongKou
Sincere Catering Co.,Ltd
208 SiPing Road
Tel:021-65211177

Pudong
Sincere Catering Co.,Ltd
7F Times Squar,500
Tel:021-58367878

Changnin
Sincere Catering Co.,Ltd
2F Maxdo Centre,8 XingYi Road
Tel:021-52081818

XuHui
Sincere Catering Co.,Ltd
1726 HuaiHai Road
(Between WanPing Road
and WuXing Road)
Tel:021-64332882

New Sincere-
Restaurant Mangement Co.,Ltd
2F, Unit109, XingGeng Road
Tel:021-33686866

BEIJING
Beijing Sincere Catering Co.,Ltd
5F LG Twin Towers ,
12 JianGuoMenWai Avenue
Tel:010-65673366

3.TOP RESTAURANT & BAR

♨ 8   🍴 8   🍷 9   🎀 9

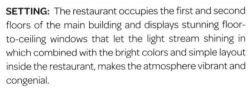

SETTING: The restaurant occupies the first and second floors of the main building and displays stunning floor-to-ceiling windows that let the light stream shining in which combined with the bright colors and simple layout inside the restaurant, makes the atmosphere vibrant and congenial.

FOOD: The dishes are authentically prepared with characteristic ingredients and methods from each of the represented countries. The highest quality salmon is selected for marinated salmon. It is wonderfully delicate, breaking apart at the slightest touch, and the marinade is equally fresh and light. Dragon roll is made by frying prawns to a light golden brown and wrapping them in vegetable strips with Spanish cherries dipped in cheese sauce. It has a sumptuous sweet flavor, with the Spanish cherry perfectly complementing the fried prawn. The Japanese style Grilled Beef is simply marvelous. First Rank Australian Scallops is a new specialty of the restaurant, and is made by stuffing prawns into Australian scallops, which are then lightly fried. A spritely curry sauce is sprinkled on the scallops, bringing out the natural sweetness of the scallops and prawns. The last dish, Goose Liver Fried Rice, is a perfect finish.

SIGNATURE DISHES

> Marinated Salmon with Spicy Raw Mango Salad
> Tom Yam Kung
> Thai Style curry-fried live crab
> Indonesian Style baked whole seabream
> Tandoori Chicken Tikka

WINE: The restaurant has its own bar and thus you can find most varieties of liquor on the wine list. A wine cellar will be built in 2011 inside the bar. The soft drinks are also attractive, especially in winter when they provide all kinds of health teas.

SERVICE: The waiters and waitresses are agile and passionate in providing good service.

47 XINLE ROAD, SHANGHAI **TEL:** 021-54038896
地址： 上海新乐路47号

RESERVATIONS: Recommended
DRESS CODE: Smart casual
LUNCH HOURS: 11:00 am-14:00 pm
DINNER HOURS: 18:00 pm-22:00 pm
LAST ORDER DINNER: 22:00 pm
WEBSITE: www.diningcity.com/shanghai/restaurantthreetop

VEGETARIAN DISHES: 10+
NO SMOKING SECTION: Yes
CAR VALET: No
CREDIT CARDS: AE, D, J, MC, UP, V
YEAR ESTABLISHED: 2009
PRICE: RMB 200/Person

100 CENTURY AVENUE

♨ 8   🍴 9   🍷 9   🎀 8

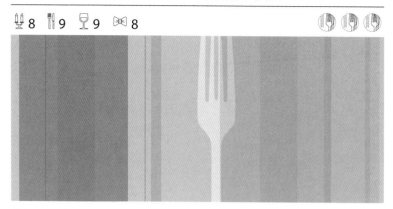

SETTING: The restaurant is located on the 91st floor of Park Hyatt, the landmark building at the Shanghai World Financial Center. The breathtaking panorama of Shanghai can be viewed through French windows with a height of 25 meters. The lamplight seems like the pearly luminescence of heaven. The scenery reaches the peak of perfection. The lively open kitchens in 100 Century Avenue Restaurant are equipped with grills, oyster and seafood bars, Woks, roast duck ovens and dessert kitchens. This is the new Eden for guests of Shanghai.

FOOD: It focuses on European cuisine, while fine Chinese and Japanese dishes menus are also provided. There is almost too much to choose.Do not miss the live oyster bar. The oysters here are from all around the world. The freshness of various kinds of raw fish and Boston langouste can with any top-ranking Japanese restaurant. Wellington goose liver, Parma ham of Italy, black pepper crab, garlic rice wrapped in lotus leaves and Australian beefsteak with sauce, which is seared on outside and tender on the inside are all spectacular. Roasted duck is roasted in the world's finest roasted duck ovens. The skin is crisp and the flesh is tender. Its quality is unmatched. The desserts and ice cream are all exquisite.

SIGNATURE DISHES
> Sashimi Platter Large
> Drunken chicken
> Beef tartar
> Beef sirloin,wagyw,Australia goog
> Chili jumbo prawns
> Roast duck

WINE: The wine cellar of Park Hyatt boasts a rich collection and it can provide over 400 varieties of wine from around the world. You can find the Japanese sake and Chinese rice wine and distilled spirits.

SERVICE: Well trained waiters can speak Chinese and English fluently, seem somewhat haughty.

100 CENTURY AVENUE, SHANGHAI **TEL:** 021-68881234-4559
地址： 上海浦东新区世纪大道100号

RESERVATIONS: Recommended
DRESS CODE: Smart casual
LUNCH HOURS: 11:30 am-14:30 pm
DINNER HOURS: 17:30 pm-22:30 pm
LAST ORDER DINNER: 22:30 pm
WEBSITE: www.parkhyattshanghai.com

VEGETARIAN DISHES: 5-10
NO SMOKING SECTION: Yes
CAR VALET: No
CREDIT CARDS: MC, V
YEAR ESTABLISHED: 2008
PRICE: RMB 500/Person

AI MEI CHINESE RESTAURANT

 8 9 8 7

SETTING: Located in the Le Royal Meridien Hotel, the restaurant welcomes you with a very impressive fish tank. Water trickles down the huge water screen, which looks magnificent and colorful when reflected by the giant crystal chandelier. Seats by the window provide a panoramic view of the landscape as people stream on to the bustling Nanjing road.

FOOD: Cantonese cuisine serves as the main choice, and is complemented by a choice of Shanghai specialties. No matter if it is a Cantonese banquet or simply Cantonese tea, every dish is exquisite and tasty. The value for money of Cantonese tea drinking at weekends is very popular and can be accompanied by nearly a hundred varieties of Cantonese dim sum, including shrimp dumpling, chicken feet, sashimi porridge and various fried rice noodles. 19 banquet rooms are available. Cantonese seafood is a specialty that the restaurant is justly proud of, which includes Double Boiled Sharks Fin Soup with Bamboo Fungus and Pigeon Eggs, Steamed Pacific Garoupa, Pan-fried Ham Scallops and particularly Crabmeat Lobster, which combines two top-level ingredients, namely lobster from Guangdong and crabmeat from Shanghai, making it a truly wonderful cuisine.

SIGNATURE DISHES
> Deep-fried fish
> Combination of barbecue platter
> Pan-fried codfish
> Pan-fried wagu beef
> Baked fish head Cantonese style in clay pot

WINE: The Restaurant provides a five-star wine list that is inclusive of Chinese white spirit and millet wine as well as imported wines of various kinds.

SERVICE: Thus, the Restaurant is far from satisfying in terms of service compared with other restaurants. Yet they defended themselves by claiming that they did not charge a service fee.

789 NAN JING ROAD E., SHANGHAI **TEL:** 021-33189999-7700
地址：上海南京东路789号

RESERVATIONS: Recommended
DRESS CODE: Smart casual
LUNCH HOURS: 11:30 am-14:30 pm
DINNER HOURS: 17:30 pm-22:00 pm
LAST ORDER DINNER: 22:00 pm
WEBSITE: www.lemeridien.com/royalshanghai

VEGETARIAN DISHES: 10+
NO SMOKING SECTION: Yes
CAR VALET: Yes
CREDIT CARDS: AE, D, J, MC, UP, V
YEAR ESTABLISHED: 2006
PRICE: RMB 400/Person

ALLURE

🍴 8   🍴 9   🍷 9   🎀 9

SETTING: The restaurant, near the lobby of the Le Royal Meridien Shanghai, has comfortable and pleasant environment with an exquisite and compact layout. Embracing a strong artistic atmosphere, the restaurant combines an open kitchen with a fine dining hall.

FOOD: The restaurant's head chef, Michael Wending, who was the apprentice of a three-star Michelin chef, is an expert at cooking advanced French cuisine, taking traditional methods and adding his own flair to make wonderfully surprising dishes. One of the famous appetizers, King Crab and Red Tuna Salad with avocado, fresh spice and fragrant spicy sauce has fresh ingredients, rich sauces and divine taste. The Cream Soup of Black Truffle and White Beans is the signature dish of the restaurant. You will be mesmerized by the flavor of the rich black truffles. A new, revolutionary masterpiece by the chef is Goose Liver Sushi with Japanese soy sauce, roasted sesame seeds and Spanish sausage; a wonderful concoction. The perfectly cooked goose liver with top-grade sushi rice work harmoniously together. The fresh and tender Australia Filet Mignon with mashed potatoes with black truffle and has a unique flavor. On the dessert list is full of French finesse and extravagance.

SIGNATURE DISHES
> King crab tartar
> Seared "sushikkinho" foie gras
> Emulsion of black truffle and white bean soup
> Butter poached boston lobster
> Baked atlantic cod fish

WINE: In the novel wine list, mostly has famous French chateau vintages. There are also many cheaper fine wines from the New World.

SERVICE: The waiters are hospitable and professional, and are very familiar with the menu. The forewoman from France is especially professional and efficient.

789 NAN JING ROAD E., SHANGHAI **TEL:** 021-33189999-7022
地址：上海南京东路789号

RESERVATIONS: Recommended
DRESS CODE: Smart casual
LUNCH HOURS: 12:00 am-14:30 pm
DINNER HOURS: 18:00 pm-22:00 pm
LAST ORDER DINNER: 22:00 pm
WEBSITE: www.lemeridien.com/royalshanghai

VEGETARIAN DISHES: 3-5
NO SMOKING SECTION: Yes
CAR VALET: Yes
CREDIT CARDS: AE, D, J, MC, UP, V
YEAR ESTABLISHED: 2006
PRICE: RMB 400/Person

AMICI ITALIAN RESTAURANT

♟ 8   🍴 9   🍷 8   🎀 9

SETTING: Set inside the longemont hotel in a wide corridor-like space, Amici restaurant is very stylish with its beige armchairs. the atmosphere is soft and relaxed, and the open kitchen and soft Italian music add a lively touch.

FOOD: Amici's new menu is a real breath of fresh air. Renewed with tantalizing detail, the selection features traditional Italian delicacies infused with taste, fantasy and an innovative verve. Start with one of the signature appetizers: the king prawns are plump and easily large enough for two. Lightly fried in the classic fritto-misto style, they are beautifully paired with a deep uyet very mellow red-onion compote. For vegetarians, the asparagus salad comes as a warm tempura mixed with crispy leaves and finished with an dash of walnut dressing. Of the entrees, the baked sole is artfully presented in triangular fillets drowned in a creamy basil-pesto potage, which complements the fish wonderfully, while the little potato chunks and green beans add a nice crunchy texture. For meat lovers, the duck breast is best superb combined with its amazing leg meat, to provide a balance of fat and lean, delicate and keen. If Amici's generous portions left some room for dessert, do try the chef's perfect tiramisu.

SIGNATURE DISHES
> Crispy fresh asparagus salad
> Crispy king prawns
> Oven baked sole fish fillet
> Grilled tuna escallop
> Roast duck breast

WINE: La carte features a selection focusing on French and Italian – the latter especially strong on the reds – but plenty of other origins too are available from both the old and new world, South Africa and Australia included.

SERVICE: The staff at Amici's does try hard to serve you well, as you would expect from any venue within a starred hotel.

2F, 1116 YAN'AN ROAD W., SHANGHAI **TEL:** 021-61159988-8230
地址： 上海延安西路1116号2楼

RESERVATIONS: Recommended	**VEGETARIAN DISHES:** 10+
DRESS CODE: Smart casual	**NO SMOKING SECTION:** Yes
LUNCH HOURS: 11:30 am-15:00 pm	**CAR VALET:** No
DINNER HOURS: 17:30 pm-23:00 pm	**CREDIT CARDS:** AE, D, J, MC, UP, V
LAST ORDER DINNER: 22:30 pm	**YEAR ESTABLISHED:** 2005
WEBSITE: www.thelongemonthhotels.com	**PRICE:** RMB 400/Person

ART SALON RESTAURANT

♨ 9   🍴 9   🍷 8   🎀 9   👐 👐 👐

SETTING: The Art Salon in downtown Shanghai shows the artist status and esthetic taste of the owner with old-style furniture, tableware and fine paintings.

FOOD: Salted chicken with scallion in hot oil is tender and delicious. Of course, the chicken is boiled in salt water and then matched with scallion in hot oil. The preserved egg matching with tofu is uncommonly good after adding dried scallop and small shrimps. Fragrant duck leg is not only delicious but the flesh is juicy and tender. The hot dishes are very tasty. The braised yellow fish with brown sauce and the braised tongue or ox tail with brown sauce are all wonderful. Its color, fragrance and taste are exquisite. The flesh is tender and it seems that the yellow fish is not fried. The braised tongue or tail with brown sauce adds pig tail and ox tail, the taste and fragrance complementing each other. The skin of ox tail melts in the mouth and is very delicious. The red rice with streaky pork is a very popular dish. The Lenten sea slug tastes like it is made from konjak, but the texture teeth is like sea slug. It is crisp on the outside and tender on the inside. It is said that the father of the owner of the restaurant is a gourmet. It proves the saying "exquisite food makes a chef and a fine chef makes a restaurant".

SIGNATURE DISHES
> Salty chicken in shallot oil
> Tofu with preserved egg and dried baby shrimps
> Duck leg in soy sauce
> Yellow fish in soy sauce
> Braised ox tongue and tail
> Braised pork with red rice

WINE: Wine, rice wine and distilled spirits are available. The selection is few but fine.

SERVICE: All waiters give clients perfect and warm-hearted service.

---

164 NANCHANG ROAD, SHANGHAI **TEL:** 021-53065462
地址： 上海南昌路164号

RESERVATIONS: Recommended for Dinner
DRESS CODE: Smart casual
LUNCH HOURS: 11:45 am-14:00 pm
DINNER HOURS: 17:30 pm-22:00 pm
LAST ORDER DINNER: 21:30 pm
WEBSITE: No

VEGETARIAN DISHES: 10+
NO SMOKING SECTION: Yes
CAR VALET: No
CREDIT CARDS: Cash Only
YEAR ESTABLISHED: 2004
PRICE: RMB 100/Person

BAI YU LAN

🍴 8　🍴 9　🍷 9　🎀 9

SETTING: Using traditional Chinese concepts and modern designs to create a unique style and furnished with a gorgeous and thick carpet, dining chairs vibrant with French passions and traditional Chinese golden eagle screens, all combine into a truly wonderful dining experience.

FOOD: The menu houses some superb Cantonese cuisine, and is complemented by several Shanghai dishes. Just from sampling the appetizers, you'll know that the skill of the chefs is top rate. The Cold Eight Vegetarian Items, one of the cold dishes, which uses many seasonal fresh vegetables, is an excellent choice for freshness. The Shredded Chicken with hot chili and ginger sauce comes straight from Sichuan influences. The sauce offsets the spiciness of the dish and really enhances the texture and delicate flavor of the chicken. Lobster is the specialty of BAI YU LAN and is well worth a try. Cheese and xo Sauce Quick-fry are all uniquely excellent, especially the latter. The aroma of the self-made xo sauce and the savory and succulent lobster meat bring out the best in each other. The desserts are very rich. Pastries and Assorted Salty Chinese Pastries are all delicious.

SIGNATURE DISHES
> Jellyfish Japanese Style
> Steamed Shanghai Crab with Sake Sauce
> Charbroiled Pork
> Sautéed Diced Japanese beef with Special Sauce
> Braised Sea Cucumber

WINE: The menu of the five-star hotel is abundant, with rich selections of white spirits, yellow wines and grape wines.

SERVICE: The waitresses all wear beautiful Cheongsam, look slim and are graceful and serve with polite courtesy.

2F, 58 MAOMING ROAD S., SHANGHAI **TEL:** 021-64151111-5215
地址： 上海茂名南路58号花园饭店2楼

RESERVATIONS: Recommended
DRESS CODE: Smart casual
LUNCH HOURS: 11:30 am-14:30 pm
DINNER HOURS: 17:30 pm-22:30 pm
LAST ORDER DINNER: 22:00 pm
WEBSITE: www.gardenhotelshanghai.com

VEGETARIAN DISHES: 10+
NO SMOKING SECTION: Yes
CAR VALET: No
CREDIT CARDS: AE, D, J, MC, V
YEAR ESTABLISHED: 1990
PRICE: RMB 400/Person

BALI LAGUNA

 8 8 8 8

SETTING: Bali Laguna is located in Jing'an Park, and features pleasant tree shaded winding paths and frogs croaking in the nearby pool.

FOOD: Indonesian cuisine-based Bali Laguna has a unique flavor, having European influences. The dishes maintain the sweet and sour taste of Southeast Asian cuisine, but combine some European tastes. Green Salad with special peanut butter is a wonderful appetizer. The taste of peanut butter is strong and the texture is smooth. The combination of the texture and the delicate fragrance of the salad has a distinctive flavor. Grilled live fish with dry onion and home-made sauces is one of specialties of Bali Laguna. The fresh and slightly crispy fish can really whet your appetite; Sautéed Crab with curried onion also deserves a mention, the well-braised onion is crispy and soft which absorbs the odor of the curry. Both the crab legs and the crab meat in the shell are good options. For the dessert, Coconut sago pudding and banana pudding are excellent choices. Sago pudding is glutinous and chewy and the accompanying syrup is smooth; the banana pudding covered in banana leaves will redefine your wildest imaginings of sweetness.

SIGNATURE DISHES
> Spicy prawn satay in Balinese style
> Old colorial recipe of oxtail soup with delicate spices
> Mixed vegetable salad
> Stir fried curry crab
> Grilled fresh fish of the day,

WINE: Special Bali Laguna cocktails and the orange juice are recommended.

SERVICE: The service here is attentive and satisfactory on the whole. But it can be busy and you may wait a long time for your dinner.

189 HUASHAN ROAD, SHANGHAI **TEL:** 021-62486970
地址：上海静安区华山路189号静安公园3号门（近南京西路）

RESERVATIONS: Recommended
DRESS CODE: Smart casual
LUNCH HOURS: 11:00 am-14:30 pm
DINNER HOURS: 18:00 pm-01:00 am
LAST ORDER DINNER: 22:30 pm
WEBSITE: www.balilaguna.com

VEGETARIAN DISHES: 10+
NO SMOKING SECTION: Yes
CAR VALET: No
CREDIT CARDS: AE, MC, V
YEAR ESTABLISHED: 2001
PRICE: RMB 300/Person

BANQUET HALL

🕯7 🍴9 🍷8 🎀8   🍽️ 🍽️

SETTING: This quaintly decorated restaurant is full of celebrity calligraphy, paintings and striped screens, which are all themed with crabs.

FOOD: With years of history, Banquet Hall, on the strength of its authentic Yangcheng Lake steamed crab, offers the "Wangbaohe Crab Banquet", which is well-known nationwide. In other months, it features Huaiyang cuisine and crab dishes. The crab dishes here are not only delicious but also varied in shape and delicate and fresh as though it were almost alive, which makes people "not bear to eat it". Removing the crab meat and frying it, then arranging it into a crab shape, the famous signature dish Plain sautéed crab meat is well recommended. It boasts a wonderful color, fragrance, flavor, and shape. You get to enjoy the delicious crab, and also avoid the hassle and inconvenience of tackling a whole crab. The featured crab meat and sautéed crab are the best choices for authentic crab. Braised Shark's Fin in Crab sauce is also a good dish. Almost every dish of Baohe Hall has the word crab, even pastry. Crab meat steamed bun has thin skin, lots of stuffing and is cooked in much liqueur. Besides its delicious crab dishes, Baohe Hall also offers delicate Huangyang cuisine and Shanghaines cuisine all year round.

SIGNATURE DISHES
> Shrimps with ginger and scallion
> Baby pigeon in special soy sauce
> Roast fish with barbecue pork
> Sautéed crabmeat
> Deep-fried crabmeat

WINE: The five-year or eight-year wines and crab feast wines with colorful and carved pots of Wangbaohe are the best matches for crab feast. In addition, all kinds of imported wines, grape wines, and white spirits are available.

SERVICE: Waiters all have a set of unique crab tools, and they will demonstrate the usage of "eight tools for crab dismantling" with the standard service.

5F, 555 JIUJIANG ROAD, SHANGHAI **TEL:** 021-53965000-80505
地址：上海九江路555号5楼

RESERVATIONS: Recommended
DRESS CODE: Smart casual
LUNCH HOURS: 11:30 am-14:00 pm
DINNER HOURS: 17:30 pm-22:00 pm
LAST ORDER DINNER: 21:30 pm
WEBSITE: www.centralhotelshanghai.com

VEGETARIAN DISHES: 10+
NO SMOKING SECTION: Yes
CAR VALET: No
CREDIT CARDS: AE, D, J, MC, UP, V
YEAR ESTABLISHED: 1999
PRICE: RMB 500/Person

BASILICO

♨ 8 🍴 9 🍷 9 🎀 8

SETTING: An elegant, classical styled dining room of warm, rich colors and beautiful features, such as inlaid marble floors and exceptional still life paintings.

FOOD: Traditional Italian dishes made with practiced finesse and the best of ingredients. Dining here is an exceptional experience for fans of fine Italian cuisine. Begin with the beautiful and generous antipasto platter, with selections such as white bean and yellow fin tuna salad that offers textures of hearty firm beans and rich oily fish, and the spicy bite of red onion. Other antipasti include coppa, mortadella and pancetta—all sumptuous meats with pure, savory aromas. Among the starters, wagyu beef carpaccio is beyond compare; the tender raw beef comes with balsamic marinated mushrooms and boasts a terrific and light lemon sauce. Rock shellfish linguini with mussels, squid and shrimp is served in a bright and tangy tomato sauce. The homemade pasta is perfectly cooked al dente. There's also a wide choice of prime meats and vegetables fresh from the grill. The rib eye is beautifully fatty and tastes wonderfully succulent when mixed with the mushroom sauce. After this hearty meal, try the housemade sorbets, like the mixed berry, which is chock-full of sweet-tart raspberries.

SIGNATURE DISHES
> Design your own platter with your favorite choice
> Wagyu beef
> Balsamic marinated mushrooms
> Pizza traditional with buffalo Mozzarella

WINE: A beautiful glass case in the dining room shows off the many wines on offer. There are whites and reds in an impressive broad list, including plenty from Italy.

SERVICE: Extremely attentive and friendly service from staff with excellent English.

3F, 1188XUEYE ROAD, SHANGHAI **TEL:** 021-38581188
地址： 上海浦东新区雪野路1188号上海世博洲际酒店3楼

RESERVATIONS: Recommended
DRESS CODE: Smart casual
LUNCH HOURS: 11:30 am-14:30 pm (Wed-Sun)
DINNER HOURS: 17:30 pm-21:30 pm
LAST ORDER DINNER: 21:00 pm
WEBSITE: www.intercontinental.com

VEGETARIAN DISHES: 10+
NO SMOKING SECTION: Yes
CAR VALET: Yes
CREDIT CARDS: AE, D, J, MC, UP, V
YEAR ESTABLISHED: 2010
PRICE: RMB 300/Person

BLD CAFE

♨ 8 🍴 8 🍷 8 🎀 9

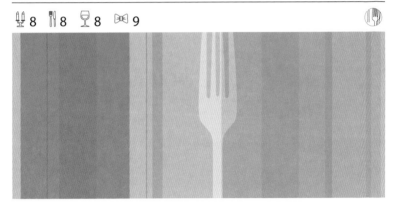

SETTING: BLD Coffee House is a buffet restaurant in Renaissance Yangtze Shanghai Hotel. The open-style restaurant has a wide sense of space and a graceful design that matches the hall of the hotel.

FOOD: The buffet here has a wide variety, including Japanese cuisine, Western style desserts, and Indian and Chinese cuisine. Among the appetizers, Classic Romaine is outstanding with moist lettuce, which tastes crisp and fresh. Accompanied with Ayu Fish and Bread Croutons, the Romaine will give you a strong appetite for the main courses. For dinner, we recommend the seafood selected by the Western Executive Chef, such as clam, oyster, razor clam and Smaragdinellidae, which are all fresh and delicious. The classic Rib Eye Steak is a little too firm and nutty for the selected sauce. Together with wine, the Steak tastes better. Another good choice is the famous Lamb Masala, which is very tender. Roti Canai becomes more delicious if you enjoy it with the curry sauce in the Lamb Masala. Pizza baked by fruitwood is a traditional hand-made dish. As the pizza is baked in a charcoal fire a unique flavor merges with the pizza. The cakes of the desserts, of which each one is delicate and wonderful, will create a perfect ending to the dinner.

SIGNATURE DISHES
> Classic Romaine
> Monte Cristo Salad
> Rib Eye Steak
> Lamb Masala

WINE: The restaurant serves all kinds of drinks, such as vodka, whiskies, gin, beer, and cocktails. Otherwise, coffee, mixed drinks and juices are also served.

SERVICE: Because it is a buffet, waiters may replace the plates from time to time.

1F, 2099 YAN'AN ROAD W., SHANGHAI **TEL:** 021-62750000-2132
地址：上海延安西路2099号扬子江万丽大酒店1楼

RESERVATIONS: Recommended	**VEGETARIAN DISHES:** 10+
DRESS CODE: Smart casual	**NO SMOKING SECTION:** Yes
LUNCH HOURS: 12:00 am-15:00 pm	**CAR VALET:** No
DINNER HOURS: 16:00 pm-22:00 pm	**CREDIT CARDS:** AE, D, J, MC, UP, V
LAST ORDER DINNER: 22:00 pm	**YEAR ESTABLISHED:** 2010
WEBSITE: www.cn.renaissanceshanghai.com	**PRICE:** RMB 308/Person

BUTTERFLY

 9 8 9 8

SETTING: Elegant wooden interiors, with heavy chandeliers and cream walls literally covered by more than 500 butterflies from 200-plus countries, plus a beautiful patio with a black-and-white tile flooring and a glass ceiling that lets plenty of natural light in. Comfortable sofas are available all along the room's sides as well as in the patio, making Butterfly a great place for an afternoon tea too.

FOOD: Butterfly's menu is typical of American venues, but with a fusion twist. Portion sizes vary substantially from one dish to another, hence it's better to check with your waiter to avoid ordering too much or too little.

We started with the indulging fondue, in which crabmeat and a creamy mix of three cheeses are served "au gratin". Dip in the large croutons that come with it, enjoy the smooth sensation, and have fun while you're at it! If you are in for burgers, the classic LAN cheese burger is very tasty and cooked to a juicy perfection, and accompanied by a mountain of fries and the usual suspects: pickles, onion, tomato and lettuce. And finally, great both as a starter or a side dish, the super-fresh Greek salad comes with feta cheese, black olives, tomato and onion chunks.

SIGNATURE DISHES
> Chicken slider
> Ahi tuna & avocado tartare
> Tortilla soup
> Memphis ribs
> Ponzu salmon
> Grilled beef tenderloin

WINE: Faithful to its affiliation to the LAN Club, Butterfly's list boasts an amazing variety of drinks, including quite a few non-alcoholic ones, which on pleasant evenings can be enjoyed on the open terrace on the top floor. There is also a separate wine list, featuring a little bit of everything from both the Old and New world.

SERVICE: Butterfly's staff is pleasant, efficient and polite.

4F, 102 GUANGDONG ROAD, SHANGHAI **TEL:** 021-63238029
地址： 上海广东路102号4楼（兰会所内）

RESERVATIONS: Recommended
DRESS CODE: Smart casual
LUNCH HOURS: 11:30 am-14:30 pm
DINNER HOURS: 18:30 pm-22:30 pm
LAST ORDER DINNER: 22:00 pm
WEBSITE: reservations@lan-global.com

VEGETARIAN DISHES: 1-2
NO SMOKING SECTION: Yes
CAR VALET: Yes
CREDIT CARDS: AE, D, J, MC, V
YEAR ESTABLISHED: 2010
PRICE: RMB 250/Person

CACHET RESTAURANT

♨ 8 ⑪ 9 ♀ 9 ⋈ 9

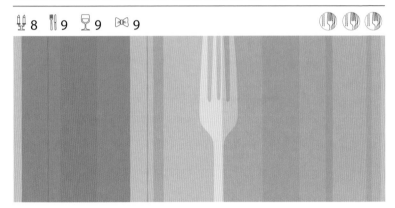

SETTING: A line of sofas adjacent to the French windows of the Xintiandi boasts fascinating scenery. The wooden tables, simple table cloth and silver tableware are match with the style cuisine here.

FOOD: The selection for food is not rich in variety but its standard surprised the guests. The starter dishes include smoked duck with salad and Australian beef slices. The duck is smoked well and is tender. The fragrance of smoked wood is absorbed by the duck breast, which displays the high degree of skills employed by the chefs. The restaurant is generous in the portions of Australian beef and it has a good flavor and tenderness. It goes very well with a glass of wine. The dish is prepared with a sprinkling of olive oil and garnished with rocket salad and a slice of Mascarpone cheese. The main dishes use rice and meat. The Italian braised rice with seasonal mushrooms is the signature dish of the restaurant and it can compare with a top Italian restaurant. The Italian rice is cooked well and is very tasty. The Australian beef comes in big portions and is best served medium rare. It comes with stuffed baked potatoes and baked peas. There are 5 or 6 choices on the dessert menu. The apple pie that we selected is baked to perfection and pastry is nice and crisp.

SIGNATURE DISHES
> Crispy suckling pig
> Gambas al ajillo Sauteed shrimps with garlic and chili
> Iberian boar ham
> Duck foie-gras terrine

WINE: For a restaurant focusing on buffet dinner and western-styled simple meal, the selection of grape wines to soft drinks is wide. The tea selection is also very rich.

SERVICE: Waiters are keen and quick; they answer all questions fluently and provide valuable help during dining.

1F, 99 MADANG ROAD, SHANGHAI **TEL:** 021-23302288
地址：上海马当路99号新天地朗廷酒店1楼

RESERVATIONS: Recommended
DRESS CODE: Smart casual
LUNCH HOURS: 11:30 am-14:00 pm
DINNER HOURS: 18:00 pm-22:30 pm
LAST ORDER DINNER: 22:00 pm
WEBSITE: www.xintiandi.langhamhotels.com

VEGETARIAN DISHES: 10+
NO SMOKING SECTION: Yes
CAR VALET: No
CREDIT CARDS: AE, D, J, MC, UP, V
YEAR ESTABLISHED: 2010
PRICE: RMB 150-250/Person

CAFÉ SWISS

🕯8 🍴8 🍷8 🎀8

SETTING: At Swissôtel Grand Shanghai, 2nd Floor, the Café Swiss features elements of Chinese design mixed with Swiss style.

FOOD: The 5 star quality restaurant offers an international buffet. The seafood bar has a wide selection of fresh shrimp, salmon, scallop and crab with all kind of sauces & dressings. Chinese and Western soups are served daily. The BBQ corner is also very popular, not surprising as it has succulent steaks, lamb chops, fish and vegetables prepared and grilled by our chef de cuisine. Other hot dishes are available in the middle of the open dining area and consists mostly of Asian flavours. The desert corner has an impressive array of sweet delights, beautifully lined. Tiramisu is the star of the show. Fresh fruits and a selection of ice cream together with a Swiss chocolate fountain that is mostly admired by children. Cold beverages such as soft drinks & iced water and also hot beverages like tea and coffee are included.

SIGNATURE DISHES
> Fresh carved salmon sashimi
> Tandoori chicken
> Roasted lamb rack
> Pigs bone broth
> Wood fired Swiss pizza
> Veal Zürichoise

WINE: A wide selection of international wines.

SERVICE: The Café Swiss offers good value for money amongst other 5 star buffets and also a perfect location in Jing An district, so no wonder it's so popular.

2F, 1 YUYUAN ROAD, SHANGHAI **TEL:** 021-53559898-6360
地址：上海愚园路1号上海宏安瑞士大酒店2楼

RESERVATIONS: Necessary
DRESS CODE: Smart casual
LUNCH HOURS: 11:30 am-14:30 pm
DINNER HOURS: 18:00 pm-22:30 pm
LAST ORDER DINNER: 22:30 pm
WEBSITE: www.swissotel.com/shanghai

VEGETARIAN DISHES: 5-10
NO SMOKING SECTION: Yes
CAR VALET: No
CREDIT CARDS: AE, D, J, MC, UP, V
YEAR ESTABLISHED: 2008
PRICE: RMB 300/Person

CATHAY ROOM

♨ 9 🍴 8 🍷 9 🎀 8 ⑪ ⑪ ⑪

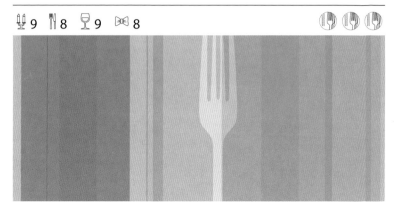

SETTING: The newly decorated Cathay Room has inherited the charming ambience and cuisine styles of the last century. The decorative dining hall creates a relaxed and elegant atmosphere for guests.

FOOD: All kinds of European delicacies are gathered together in the Cathay Room, which has help create a legendary restaurant in Shanghai. It is an ideal place for locals and tourists to revel in nostalgia. The Australian executive chef, Anthony Hannan, has introduced various and numerous ingredients and dishes such as European seafood, American organic pork and superior Australian beef. He has an ambition to satisfy even the most picky guests. High quality ingredients are used for the appetizers. The organic vegetable salad, with the self-made yogurt dressing, is unusually fine; In addition, the Maine lobster salad is also a good choice. The oxtail broth is also one of its specialties. It has a clear color and strong taste. The signature main dish is a 5 ounce lean, pure fed beef tenderloin from Australian with summer squash, asparagus, smoked dried mushroom and subtle vinaigrette. The desserts are of relatively less variety but each one is has a wonderful color, smell and taste.

SIGNATURE DISHES
> Maine lobster salad
> Buffalo Mozzarella
> Oxtail Consomme
> Lean Australia Grain Fed Beef tenderloin
> Slow baked herb crusted cod

WINE: More than 200 top ranked wines selected from Europe and the New World picked by the resident wine taster.

SERVICE: Courteous, excellent service of 5-star restaurant.

9F, 20 NANJING ROAD E., SHANGHAI **TEL:** 021-63216888-6881
地址：上海南京东路20号和平饭店9楼

RESERVATIONS: Recommended	**VEGETARIAN DISHES:** 3-5
DRESS CODE: Smart casual	**NO SMOKING SECTION:** Yes
LUNCH HOURS: 12:00 am-14:30 pm	**CAR VALET:** No
DINNER HOURS: 18:00 pm-22:00 pm	**CREDIT CARDS:** AE, D, J, MC, UP, V
LAST ORDER DINNER: 22:00 pm	**YEAR ESTABLISHED:** 2010
WEBSITE: www.fairmont.com	**PRICE:** RMB 400/Person

CHICAGO STEAK HOUSE

🕯 8　🍴 7　🍷 8　✉ 8

SETTING: Set inside the Eton hotel in Pudong, Chicago Steak house presents itself with an open space overlooking a lively kitchen.

FOOD: Chicago's menu is typical of any steakhouse, but even though the spotlight is undoubtedly on the grill, there are indeed quite a few appetizers that can very well stand alone and look good doing it. Apart from these entrees, the menu offers salads, soups, and side dishes, while the grill features Australian "Wagyu" beef (marble 8+), Black Angus beef and seafood, all accompanied with your favorite choice of Chicago's wonderful sauces. For starters, the king prawns were particularly tasty, and nicely flavored and broiled; but we appreciated much more the artistic verve put into the scallop ceviche, beautifully presented. And then we moved to the main feature. The imported "Wagyu" rib-eye steak came perfectly done (medium-rare, as suggested on the menu), with just a touch of veggies on the side, and ready to be dipped in a nostalgic Béarnaise sauce and enjoyed with a classic, steaming baked potato topped with cream and crispy bacon bits. The marbling of the meat provided for outstanding tenderness, and the aging for a decisive yet pleasant flavor.

SIGNATURE DISHES
> "Foie gras" terrine
> Ceviche of scallops
> King prawns cocktail with mango and wasabi mayonnaise
> Australian "Wagyu" beef
> Aged certified Black Angus
> Boston lobster

WINE: A large selection of liquors, plenty of cocktails, aperitifs, soft drinks and the likes. On the other hand not so many wines, but the ones available are reasonably priced and some can be ordered by the glass.

SERVICE: Friendly and affable, the staff here will help you enjoy a casual dinner and forget the hassle of a busy day.

4F, 535 PUDONG AVENUE, SHANGHAI **TEL:** 021-38789888
地址：上海浦东大道535号4楼

RESERVATIONS: Recommended
DRESS CODE: Smart casual
LUNCH HOURS: 12:00 am-14:00 pm
DINNER HOURS: 18:00 pm-22:00 pm
LAST ORDER DINNER: 22:00 pm
WEBSITE: www.etonhotelshanghai.cn

VEGETARIAN DISHES: 5-10
NO SMOKING SECTION: Yes
CAR VALET: Yes
CREDIT CARDS: AE, D, J, MC, UP, V
YEAR ESTABLISHED: 2007
PRICE: RMB 400/Person

CHINA BISTRO

🕯8　🍴8　🍷8　🎀9

SETTING: Set inside a 5-star hotel in Yuyuan Business District, the China Bistro is an inviting interplay of nostalgia and vogue that deftly hovers between minimalism and grandness.

FOOD: China Bistro specializes in Cantonese cuisine, with a dash of local Shanghai dishes. The Deep Fried Shrimp, a cold dish, is first sweet and then salty, with a crunchy outside and tender inside, and is a great starter. The short and thick Jellyfish with Soy Sauce comes in generous portions, and while it's not particularly flavorsome, it comes with an array of delicious savory sauces and is wonderfully crispy. The Cantonese Goose is another fabulous local option. Of the hot dishes, the Shanghai Shrimps are full of flavor, succulent and satisfyingly plump. The Black Pepper Beef is an entertaining dish: the hot plate sizzles and pops as the waiter pours black pepper sauce it. The fresh beef, eaten with knife and fork in the western style, is moist and tender and carries quite a kick from the sauce. Quick-Fried Diced Beef in Bean Sauce is very popular, though bizarrely the plate is far too big for this dish. Mixed seafood soup followed by Fried Rice with Egg White and Shredded Conpoy is a great combination.

SIGNATURE DISHES
> Jellyfish
> Grilled Goose
> Grilled beef with bone
> Shanghai shrimps
> Black pepper beef

WINE: There are many vintage wines from different countries. New World wines are prevalent. There are some homemade spirits and yellow wine.

SERVICE: The service is professional and efficient, yet also pleasant and helpful. Waitresses happily answer questions, but never speak out of turn. All in all, the service is considerate and professional.

159, HENAN ROAD S., SHANGHAI **TEL:** 021-23218977
地址：上海豫园万丽酒店3楼，河南南路159号

RESERVATIONS: Recommended
DRESS CODE: Smart casual
LUNCH HOURS: 11:00 am-14:30 pm
DINNER HOURS: 17:00 pm-22:00 pm
LAST ORDER DINNER: 22:00 pm
WEBSITE: www.renaissanceyugarden.com

VEGETARIAN DISHES: 10+
NO SMOKING SECTION: Yes
CAR VALET: No
CREDIT CARDS: AE, D, J, MC, V
YEAR ESTABLISHED: 2007
PRICE: RMB 200/Person

CIAO DINING ROOM AND CIAO BAMBINO

♨ 8 🍴 8 🍷 8 🎀 9

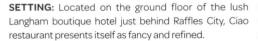

SETTING: Located on the ground floor of the lush Langham boutique hotel just behind Raffles City, Ciao restaurant presents itself as fancy and refined.

FOOD: With a menu somewhere between Portuguese and Venetian, Ciao's offerings range from pizza to cheese platters, quite a few main courses as well as a couple of vegetarian dishes. The lavish antipasti buffet features cold cuts and preserved veggies, smoked salmon and all sorts of other treats, for a light lunch with plenty of variety or a dinner just the way you like it. One of Ciao's signature dishes, the warm cod salad, is served with intense accents of cured ham and a sweet balsamic reduction. From the pasta courses, the potato gnocchi is served in a potage of asparagus with shrimps and tomatoes, which are cute in shape and very delicate in flavor. Moving on to the main courses, the grilled king prawns come on a palette of brushstrokes of colorful sauces, accompanied by baked veggie sticks, while the rib-eye steak is an abundant, flavorful portion with greens and baked potato wedges. The dessert list is somehow short, but Ciao Bambino in the room just next door boasts a full range of pastries for all tastes. The Tiramisu we tried did make quite an impression.

SIGNATURE DISHES
> Caesar salad
> Tomato and buffalo mozzarella cheese salad
> Madrilene spicy codfish salad
> Grilled bacalau codfish
> Grilled king prawns
> Grilled rib-eye steak

WINE: Ciao's wine list offers few choices but has all the basics: a few champagnes, reds and whites mainly from the New World, which are available by the glass, as well as fresh juices and even smoothies.

SERVICE: Staff here try their best and will definitely make you feel at ease.

1F, 740 HANKOU ROAD, SHANGHAI **TEL:** 021-60800743
地址：上海汉口路740号朗廷扬子精品酒店1楼

RESERVATIONS: Recommended	**VEGETARIAN DISHES:** 10+
DRESS CODE: Smart casual	**NO SMOKING SECTION:** Yes
LUNCH HOURS: 6:30 am-18:30 pm	**CAR VALET:** No
DINNER HOURS: 18:30 pm-23:00 pm	**CREDIT CARDS:** AE, D, J, MC, UP, V
LAST ORDER DINNER: 22:30 pm	**YEAR ESTABLISHED:** 2009
WEBSITE: www.langhamhotels.com	**PRICE:** RMB 350/Person

CLUB JIN MAO

🕯9 🍴9 🍷9 ✉9

SETTING: This grand restaurant can be found on the 86th floor of the famed Jin Mao Tower. Originally opening only to guests and club member, the exquisite Chinese style private club has rooms named after prominent Chinese figures and a striking lobby from which the beautiful Pudong skyline cab be seen.

FOOD: Featuring very authentic Shanghai cuisine and a scintillating new menu masterminded by Chef Chen Hua, who has won countless international awards. The exquisite seasonal dishes are bursting with flavor and color. The signature dishes are the fragrant one-thousand layer potherb rolls, Maotai bean sprouts with distilled spirits. vegetable leaves, fragrant garlic mutton and toasted cuttlefish. The more regular fare, such as steamed dumpling with crab meat and "Zhendehao" wonton, are all equally exquisite. My European guest instantly fell in love with the delicious Shanghai Braised Duck. The restaurant always garners great renown from media both at home and aboard, including *The New York Times* and *Shanghai Tatler*.

SIGNATURE DISHES
> Crispy shrimps
> Drunken chicken
> Sautéed fresh water shrimps
> Boiled minced pork ball with hairy crab meat and roe
> Steamed Shanghainese pork dumplings with crab meat

WINE: Various rice wine and Chinese distilled spirits are on selection. The wine list also has a wide selection.

SERVICE: Well trained waiters can speak Chinese and English fluently. Even with insufficient waiters, services such as pouring wine, serving tea and dishes and changing plates is provided well and timely.

86F, GRAND HYATT SHANGHAI, 88 CENTURY ANVENUE, SHANGHAI **TEL:** 021-50491234
地址：上海市浦东新区世纪大道88号金茂君悦大酒店86楼

RESERVATIONS: Recommended
DRESS CODE: Smart casual
LUNCH HOURS: 11:30 am-14:30 pm
DINNER HOURS: 17:30 pm-22:00 pm
LAST ORDER DINNER: 22:00 pm
WEBSITE: www.shanghai.grand.hyatt.com

VEGETARIAN DISHES: 10+
NO SMOKING SECTION: Yes
CAR VALET: No
CREDIT CARDS: AE, J, MC, V
YEAR ESTABLISHED: 1999
PRICE: RMB 400/Person

CLUB VIETNAM

🍴 8 🍴 8 🍷 8 🎀 8

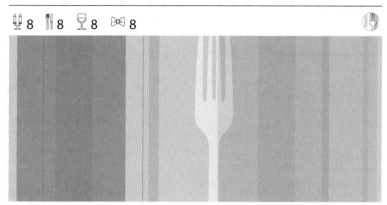

SETTING: Its chiefly white decor is minimal and comfortable. The environment is so elegant, however, that you will feel comfortable even if the sun is hiding.

FOOD: Club Vietnam's cuisine is highly regarded for its authenticity and freshness. Ripe mango and prawn scroll includes fresh vegetable, mango, prawn and other 'secret' ingredients. This is a true 'appetizer' as so delicious it will stimulate any appetite. The Vietnamese king prawn soup is thick yet not oily and also has one wanting more. The Vietnamese roasted sugar cane consists of mashed prawn wrapped around a cane-splint. It holds well and tastes wonderful, crisp outside and tender inside. Roast chicken with red preserved bean curd is characterized by a crispy skin and fragrant taste and is soft and smooth to the mouth. Slowly stewed curry of beef brisket with coconut milk features thick milk and a rich fragrant flavor that is set off with accompanying French bread. The curry doesn't tastes too spicy and the beef brisket is not tough. Salmon grilled with vanilla and fish sauce is different and quite satisfying. Like the dishes, dessert is generous. Hmm - Vietnamese cream caramel steamed with coffee, homemade chocolate cake, hot grated apples with appled-flavored caramel, all well worth recommending.

SIGNATURE DISHES
> Fresh rice paper rolls with mango and prawns
> Pomelo salad with prawns
> Classically Vietnam spring rolls
> Vietnam grilled chicken
> Grilled mandarin fish

WINE: There are a variety of beverages to satisfy all tastes.

SERVICE: Waiters are polite and attentive.

889, JULU ROAD, SHANGHAI **TEL:** 021-64458082
地址：上海巨鹿路889号11-12幢1-2层

RESERVATIONS: Recommended
DRESS CODE: Smart casual
LUNCH HOURS: 11:30 am-14:30 pm
DINNER HOURS: 17:30 pm-23:00 pm
LAST ORDER DINNER: 22:30 pm
WEBSITE: www.FCCshanghai.com

VEGETARIAN DISHES: 5-10
NO SMOKING SECTION: Yes
CAR VALET: No
CREDIT CARDS: AE, D, J, MC, UP, V
YEAR ESTABLISHED: 2006
PRICE: RMB 200/Person

DANIELI'S ITALIAN RESTAURANT

♨ 8 🍴 9 🍷 9 🎀 9

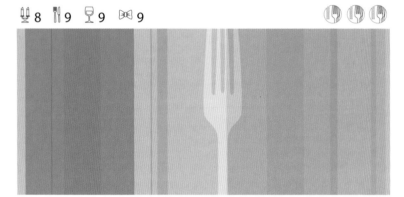

SETTING: From the very top of the luxurious 5-star St.Regis hotel, the very sophisticated Danieli's restaurant cradles you throughout the whole experience with its smooth atmosphere, classic silverware, and stunning views of Lujiazui's skyline and its imposing World Financial Center.

FOOD: From the starters, the beautiful chef's mixed Antipasto is a great way to begin, with its colorful array of seasonal and year-round ingredients tastefully arranged on the plate. The Wagyu carpaccio is quite amazing too, with its super-thin slices topped with crispy, bitter arugula leaves balanced by a mild-sweet dressing of mustard.

First courses is where we found most of Danieli's creativity at work: in the Sardinian-style potato gnocchi, dressed with a velvety, sweetish sauce of bell peppers, saffron and sea urchins; or in the round ravioli filled with a surf-n-turf mix of goose liver and crab, and dressed with mushrooms and fresh hints of oregano.From among the suggested Mains, the sea bass is a total feast for seafood lovers, with an earthy portion of fish, plum king prawns and clams, all soaked in plenty of garlic-flavored tomato jus. To complete the dining experience, enjoy the pastry chef's dessert selection.

SIGNATURE DISHES
> Wagyu beef carpaccio
> Braised asparagus
> Danieli's chef Roberto's antipasto
> Sea bass "en papillotte"
> Breaded Australian veal tenderloin

WINE: A wide selection of champagnes, reds and whites from both the Old and New world, famous entries as well as rare vintages, and quite a few can be enjoyed by the glass. The setting within a five-star hotel also provides for a vast variety of soft drinks, liquors, cocktails, teas and the like.

SERVICE: The staff at Daniel's are welcoming and very friendly.

---

889 DONGFANG ROAD, SHANGHAI **TEL:** 021-50504567-6370
地址：上海浦东东方路889号

RESERVATIONS: Recommended
DRESS CODE: Smart casual
LUNCH HOURS: 11:30 am-14:00 pm
DINNER HOURS: 18:00 pm-22:30 pm
LAST ORDER DINNER: 22:30 pm
WEBSITE: www.stregis.com/shanghai

VEGETARIAN DISHES: 5-10
NO SMOKING SECTION: Yes
CAR VALET: No
CREDIT CARDS: AE, D, J, MC, V
YEAR ESTABLISHED: 2001
PRICE: RMB 400/Person

DINING ROOM

♨ 9 🍴 9 🍷 9 🎀 8   🖐 🖐 🖐

SETTING: Lobby restaurant on the 87th floor of Park Hyatt is a fine dining western restaurant. It features a huge glass wine cabinet and mother of pearl embedded in the wall that resonates the luxury of the venue. The dining environment is graceful, comfortable and private. The beautiful scenery on both banks of the Pujiang River can be viewed through French windows of a great height.

FOOD: It offers traditional European cuisine and various set meals matched with a wine selection. "Chef Tables" for ten persons are equipped for grand banquets. The western cuisine is made of high quality ingredients such as black truffles, caviar, langouste, and goose liver and fully deserves its high praise. The fried goose liver with truffles is extraordinary. The fried cuisine is neither soft nor hard. Recommended dishes are the raw beef salad with black truffles, fresh langouste salad with avocado tomato and basil, slow steamed salmon with caviar, coal-baked Dover soles, slow fire oil-stewed beef filet with lily chanterelle, and duck breast matching with horsebean. The food and wine in the set meals are matched perfectly by the chefs and sommeliers. However, it is not easy to find a wine with three digits on the wine list. The set meals provide a more cost effective solution.

SIGNATURE DISHES
> Home smoked salmon,potato salad,Willians pear sauce
> Roasted veal
> Foie gras
> Boston lobster
> Digs cheek
> Lamp loin

WINE: The hotel's glasshouse cellar collects hundreds of vintage wines from across the world, of which sommelier give useful advice.

SERVICE: The well trained waiters can speak Chinese and English fluently.

100 CENTURY AVENUE, SHANGHAI **TEL:** 021-68881234
地址：上海浦东新区世纪大道100号

RESERVATIONS: Recommended
DRESS CODE: Smart casual
LUNCH HOURS: 12:00 am-14:30 pm
DINNER HOURS: 17:30 pm-22:30 pm
LAST ORDER DINNER: 22:30 pm
WEBSITE: www.parkhyattshanghai.com

VEGETARIAN DISHES: 5-10
NO SMOKING SECTION: Yes
CAR VALET: No
CREDIT CARDS: MC, V
YEAR ESTABLISHED: 2008
PRICE: RMB 700/Person

DRAGON PHOENIX

♨ 9   🍴 8   🍷 9   🎀 8   👏 👏 👏

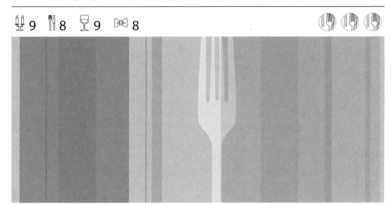

SETTING: The name of the Restaurant comes from the fact that the ceilings are decorated with embossments of patterns of dragons and phoenixes embracing red vertical columns with distinct Chinese characteristics. The dining experience is enhanced by accompanying Chinese folk music. Brimming with antique luxury and elegance, as if time and space had returned to the past, the newly renovated Peace Hotel is one of the most attractive landmarks in Shanghai and the Dragon-Phoenix Restaurant is an ideal resort that cannot be missed by gourmets.

FOOD: Being famous for its Shanghai cuisine and complemented by a selection of Cantonese Sichuan cuisine, the Dragon-Phoenix Restaurant provides a wide array of choices. Having been in personal charge of the master chef Gu Delong, who has served for 40 years for the Jinjiang Group, the Restaurant serves many extraordinarily Shanghai local dishes such as Crab Roe Tofu, Stir-fried Shredded Finless Eel and Stir-fried Shrimp. Cantonese dishes ranging from Marinated Dishes to Coral Grouper Shark Fin are of high quality while the Sichuan dishes, such as authentic Chicken Pieces with Black Fungus and Hot Pepper in Geleshan Spicy Sauce, are very popular.

SIGNATURE DISHES
> Braised wheat bran tofu
> Peace Hotel chicken pickeled in rice winesauce
> Marinated slices of poached goose liver
> Crystal sautéed river shrimps
> Braised sea cucumber

WINE: The Restaurant provides a rich collection of wines ranging from Chinese white spirits to grape wines from France and the New World together with various famous teas.

SERVICE: Service here is mediocre compared with the Peace Hotel.

8F, 20 NANJING ROAD E., SHANGHAI **TEL:** 021-63216888-6880
地址： 上海南京东路20号和平饭店8楼

RESERVATIONS: Necessary
DRESS CODE: Smart casual
LUNCH HOURS: 11:30 am-14:30 pm
DINNER HOURS: 17:30 pm-22:00 pm
LAST ORDER DINNER: 21:45 pm
WEBSITE: www.fairmont.com

VEGETARIAN DISHES: 10+
NO SMOKING SECTION: Yes
CAR VALET: No
CREDIT CARDS: AE, D, J, MC, UP, V
YEAR ESTABLISHED: 2010
PRICE: RMB 400/Person

DYNASTY

 8 9 9 9

SETTING: Being the Chinese restaurant of five-star Renaissance Yangtze Hotel, Dynasty boasts antique décor and design, with a vase-like screen door and china furnished quite differently from modern buildings, forming a delightful contrast.

FOOD: Cantonese cuisine is specialty, while the signature dish is Chilled Red Crab "Chao Zhou" Style, which tastes delicate and sweet. Marinated Mandarin Fish is fresh and tasty as the fish is killed when ordered. For the hot dishes, Braised Duck with White Gourd and Pearl Barley is a strong recommendation for autumn that tastes delicate and helps to maintain health. Classic Crispy Roasted Chicken, after being cooked in a "Deep-fried Spring Chicken" method and mashed garlic is added, tastes delicious and fresh. Braised Mushrooms with Seasonal Vegetables is also a delicacy. Elongated Deep-fried Shrimp Spring Rolls has a great freshness and is delicious beyond description. It is stuffed with shrimp dumplings and tastes better when dipped in catsup. Steamed Shrimp dumpling "Har Kau" is recognized as a classic of Cantonese dim sum. Placed in a small pan, Steamed Chicken Paws with Black Bean Sauce tastes crisp and succulent. The Braised Bird's Nest with Papaya is delicious and helps maintain a good complexion.

SIGNATURE DISHES
> Marinated mandarin fish
> Classic crispy roasted chicken
> Chilled red crab"Chao Zhou" style
> Braised cod fish with scallion and garlic in stone pot

WINE: Features a rich collection of wines, including grape wines from the New and Old world, Chinese wines like Shao Xing wine and white spirits, Japanese sakes and German draft beers and cocktails.

SERVICE: Qualified five-star hotel and experienced waiters change plates frequently and provide prompt answers with a smile.

2F, 2099 YAN'AN ROAD W., SHANGHAI **TEL:** 021-62750000-2282
地址： 上海延安西路2099号扬子江万丽大酒店2楼

RESERVATIONS: Recommended
DRESS CODE: Smart casual
LUNCH HOURS: 11:00 am-14:30 pm
DINNER HOURS: 18:00 pm-22:30 pm
LAST ORDER DINNER: 22:30 pm
WEBSITE: www.cn.renaissanceshanghai.com

VEGETARIAN DISHES: 5-10
NO SMOKING SECTION: Yes
CAR VALET: Yes
CREDIT CARDS: AE, D, J, MC, V
YEAR ESTABLISHED: 1992
PRICE: RMB 150-300/Person

EEST THE CRYSTAL GARDEN RESTAURANT

♨ 8   🍴 8   🍷 9   🎀 9   🖐 🖐

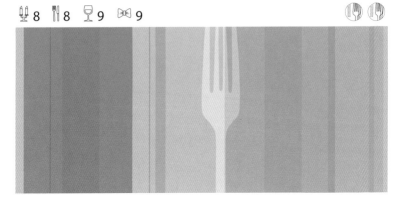

SETTING: The Restaurant is located on the fifth floor of Westin Hotel. Against a background of blue sky and the white cloud, customers seated near the windows may overlook the bustling Yan'an Road and the Bund.

FOOD: Marinated Cucumber with Ginger tastes a little hot and has good quality sauces and fragrant seasonings. Kani Salada Miso Dressing – Crabmeat Asparagus Salad with Miso Dressing smells delicious and tastes fresh and tender. After the appetizer, the Gyu Hire Niku is served, of which the tender niku and delicious toasted garlic slices are wonderful choices. Kong Po Chicken with Dried Chilli and Macademia Nuts is neither of the Guizhou or Sichuan style, which are the typical Cantonese styles. The chilli in slices is not too hot and the chicken tastes slightly sweet, which means that the dish is not sauté but fried. Meanwhile, the sauce in the dish is macademia nuts instead of peanuts, which has a pleasant flavor. Tom Yum Soup, known as the national soup of Thailand, is made of Tom Yum and shrimps that are large and succulent with various seasonings, such as citronella and myrcia. This is the traditional and authentic dish but without coconut, which is exciting and comforting.

SIGNATURE DISHES
> Marinated cucumber
> Kong po chicken
> Gyu hire niku
> Pomelo and prawn salad
> Gaeng karie talay yellow curry with seafood and potato

WINE: The restaurant serves various grape wines of the Old and New World, but are mostly of the New World.

SERVICE: Waiters here are diligent and considerate, and will answer any question without being obtrusive.

5F, 88 HENAN ROAD M., SHANGHAI **TEL:** 021-63351787
地址： 上海河南中路88号威斯汀大饭店5楼

RESERVATIONS: Recommended
DRESS CODE: Smart casual
LUNCH HOURS: 10:30 am-14:30 pm
DINNER HOURS: 17:30 pm-22:30 pm
LAST ORDER DINNER: 22:30 pm
WEBSITE: www.westin.com/Shanghai

VEGETARIAN DISHES: 10+
NO SMOKING SECTION: Yes
CAR VALET: Yes
CREDIT CARDS: AE, D, J, MC, V
YEAR ESTABLISHED: 2002
PRICE: RMB 300/Person

EL WILLY SPANISH RESTAURANT

🍴 8   🍴 9   🍷 8   🎀 8   🍷 🍷 🍷

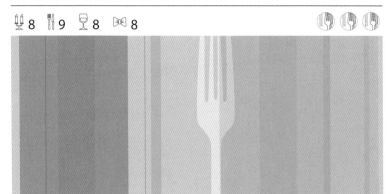

SETTING: The restaurant is named after Guillermo Willy Trullás Moreno, who has a distinct personal magnetism and charisma that is one of the main drawing points of the restaurant. Its layout embodies a romantic Mediterranean style. The decoration is soft and inviting. The various vivid oil paintings and water colors that adorn the walls and are very captivating.

FOOD: Willy, from Barcelona, Spain serves dishes that integrate traditional and modern elements. The menu includes Spanish snack "tapas" and Spain braised rice (risotto), which comes in many styles. The starter dish oyster oil and fresh scallop with beef tallow fruit jam and crisp shallot slices has a magnificent color. Tender stewed oyster with garlic sauce and Iberian Ham are also great choices from the TAPAS menu. The tender stewed oyster and the savory sweetness of the Iberian Ham complement each other wonderfully. Full-flavored barbecued roast suckling pig with snow pear jam and strong peppertree sauce is a divine dish. After several hours cooking, the skin is crisp and the flesh tender. It is delicious and the fragrance of the oil is rich. The signature dish of braised rice with lobster, boiled seafood and rice with cuttlefish juice and lobster seafood rice is a must try.

SIGNATURE DISHES
> Iberian Ham
> Scallop ceviche
> Crispy suckling pig
> Lobster juice paella
> Cuttlefish and squid ink juicy paella
> Willy's dry paella

WINE: The variety on the wine list is rich and focuses on Spanish vintage wines.

SERVICE: It provides a warm and sound service.

20, DONGHU ROAD, SHANGHAI **TEL:** 021-54045757
地址：上海东湖路20号

RESERVATIONS: Necessary for Dinner
DRESS CODE: Smart casual
LUNCH HOURS: 11:00 am-14:30 pm
DINNER HOURS: 18:00 pm-22:30 pm
LAST ORDER DINNER: 22:30 pm
WEBSITE: www.el-willy.com

VEGETARIAN DISHES: 3-5
NO SMOKING SECTION: Yes
CAR VALET: No
CREDIT CARDS: AE, J, MC, V
YEAR ESTABLISHED: 2008
PRICE: RMB 400/Person

EPICTURE ON 45 REVOLVING RESTAURANT

8 8 8 8

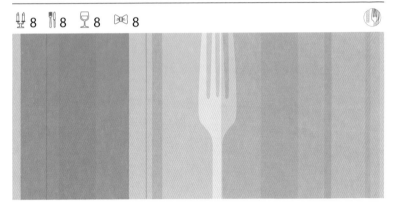

SETTING: Set inside the "UFO" on People's Square's Radisson New World hotel, this venue on the move offers one of Shanghai's best views.

FOOD: A very mixed concept to appeal to all diners, you can either have your European, Chinese, Indian or Japanese full-course menu, or create your own fusion menu jumping from one to the next style, with a choice ranging from sushi and sashimi, to tandoori meat, to Shanghainese dishes and Western creations. The Philippine mango salad goes beautifully with the tender shrimps, though you may want to ask to go easy on the mayonnaise it is lavishly topped with. Another cold starter, the tuna tartare, is beautifully layered, and comes with crunchy, colorful veggies and a sweet sauce.If you are on a diet, but not too much, the tortilla rolls come with the right healthy look to cover it all up. The dish is very clean and light, while the lightly spiced chicken filling provides plenty of real flavors. For more hot dishes, the crisp tempura comes in a traditional lacquered tray and its dip. For something more exotic, the classic tandoori mixed platter features seafood as well as meat, marinated in mild concoctions and then baked slowly.The dessert list is very international too, ranging from French pastry to Asian.

SIGNATURE DISHES

> Steamed lobster and mango salad
> Onion and spinach fritters
> Chicken piccata with scallop
> Tandoori combination
> Mixed vegetable curry

WINE: Very balanced between wines and other drinks from the New and Old Worlds as well as sake and Chinese spirits, including plenty of cocktails, wines by the glass and even a special menu of pairing between magical wineries and dishes.

SERVICE: Affable and easy going, the staff at Epicure make you feel at home.

45F, 88 NANJING ROAD W., SHANGHAI **TEL:** 021-63599999-4212
地址：上海南京西路88号45楼

RESERVATIONS: Recommended for Dinner
DRESS CODE: Smart casual
LUNCH HOURS: 11:30 am-14:30 pm
DINNER HOURS: 18:00 pm-22:30 pm
LAST ORDER DINNER: 22:15 pm
WEBSITE: www.radisson.com/shanghai-newworld

VEGETARIAN DISHES: 10+
NO SMOKING SECTION: Yes
CAR VALET: No
CREDIT CARDS: AE, D, J, MC, V
YEAR ESTABLISHED: 2005
PRICE: RMB 400/Person

FAMILY LI IMPERIAL CUISINE

🍴 9   🍴 9   🍷 9   🎀 9

SETTING: Located in the depths of the Huangpu Park, the restaurant is elegant and luxurious. The main building of the restaurant integrates a bridge, running water, booths and windowed veranda.

FOOD: All the set meals consist of three parts: a hand plate, hot dish and desserts. The hand plate consists of ten kinds of exquisite pickled vegetables. The Jumbo Shrimp is crisp and juicy. The Braised Jade Tofu is cooked with imported scallop and green soy bean after being mashed. The taste of the scallop is enhanced with capsicum. It is fresh and tasty. The traditional Beijing snack Zhagezha is crisp and delicious. Beijing smoked meat uses high-grade streaky pork and is boiled in an elaborate soup and then is smoked with fruit wood. The main dish, bird's nest in broth, uses only the finest ingredients and it is cooked very well.. It has comes in two styles: salty or sweet. Fried Lobster uses imported Australian lobster and the texture is supple. It is a fusion of traditional palace cuisine and of modern ingredients prepared using traditional methods. Braised sea cucumber with shallot made using Guandong sea cucumber is cooked in this traditional style and the resulting taste is very authentic. The three non-sticky sweet desserts were the favorite desserts of Queen Mother Cixi.

SIGNATURE DISHES
> Stir-fried fresh green bean paste with fresh scallop
> Deep-fried duck with shrimp paste and sesame
> Well-stewed superipr shark's fin
> Braised abalone

WINE: The wine list is rich and the selection is wide.

SERVICE: The waiters wear elegant uniforms. The cuisine introduction before the meal and the considerate service of changing napkins 4 times are both nice touches.

500 ZHONGSHAN NO.1 ROAD E., (INSIDE HUANGPU PARK) SHANGHAI **TEL:** 021-53088071
地址： 中山东一路500号（黄浦公园内）

RESERVATIONS: Necessary
DRESS CODE: Smart casual
LUNCH HOURS: 11:00 am-14:30 pm
DINNER HOURS: 17:3 pm-21:30 pm
LAST ORDER DINNER: 20:30 pm
WEBSITE: www.familylishanghai.com

VEGETARIAN DISHES: 5-10
NO SMOKING SECTION: No
CAR VALET: No
CREDIT CARDS: AE, D, J, MC, V
YEAR ESTABLISHED: 2006
PRICE: RMB 600-800/Person

FAVOLA ITALIAN RESTAURANT

♨ 8   🍴 9   🍷 9   🎀 8

SETTING: Housed at the 8th floor of Le Royal Meridien Hotel, Favola is designed in a refined style and divided into three dining areas and a unique glass cellar area. The open kitchen unveils the Chef's operation while the French windows gather a panoramic view of the Peoples' Square and park.

FOOD: Favola provides traditional Italian dishes, including authentic risotto, pasta and pizzas (Frutti di mare, Margherita and Napoli flavors) made with a charcoal oven. Appetizers include such traditional favorites as Italian Ham, Goose Liver Risotto and Organic Vegetable Salad accompanied by Italian balsamic vinegar. For main courses, Favola serves Lobster Pasta, T-bone, Caviar and Salmon Pasta, and Roasted Codfish sprinkled with saffron crocus juice, to name but a few. The buffet lunch is a cheaper but still appetizing option. If you're feeling adventurous, \cooking lessons are also given by the Italian Chef.

SIGNATURE DISHES
> Buffalo mozzarella
> Carpaccio of beef tenderloin
> Seared veal t-bone, gorhonzola polenta, roasted potato
> Soup with Beef Tendon and Mushroom

WINE: Favola has a rich cellar of collection featuring \vintages from Tuscany and other regions in Italy as well as wines from France and the New World.

SERVICE: Waiters in Favola are well-trained and in place to offer effective suggestions in fluent English.

789 NANJING ROAD E., SHANGHAI **TEL:** 021-33189999-7778
地址：上海南京东路789号

RESERVATIONS: Recommended
DRESS CODE: Smart casual
LUNCH HOURS: 10:00 am-14:30 pm
DINNER HOURS: 18:00 pm-22:30 pm
LAST ORDER DINNER: 22:30 pm
WEBSITE: www.lemeridien.com/royalshanghai

VEGETARIAN DISHES: 5-10
NO SMOKING SECTION: Yes
CAR VALET: Yes
CREDIT CARDS: AE, D, J, MC, UP, V
YEAR ESTABLISHED: 2006
PRICE: RMB 400/Person

FU 1039

9 8 9 9

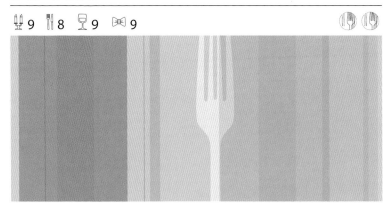

SETTING: A multitude of antiques demonstrate the owner's taste and social status, while sophisticated tableware and delicate dishes immerse Shanghai natives in a bliss of dining.

FOOD: FU provides Shanghai dishes blended with tradition with innovation. For cold dishes, Sweet Lotus Root-filled with Glutinous Rice, which was acknowledged as the favorite sweet dish in ancient Shanghai, has a charm that does not lie in its sweetness but in the combined stickiness of rice and lotus root and the fragrance of osmanthus. Crispy Eel Strips with Roasted Sesame Seeds is another dish that tastes sweet and fresh and is made by frying pickled finless eels in hot oil. The Braised Sea Cucumber in Sweet Soy Sauce is quite different as the dish "takes ingredients from the South to cook in a Northern way", namely using big black sea cucumbers from the South and cooking them with the culinary skills of Shangdong cuisine, braising the black sea cucumbers with chicken and meat gravy. Sautéd River Crab Meat Served with Baked Sesame Tie is a seasonal dish of "September Female, October Male", which is a perfect combination of freshness and deliciousness complemented by sesame ties.

SIGNATURE DISHES
> sweet lotus root-filled with slutinous rice
> Marinated drunken chicken
> Crispy eel strips with roasted sesame seeds
> Hairy crab meal cuisine combination

WINE: FU provides a great variety of wines, including various vintage wines, first-class Chinese white spirits, Shao Xing wine, etc, which offers guests an abundant choices.

SERVICE: Waiters wearing black uniforms serve dishes with great courtesy. Their service is helpful yet not overwhelming, which allows guests to enjoy their dining.

1039 YUYUAN ROAD, SHANGHAI **TEL:** 021-52371878
地址：上海愚园路1039号

RESERVATIONS: Recommended
DRESS CODE: Smart casual
LUNCH HOURS: 11:00 am-14:00 pm
DINNER HOURS: 17:00 pm-24:00 pm
LAST ORDER DINNER: 24:00 pm
EMAIL: fu1039@gmail.com

VEGETARIAN DISHES: 10+
NO SMOKING SECTION: Yes
CAR VALET: Yes
CREDIT CARDS: AE, D, J, MC, UP, V
YEAR ESTABLISHED: 2006
PRICE: RMB 200/Person

FU 1088

9 | 9 | 9 | 9

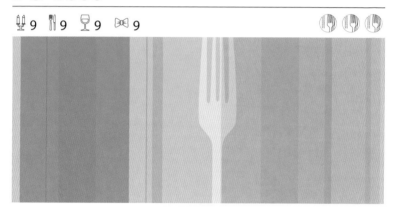

SETTING: Owned by former Shanghai nobles, FU 1088 has been renovated from a house into a clubhouse decked out in pieces of the past owners – a chandelier, piano with ivory-made keys, tablets 80 years in age, etc.

FOOD: FU 1088, compared with its sister restaurant FU 1039 at Yu Yuan Lu, is more sophisticated and elegant despite that they provide similar, nostalgic dishes. Deep-fried Fish in Sweet Soy Sauce, a cold dish that is made with herring, has a taste very much of the old flavor from 60 years ago, namely not too sweet yet with a perfect crispness and softness. Shanghainese Tea Smoked Egg with Caviar is cooked with excellent culinary skill; the exterior of the smoked egg is a very deep color while the interior remains yellow. Slow Baked Beef Rib, Crisp Garlic indeed achieves a "crisp outside and tender inside" after baking the beef rib on a slow heat, boiling it in low temperature water and lightly baking its skin. Stemmed Egg white Custard with Sautéed Hairy Crab Meat, served in the shell, uses only egg white and has just the right amount of crab. Sautéed Sweet Pea with Minced Ham, fried with minced ham and small peas is a firm favorite with guests.

SIGNATURE DISHES
> Deep-fried fish
> Shanghainese tea smoked egg with caviar
> Braised shark's fin
> Slow baked beef rib
> Steamed egg white custard with sautéed hairy crab meat

WINE: FU 1088 provides a rich collection of wines from the New and Old Worlds with top-grade Chinese white spirits and Shao Xing wines also available.

SERVICE: FU 1088 provides hotel-style service, namely no interruption if not strictly necessary, so as to guarantee sufficient privacy for customers.

375 ZHENNING ROAD, SHANGHAI **TEL:** 021-52397878
地址：上海镇宁路375号

RESERVATIONS: Recommended
DRESS CODE: Smart casual
LUNCH HOURS: 11:00 am-14:00 pm
DINNER HOURS: 17:30 pm-24:00 pm
LAST ORDER DINNER: 24:00 pm
WEBSITE: www.fu1088.com

VEGETARIAN DISHES: 10+
NO SMOKING SECTION: Yes
CAR VALET: Yes
CREDIT CARDS: AE, D, J, MC, UP, V
YEAR ESTABLISHED: 2007
PRICE: RMB 300-500/Person

GIOVANNI'S ITALIAN RESTAURANT

🕯 8 🍴 9 🍷 8 🎀 9

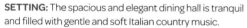

SETTING: The spacious and elegant dining hall is tranquil and filled with gentle and soft Italian country music.

FOOD: From style to taste, Giovanni's authentic Tuscan delicacies are a feast for the senses, from the appetizers right through to the desserts, all being prepared by Italian chefs. The Beef Salad appetizer lusciously melts in the mouth, blending the savory, thinly-cut raw beef with sour cream vanilla syrup. The goose liver Foie Gras with Apple and Cranberry is an absolute must try. The delightfully creamy goose liver accompanied with the sweet flavor of cranberry and apple is a divine combination. As to soups, we ordered the Potato Bread Soup that is rich in natural flavors and very authentic. The waiter divided the soup into two bowls for us, which is quite considerate. There are many other choices of soup beside this, such as seafood soup and Tomato soup. For main courses, Spinosini with Hot Salmon Caviar Sauce is a firm favorite. It's a traditional Tuscan recipe that reveals all the best features of Italian cuisine. This rich fish pasta differs from the usual tomato based pasta dishes as the salmon sauce is a bit spicy. Of the desserts, Tiramisu and chocolate are the stand out choices. You'll find everything you could wish for in an Italian restaurant at Giovanni's.

SIGNATURE DISHES
> Tuna Carpaccio
> Seafood Soup
> Tomato Soup
> Veal Cutlet Milanese Style With Arugula Cherry Tomato
> Lamb Ragout
> Salmon Beet Root Salad

WINE: Giovanni's provides a rich collection of wines ranging from exported wines to various drinks, juices and coffee.

SERVICE: Waiters serve with hospitality and sincerity.

27F, 5 ZUNYI ROAD S., SHANGHAI **TEL:** 021-62758888-4276
地址： 上海遵义南路5号虹桥喜来登上海太平洋大饭店27楼

RESERVATIONS: Necessary for Dinner
DRESS CODE: Smart casual
LUNCH HOURS: 12:00 am-14:00 pm
DINNER HOURS: 18:00 pm-22:30 pm
LAST ORDER DINNER: 22:15 pm
WEBSITE: sheraton.com/hongqiao

VEGETARIAN DISHES: 3-5
NO SMOKING SECTION: Yes
CAR VALET: Yes
CREDIT CARDS: AE, D, J, MC, UP, V
YEAR ESTABLISHED: 1999
PRICE: RMB 500/Person

GUAN YUE TAI

♨ 9 🍴 9 🍷 8 🎀 9

SETTING: Its Neoclassical, verging on post-modern, decorative style belongs to, lends the restaurant an elegant atmosphere.

FOOD: The dishes are a fusion of Shanghai and Guangdong Cuisine and dishes. We tried the set meal. The appetizer was a plate of three cold delights, which is made of sautéed shrimps, snow bean and shredded pig's ears. The sautéed shrimps have a delightful fragrance of lemon, which are neither oily nor sweet, and the snow beans are lightly salted. The fresh, simple fragrance of the ingredients is delightful. The hot dishes are Sautéed scallops and cuttlefish with caviar, which are chewy due to the freshness of the ingredients. The scallop and herring roes (red and black) that make caviar is an extraordinary flavor and not to be missed. Australian Wagyu beef in barbecue sauce is a dish pan-fried in a Western style, which is an innovation in Chinese food. The beef is lightly seared and very tender, and is first pan fried before the sauce and asparagus are added. The excellent steamed mandarin fish with ham is first steamed and then sprinkled with soya sauce. The accompanying hot plate envelops the fish and keeps the dish warm and extends its flavor. The meat of the abalone in Braised Abalone with Spinach is fresh and tender.

SIGNATURE DISHES
> Four-happiness Kou Fu
> Deep-fried shrimp
> Australian Wagyu beef in barbecue sauce
> Wok-fried lobster
> Braised shark's fin soup with sea urchin in stone casserole

WINE: The wines are varied and plentiful, including ones from the Old and New World. The notable wines are from the Old World of France and Italy. The yellow wine is also famous and you can order "Baolong Moutain" yellow wine of both ten and twenty years old.

SERVICE: All the waitresses often serve a dish immediately after you finish one and control the service very well.

26F, 1200 CAOXI ROAD N., SHANGHAI **TEL:** 021-64391000-3011
地址： 上海漕溪北路1200号华亭宾馆26楼

RESERVATIONS: Recommended
DRESS CODE: Smart casual
LUNCH HOURS: 11:30 am-14:30 pm
DINNER HOURS: 17:30 pm-22:00 pm
LAST ORDER DINNER: 21:30 pm
EMAIL: F&B@huating-hotel.com

VEGETARIAN DISHES: 10+
NO SMOKING SECTION: Yes
CAR VALET: No
CREDIT CARDS: D, MC, V
YEAR ESTABLISHED: 2006
PRICE: RMB 400/Person

GUI HUA LOU

SETTING: It is located at the end of the lobby on the first floor in the Pudong Shangri-La Hotel. Under the red lanterns there is Chinese decoration divided by red chairs with backrests and antique ebony screens. The entire scenery of Binjiang Park can be viewed through big French windows.

FOOD: There are two menus focusing on Huaiyang cuisine and Sichuan cuisine. Both are top-ranking. In particular, the Huaiyang cuisine is so authentic and exquisite that it can easily compare beauty the best Yangzhou restaurant. Sea slug with abalone, shark's fin and fish maw are very delicious. The Noodles in Fish Broth with dense broth boiled with crucian and yellow ell are very popular among guests. The delicious and attractive stewed crab and pork balls with green vegetables highlights the authentic skills of the chef. The roasted live weever with shallot served on a bamboo plate boasts crisp skin and tender meat, while the shallots are fragrant and the fish is delicious. It is a rare treat to taste the tea-smoked duck with fragrance, roasted crispy goose, dainty Nanjing boiled salted duck, baked cake with roasted duck, Chrysanthemum duck with fine shape and various goose and ducks with various tastes. All of them are unique and the aftertaste is wonderful.

SIGNATURE DISHES
> Stuffed lotus root
> Salty duck Nanjing Style
> Chilled crystal pork
> Deep-fried spicy chicken
> Curry prawns with deep-fried bun
> Stew pork ribs with cloves

WINE: Tea list with wide selection, rich Chinese distilled spirits and local rice wine as well as French wine and various New World wines are offered.

SERVICE: Well trained top waiters can speak Chinese and English fluently. They provide warm-hearted service and pour wine and change dishes quickly.

33 FUCHENG ROAD, SHANGHAI **TEL:** 021-68828888-220
地址： 上海富城路33号浦东香格里拉大酒店浦江楼一层

RESERVATIONS: Recommended
DRESS CODE: Smart casual
LUNCH HOURS: 11:30 am-15:00 pm
DINNER HOURS: 17:30 pm-22:30 pm
LAST ORDER DINNER: 22:15 pm
WEBSITE: www.shangri-la.com

VEGETARIAN DISHES: 10+
NO SMOKING SECTION: Yes
CAR VALET: Yes (7:00-23:30)
CREDIT CARDS: AE, D, J, MC, UP, V
YEAR ESTABLISHED: 2005
PRICE: RMB 400/Person

GUI LIN GARDEN 1931

♨ 9　🍴 9　🍷 9　🎀 9

SETTING: Located on the site of the former private garden of Huang Jinrong in Guilin Park, Guilin Garden is one of the best Chinese restaurants and residences in Shanghai, with a history spanning nearly 80 years. The design of the building is a wonderful example of private gardens south of the Yangtze River, with waterside pavilion, veranda and tower in correspondence with bliss, money, longevity, happiness and immortality.

FOOD: Specialty dishes focus on sauces related to promoting health, including Cantonese cuisine, Benbang cuisine and set dishes that vary according to season. In particular, Stir Fried Pramn with Longjing Tea tastes crisp and fragrant, and Braised Pork in Brown Sauce Soaked in aged Pu'er Tea is refreshing and delicious; the signature dish, the Shark Fin with Perigord truffle with soup, is authentic and appetizing. The unique "Buddha Jumps Over the Wall" is the famous specialty of the restaurant and is a must try. The steaming Cxyeleotris marmoratus and the Australian Meat Baked with Rose Salt are also outstanding. Moreover, you must not miss the seasonal dishes, such as Indian Knifefish. We strongly recommend you try Cubilose Boiled with sweet-scented osmanthus, which requires a reservation.

SIGNATURE DISHES
> Vegetable salad
> Slow fried French goose liver
> Braised boiled birds nest
> Sea cucumber stewed Japanese Yoshihama abalone
> Japanese kobe beef & goose liver

WINE: Customers may order drinks from an abundant wine list or choose grape wine provided by sommeliers to match the dishes during the order. Also, customers can choose from one of the best tea lists in Shanghai.

SERVICE: The service here is hospitable from greeting customers to seeing customers off.

188 CAOBAO ROAD, SHANGHAI **TEL:** 021-64515098
地址：上海漕宝路188号（桂林公园内）

RESERVATIONS: Necessary	**VEGETARIAN DISHES:** 10+
DRESS CODE: Smart casual	**NO SMOKING SECTION:** Yes
LUNCH HOURS: 11:00 am-14:00 pm	**CAR VALET:** Yes
DINNER HOURS: 17:00 pm-23:00 pm	**CREDIT CARDS:** AE, D, J, MC, UP, V
LAST ORDER DINNER: 22:00 pm	**YEAR ESTABLISHED:** 2007
WEBSITE: No	**PRICE:** RMB 1000/Person

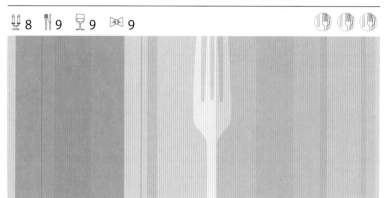

HAIYI HARBOUR PLAZA

8 9 9 9

SETTING: The magnificent hall and the gorgeous crystal chandelier hanging overhead make this a elegant, stylish and grand dining environment.

FOOD: Harbour Plaza mainly serves Chiuchow cuisine and Cantonese cuisine, accompanied with some Sichuan and Hunan cuisine. The ingredients that Harbour Plaza use are fresh and the portions are large. The Roast Spring Pigeon, that boasts low fat and high energy, is ordered by almost every table for its crispy skin and tender meat. So you can see how popular the dish is. Agaric Fried with Lily Leaf is also cooked with fresh ingredients. It is rich in nutrition and the delicate agaric with sweet lily leaf really works up an appetite. Shunde cuisine is famous for its Cantonese cuisine. The Shunde Pan-Fried Fish Heat in Clay Pot is also fresh is a popular choice. The golden yellow fried fish head is crisp and full of delicate flavors that will immerse your taste buds in delight. The dim sum here is varied and delicious. Pyramid dumplings made of orange powder are so semi-transparent that the mushroom inside can be seen. They taste delicious. Although many people dislike the taste of Crispy Durian Cake, people who like Durian will love them here. It has a very intricate cooking method, with over 50 layers. It leaves a lingering flavor in the mouth.

SIGNATURE DISHES
> Crispy Cucumber
> Cold jellyfish with brown Vin
> Pan-fried Fish Head
> Braised Bird nest with rock Suger sauce
> Braised Fish Maw in Oyster sauce

WINE: Vintage wines from Europe and United States are available. There are also good Chinese spirits and yellow wines.

SERVICE: The waiters here are enthusiastic. They are diligent in changing dishes. When customers leave, they often remind them to stamp their parking coupon and show them to the gate.

2635 YAN'AN ROAD W., SHANGHAI **TEL:** 021-62701998
地址：上海延安西路2635号

RESERVATIONS: Recommended
DRESS CODE: Smart casual
LUNCH HOURS: 11:00 am-14:30 pm
DINNER HOURS: 17:00 pm-21:30 pm
LAST ORDER DINNER: 21:00 pm
WEBSITE: www.harbour_plaza.com

VEGETARIAN DISHES: 10+
NO SMOKING SECTION: Yes
CAR VALET: Yes
CREDIT CARDS: J, MC, V
YEAR ESTABLISHED: 1998
PRICE: RMB 300/Person

HANANO JAPANESE RESTAURANT

🕯️ 8   🍴 8   🍷 8   🎀 9

SETTING: The Hanano Japanese Restaurant is exquisite, unassuming and peaceful.

FOOD: The succulent slices of raw fish come from many seasonal fish, which are all fresh and can be enjoyed simply with wasabi. The sweet shrimp sashimi and sea urchin sashimi are the most popular choices. Beside the sashimis, the specialty is on grilled prawns, grilled king crabs and grilled sanma and mackerel with salt. The prawns small size but big in taste; with pleasant seasoning that expertly brings out the natural flavors, the sanma and mackerel are expertly grilled. The beef teppanyaki is roasted to a perfect, juicy medium rare and is very tender. The Teriyaki chicken is succulent, comes in big portions and tastes sweet with the added Mirin. As for the California rolls, they are both sweet and sour, with soft stuffing and a crispy outer wrap, and the roes scattered across it are juicy and burst with flavor. Assorted Tempura, a fried Japanese cuisine, stands out above all, and uses flour, eggs, fish, shrimps and seasonal vegetables as the ingredients. The vegetables in it include eggplant, winter mushroom, green pepper, taro and sweet potato. It's crisp and fragrant but not greasy; dip it in the soy sauce and ginger paste and it is even better. The desserts feature tasty puddings ice cream.

SIGNATURE DISHES
> Vegetable Salad
> Potato Salad
> California Roll
> Assorted Sushi
> Miso Silver Pout
> Assorted Tempura

WINE: Only tea and water is offered for free. Other drinks are expensive and should be ordered separately. There's a wide selection of wines.

SERVICE: Waiters are busy, but are warm, kind and helpful.

2F, 5 ZUNYI ROAD S., SHANGHAI **TEL:** 021-62758888-4920
地址：上海遵义南路5号虹桥喜来登上海太平洋大饭店2楼

RESERVATIONS: Necessary for Dinner
DRESS CODE: Smart casual
LUNCH HOURS: 11:30 am-14:00 pm
DINNER HOURS: 17:30 pm-22:00 pm
LAST ORDER DINNER: 22:00 pm
WEBSITE: www.sheraton.com/hongqiao

VEGETARIAN DISHES: 10+
NO SMOKING SECTION: Yes
CAR VALET: Yes
CREDIT CARDS: AE, D, J, MC, UP, V
YEAR ESTABLISHED: 1990
PRICE: RMB 250/Person

HANG YUEN HIN

🕯9 🍴9 🍷8 🎀9

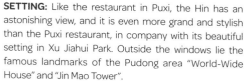

SETTING: Like the restaurant in Puxi, the Hin has an astonishing view, and it is even more grand and stylish than the Puxi restaurant, in company with its beautiful setting in Xu Jiahui Park. Outside the windows lie the famous landmarks of the Pudong area "World-Wide House" and "Jin Mao Tower".

FOOD: Jelly fish is comprised of the heads of the jelly fish instead of the skin, so it is very crisp. Snow pea & morel is fresh and cool, while Honey BBQ pork, "Red Roast Pork" with an enticing red color, tastes crisp and soft and is lightly sweet.Super shark's fin is simmered in chicken, pork and ham broth for 12 hours with authentic brown shark's fin as the sauce; the fin is glutinous and the soup is perfect. Roasted baby pigeon uses pigeon of 18 days (400g/pigeon), and is plump and fresh. The soup is enhanced with lobster slices which eliminates any greasiness. Beef with garlic has tender cubes of beef with a light fragrance of garlic. The vegetables in the dish provide a nice balance to the oil of the beef. The dessert is Shrimp rolls & almond. After being wrapped in Wafer paper, the shrimp meat is fried with apricots. A great dish to share.

SIGNATURE DISHES
> Jelly fish
> Japanese abalone
> sliced chicken with salt & ginger sauce
> snow pea&morel
> Braised shark's fin with crab meat

WINE: The restaurant has French and Italian wines of the Old World, and wines from Australian and South America. The restaurant also offers Chinese wine and yellow wines.

SERVICE: The service here is warm and not oppressive. Also, the waiters will serve you only when you require it.

3F, 201 CENTURY AVENUE;290/292, WAN PING ROAD, SHANGHAI **TEL:** 021-68809778
地址：上海浦东新区世纪大道201号渣打银行大厦3楼

RESERVATIONS: Recommended
DRESS CODE: Smart casual
LUNCH HOURS: 11:30 am-14:30 pm
DINNER HOURS: 17:30 pm-22:00 pm
LAST ORDER DINNER: 22:00 pm
WEBSITE: www.hengyuexuan.com.cn

VEGETARIAN DISHES: 5-10
NO SMOKING SECTION: No
CAR VALET: No
CREDIT CARDS: AE, J, MC, V
YEAR ESTABLISHED: 2009
PRICE: RMB 400-600/Person

HENG SHAN CAFE & CHINESE CUISINE

🕯 7 🍴 8 🍷 8 🎀 9

SETTING: Heng Shan Cafe & Chinese Cuisine is inconspicuous but it attracts many more regular guests due to its convenient location, popular decoration and, above all, the excellence of its food.

FOOD: The most popular dish is barbecued pork, with both the honeydew and crackling good choices. The pork neck barbecued in honey after barbecuing is a nice mix of fattiness and leanness. The Barbecued Pork with crackling is not served at noon and is only available in the evening. Any pork lover cannot miss this, it tastes fantastic when the pork is mixed in with the juices. Among hot dishes, the fried silvery pout, undoubtedly, is a healthy choice that is suitable for the young and the old. The egg yolk and flour wrapped silvery pout is lightly fried. After it is fried on a medium heat it becomes golden, and then the oil that was absorbed will be extracted. Therefore, the soft meat is crisp and not very oily.There are also dozens of varieties of steamed vermicelli roll and congee. The soup is also a must try. The delicious soups of Heng Shan Cafe & Chinese Cuisine, such as the hot pot of pork lung with needle mushroom, cabbage and almond, the hot pot of free range chicken with snow pear, and American ginseng and fig are very healthy and delicious.

SIGNATURE DISHES

> House special crispy pork belly
> Shrimp skewers baked in sea salt and served in alini wooden barrel
> Female crab and vermicelli
> Pan-fried cod fish

WINE: It offers many varieties of wines and ginger ale and fresh pressed juice. The juice mixed by the restaurant is worth trying.

SERVICE: Waiters are capable and experienced and announce the names of dishes to guests upon serving. The service is not formal but is still efficient.

1F, 719 YAN'AN ROAD W., SHANGHAI **TEL:** 021-62260525/62265517
地址： 上海延安西路719号佳都大厦首层

RESERVATIONS: Recommended
DRESS CODE: Smart casual
LUNCH HOURS: 9:00 am-18:00 pm
DINNER HOURS: 18:00 pm-23:30 pm
LAST ORDER DINNER: 23:00 pm
WEBSITE: www.hengshancafe.com.cn

VEGETARIAN DISHES: 10+
NO SMOKING SECTION: Yes
CAR VALET: No
CREDIT CARDS: AE, D, J, MC, UP, V
YEAR ESTABLISHED: 2005
PRICE: RMB 150-200/Person

HISAGO

♨ 8   🍴 9   🍷 9   🎀 9

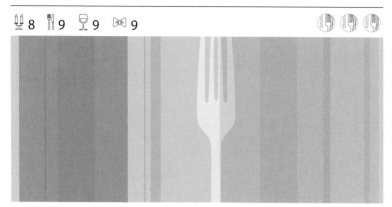

SETTING: The mural on the wall is a partial 12th-century painting of animals and figures. The restaurant acquired its name from Japanese who often use pickled cucurbit skin as their last dish after eating Sushi.

FOOD: The specialty Sushi restaurant before Edo (with Tokyo style) serves Sushi of Kaiseki cuisine. Appetizers include: abalone, Octopus, steamed North Sea Red hairy crab. The abalone goes best with Japanese sea salt. The appetizers can be had with a nice cup of sake. Dishes that go well with wine: Snow crab roe & meat from North Korea is delicious. Soup: Clam Broth with Mushrooms in liqueur, with a side dish of spinach and diced lemon, is cooked with "cram". Sashimi: the way of cutting fish for sashimi is different from that of sushi. Recommended are tenderloin, sea breams and arkshell of tuna. The side of arkshell is very crisp and tender.The side dish is wakame, a Japanese sea vegetable. Roast food: Grilled Sea Breams in yuuannyaki style is made by pickling Mirin in soy sauce half a day. The gingko is strung up with pine needles. Sushi: ginger with white trevally from Japan is served, followed by arkshell, tuna pickled with soy sauce, squid, sea urchin and half grilled Fatty Tuna (O-Toro). Also recommended is tuna tenderloin with onion roll and hisago dry roll.

SIGNATURE DISHES
> Steam Abalone
> Kelp marinated Sea bream
> Snow crab roe & meat
> Marinated Tuna
> Half grilled Fatty Tuna (O-Toro)
> Ark Shell

WINE: The sake from Japan is very authentic. The wine can be sold by glass or bottle. The tea here is also very unique and tastes pure. Viridescence tea (different from Matcha) is steamed delicious.

SERVICE: The service here is quiet and very considerate, which is the formal Japanese style. The service is up to "huaishi" level.

372 XINGGUO ROAD, SHANGHAI **TEL:** 021-52082873
地址： 上海兴国路372弄1号

RESERVATIONS: Recommended
DRESS CODE: Smart casual
LUNCH HOURS: 12:00 am-14:00 pm
DINNER HOURS: 18:00 pm-22:00 pm
LAST ORDER DINNER: 22:00 pm
WEBSITE: No

VEGETARIAN DISHES: 2-3
NO SMOKING SECTION: Yes
CAR VALET: No
CREDIT CARDS: MC, V
YEAR ESTABLISHED: 2010
PRICE: RMB 600/Person

HONG RUI XING

♕ 8   🍴 8   🍷 8   🎓 9

SETTING: The Chinese restaurant, on the first, second and third floors of East Asia Sport Hotel, boasts private rooms named with after Suzhou Garden and ten scenes of the West Lake, portraits of emperors of the Qing Dynasty, cornice and rake. It strongly displays a royal style.

FOOD: The choice of ingredients for the nostalgic and homely authentic Shanghai Cuisine is wide and seasonal. Soviet-styled noodles and pastries are served on the first floor. Cold dishes: Needle Mushroom with Holland Bean is cut beautifully and tastes sweet. Farmer's local chicken is different from common white cut chicken (Pinyin name Bai Zhan Ji). Hot dishes: sweet crisp beef is crisp and delicious. The steamed squid in chili sauce is wonderfully rubbery and the diced chili is perfect. The Fried Stinky Tofu is from Zhejiang. After frying, it is matched with chili sauce or sweet flour paste. Hot and Sour dishes are also offered. Preserved Short Rib with Taro Hot Pot and Short Rib with Chaozhou Taro Hot Pot are delicious. Braised egg dumpling with three kinds of ingredients such as pork skin or cabbage is an old delicacy of Shanghai. The dried fish of Braised Eel with Soy Sauce are saturated with each other and the softness and stickiness beautifully combined.

SIGNATURE DISHES
> Fish Head Soup
> Featured shrimp
> Steamed Onion
> Scalded Black Fungus
> Deep-Fried Small Yellow Croakers
> SUZHOU Tofu

WINE: Various high grade distilled spirits and rice wines specially brewed in Hong Rui Xing Restaurant are served. Middle and high grade new and old world wines are also offered.

SERVICE: It provides warm-hearted and considerate service.

1500 ZHONGSHAN NO.2 ROAD S., SHANGHAI **TEL:** 021-64275177
地址：上海中山南二路1500号

RESERVATIONS: Necessary
DRESS CODE: Smart casual
LUNCH HOURS: 11:00 am-14:00 pm
DINNER HOURS: 17:00 pm-21:00 pm
LAST ORDER DINNER: 20:30 pm
WEBSITE: www. hongruixing.com

VEGETARIAN DISHES: 10+
NO SMOKING SECTION: Yes
CAR VALET: Yes
CREDIT CARDS: MC, V
YEAR ESTABLISHED: 2002
PRICE: RMB 100/Person

ISSIMO

♨ 8   🍴 9   🍷 8   🎀 9

SETTING: Old timber flooring, solid wood round tables, diamond-shaped glass, ornaments that can be seen everywhere, and a wood burning oven transported from Naples.

FOOD: The delicious cuisine on offer at ISSIMO is genuine rustic Italian. Indeed, the authentic cuisine, fresh ingredients and wonderful throwback copper grill wood burner create a dreamlike atmosphere. Appetizers include Parma Ham with cherry tomatoes and cheese that delivers a great burst of rich flavors. The cheese is fragrant and can be enjoyed all by itself. The sweet and velvety chicken liver pate is simply divine. There are almost too many choices for the many main courses. The tender and juicy T-bone steak is cooked perfectly to order, while the pizza here comes fresh from a brick oven, with a perfect thin base, crispy crust and a wonderful selection of toppings. The mushroom and basil pizza, stuffed with buffalo cheese, is delicious. The pesto clam pasta is awash with the delicate taste of basil and seafood, and the pasta is a perfect al dente ("to the tooth" firmness). Ice cream is offered as dessert, the highlight being chocolate marsh mellow, and the indulgently rich will blow you away.

SIGNATURE DISHES
> Selection of antipasti
> D.O.P.Parma ham with burrata cheese
> Deep-fried green olives stuffed with pork and beef
> Australian grain-fed T-bone steak "Fiorentina" style,800gr

WINE: ISSIMO provides various wines, including red wine, white wine and sparkling wine.

SERVICE: Hospitable waiters, diligent and deft, provide considerate service to the guests and show them the oven after dinner.

931 NANJING ROAD W., SHANGHAI **TEL:** 021-33024997
地址： 上海南京西路931号

RESERVATIONS: Recommended
DRESS CODE: Smart casual
LUNCH HOURS: 12:00 am-14:30 pm
DINNER HOURS: 18:30 pm-22:30 pm
LAST ORDER DINNER: 22:30 pm
WEBSITE: www.jiashanghai.com

VEGETARIAN DISHES: 10+
NO SMOKING SECTION: Yes
CAR VALET: Yes
CREDIT CARDS: AE, D, J, MC, UP, V
YEAR ESTABLISHED: 2008
PRICE: RMB 400/Person

JADE

8 | 9 | 8 | 9

SETTING: Jade boasts a large, elegant dining space.

FOOD: It's quite a shock that a five-star hotel can provide such reasonable value for money while maintaining its reputation for excellence with its Cantonese, Shanghai and Sichuan cuisine. The Soup of the Day tests the chef's masterful culinary skills and displays the restaurant's mantra: fresh ingredients cooked to perfection. Cantonese Stir-fried Mango Veal Rib Dice, a dish made with the tenderest beef, is dotted with yellow, red and green peppers and is an utter delight. The dish is finished with a quick-fry of the veal rib and mango and cooked to perfection without the use of even a meat tenderizer. Non-Shanghainese are very impressed by Western-style dishes. Seizing this opportunity, Shanghai natives have racked their brains to treat guests to so-called "authentic" Western dishes. At the same time the, original Shanghai dishes of heavy oils and sauces have been gradually weakened, with only a few famous dishes now remembered by a nostalgic few. Jade offers Caviar Dry-fried Steamed Pork Dumplings, which tastes better than those that are over-steamed to transparency, such as crab roe. The meat in Steamed Pork Dumplings is tender and succulent, with a texture that will leave you wanting more and more.

SIGNATURE DISHES
> Roasted Crispy Goose
> Jellyfish in Vinegar Sauce
> Spinacia with Pine Nuts
> Crab Meat and Shark's Fin in Pot
> Crispy Papaya Puff

WINE: Complete range of white spirits and yellow rice wines with clear classification.

SERVICE: Jade provides hospitable and warm service. Waiters are familiar with the cuisine and change dish plates promptly.

5F, 500 HENGFENG ROAD, SHANGHAI **TEL:** 021-52539999-6398
地址：上海恒丰路500号5楼

RESERVATIONS: Recommended
DRESS CODE: Smart casual
LUNCH HOURS: 11:30 am-14:30 pm
DINNER HOURS: 17:00 pm-22:00 pm
LAST ORDER DINNER: 22:00 pm
WEBSITE: www.intercontinental.com

VEGETARIAN DISHES: 5-10
NO SMOKING SECTION: Yes
CAR VALET: Yes
CREDIT CARDS: AE, J, MC, V
YEAR ESTABLISHED: 2009
PRICE: RMB 200/Person

JADE MANSION

🕯 8 🍴 9 🍷 9 🎀 9

SETTING: The tables are furnished and decorated to a simple taste. Interlaced black and white chandeliers hang from the ceiling and are a touch of majesty amongst the simplicity.

FOOD: Before the meal waiters present a hospitality fruit plate; a nice little gesture. The cold dish of Cubed Squid and Shallots comes highly recommended and is decorated with shredded shallot and pimiento and has a fresh, salty sauce with a slight sweetness that brings out the natural flavor of the squid. The signature dish Braised Boning fish's head with orchid and fish's lip requires one day advance booking as 3 hours are needed to bone the head of the silver carp. Not a single, tiny fishbone is allowed in this dish while the full shape must be maintained. No easy feat. The fish's lip, ham, rape core, orchid and mai dong are added later. The clear, fragrant soup is full of collagens and is a nutritious and delicious Kung Fu dish suitable for all ages. A dash of pepper really enhances its delicate flavor. Another signature dish is seafood duck in capsicum. This new dish is served at a very reasonable price and is a reinvention of the revised traditional Sichuan dish.

SIGNATURE DISHES
> Braised duck in jujube flavor Shanghai style
> Truffle goose liver wrapped with lettuce
> Braised fish head with gastrodia tuber and fish lips
> Braised duck with hot chilli oil

WINE: A lot of liquors to choose from, especially grape wines at a moderate price. The signature dishes on the menu are matched with recommended wines.

SERVICE: The waiters and waitresses are warm and considerate and help divide dishes for all guests.

4F, 8 CENTURY BOULEVARD, SHANGHAI **TEL:** 021-50127728
地址： 上海浦东新区世纪大道8号国金中心4楼

RESERVATIONS: Recommended
DRESS CODE: Smart casual
LUNCH HOURS: 10:00 am-16:00 pm
DINNER HOURS: 18:00 pm-23:00 pm
LAST ORDER DINNER: 23:00 pm
WEBSITE: www.jade388.com

VEGETARIAN DISHES: 10+
NO SMOKING SECTION: Yes
CAR VALET: No
CREDIT CARDS: MC, V
YEAR ESTABLISHED: 2010
PRICE: RMB 500/Person

JADE ON 36 RESTAURANT

♨ 9   🍴 9   🍷 9   🎀 9

SETTING: The restaurant is a masterpiece of Chinese features in a futuristic concept. As its name implies, it is located on the top floor, the 36th. Guests can enter the restaurant through a traditional 4.3-meter bowl made of metal and porcelain and then will be surrounded by emerald glass and gems. The huge French glass window designed with special materials brings a spectacular view.

FOOD: The restaurant is one of best and most famous restaurants in Shanghai. After chef PAUL PAIRET left, it became unknown for a brief period. Fabrice Giraud from Saint-Emilion Ville Castle Hotel brings the epicure a refreshing surprise with both traditional and modern French cuisine. Most dishes in the new menu are classic French dishes. Pastoral series includes smoked duck breast, boiled goose liver with fresh soup, stewed snail with vanilla and cream and Tasmania beef filet with bone marrow. The Seafood series includes scallop with the taste of fruit, crab with fruit and vegetables in frozen soup and inky liquor silvery pout; they all reach perfection in taste and vision. Giraud uses fresh, organic ingredients and refuses to use any man-made artificial spices in the dishes. The harmony of man and nature is well showcased here.

SIGNATURE DISHES

> Snails in creamy persillade, paprika tuile & champagne foam
> Asparagus soup
> Pan fried black cod
> Pyrenees soured Australian lamb rack

WINE: The wine list is rich, especially in Bordeaux wines. Waiters and sommeliers can give you useful advice

SERVICE: Waiters are very warm-hearted and professional and they can provide guests with good all round service. Chef recommendation: lobster salad, inky liquor silvery pout, mutton chop with truffle and lemon tart.

36F, 33 FUCHENG ROAD, SHANGHAI **TEL:** 021-68828888-280

地址：上海浦东富城路33号上海浦东香格里拉大酒店紫金楼36层

RESERVATIONS: Recommended
DRESS CODE: Smart casual
LUNCH HOURS: 11:30 am-15:00 pm (Only Sunday)
DINNER HOURS: 18:00 pm-22:30 pm
LAST ORDER DINNER: 22:15 pm
WEBSITE: www.shangri-la.com

VEGETARIAN DISHES: 3-5
NO SMOKING SECTION: Yes
CAR VALET: Yes (7:00-23:30)
CREDIT CARDS: AE, D, J, MC, UP, V
YEAR ESTABLISHED: 2005
PRICE: RMB 600/Person

JEAN GEORGES

 9 9 9 9

SETTING: Jean Georges somehow resembles the perfect fine-dining experience that is pictured in every diner's mind. The retro` chairs, the massive vault and views over Lujiazui's skyline all contribute to this "chateau ambience", and the well-dosed lights and high ceiling balance out this imposing yet very comfortable atmosphere.

FOOD: Jean Georges' carte features a fixed-price menu, a JG menu, and a seasonal menu. Fairly clear and straightforward, and all extremely French and rich with well-thought out delicacies to please even the most demanding of palates. Every detail, from the silver cloche for butter to the refined amuse-bouche, is treated with the outmost care, and attention to elegance simply dominates.From the starters, the classic foie gras brule` is a concoction of textures and flavors you won't forget, and the dried sour cherries and crunchy pistachios complement the melt-in-the-mouth liver with pleasantly sweet notes.Moving on to the main courses, the generous beef tenderloin rests on a bed of chunky tomato compote with an unusual but well-thought smoked aroma, and the side of spinach and crunchy-baked potato complements the whole.The dessert plate completes the meal in style, with a very elegant composition of seasonal flavors and colors.

SIGNATURE DISHES
> Ribbons of tuna
> Sea scallop
> Egg caviar
> Red snapper
> Parmesan crusted organic chicken
> Lobster tartine

WINE: JG's wines list has got it all, and very much in line with the menu, is presented first as a condensed array of highly targeted suggestions, including fine reds and whites and even champagnes by the glass, and JG's signature cocktails.

SERVICE: Service gets close to impeccable at Jean-Georges, from the phone reservation all the way to the runners in the hall.

4F, 3 ZHONGSHANG NO.1 ROAD E., SHANGHAI **TEL:** 021-63217733
地址： 上海中山东一路3号4楼

RESERVATIONS: Necessary for Dinner
DRESS CODE: Suit and tie/Smart casual
LUNCH HOURS: 11:30 am-14:30 pm
DINNER HOURS: 18:00 pm-23:00 pm
LAST ORDER DINNER: 23:00 pm
WEBSITE: www.threeonthebund.com

VEGETARIAN DISHES: 5-10
NO SMOKING SECTION: Yes
CAR VALET: Yes
CREDIT CARDS: AE, D, J, MC, V
YEAR ESTABLISHED: 2004
PRICE: RMB 400/Person

JIN XUAN

🕯8 🍴9 🍷9 🎀9   🖐 🖐 🖐

SETTING: The restaurant commands a beautiful panoramic view of Shanghai. The interior decorations are elegant and grand, which makes diners feel elegant and grand in turn.

FOOD: Jin Xuan offers mainly authentic Guangdong Cuisine, made by gourmet Hong Kong chefs, and selected signature dishes from each province. Appetizers consist of three dishes. The first is chilled river shrimps in a delightful mix of wasabi & mayonnaise sauce. The peeled prawns are simmered on a low heat with just a dash of wasabi, resulting in a smooth taste with a slight kick. The second dish is shredded salted duck and marinated duck tongue, with a sweet-scented osmanthus that wonderfully complements the duck. The duck tongue will, quite fittingly, really get your taste buds working. The last dish is black fungus with fragrant garlic and vinegar, which is crispy, refreshing and delicious. The soup, Liao sea cucumber with pumpkin and millet, is a delicate and healthy choice. For the main courses, the Pan-fired beef short ribs with honey pepper sauce is so tender teeth go through it like butter. There are two equally delicious rice dishes to choose from: the tossed fried rice with diced chicken, shrimps and abalone sauce and the Abalone sauce rice with seafood.

SIGNATURE DISHES
> Chilled river shrimps, wasabi & mayonnaise sauce
> Liao sea cucumber with pumpkin and millet sauce
> Pan-fired beef short ribs with honey pepper sauce

WINE: There are more than 400 kinds of wine from the Old and New World, and it is rare and commendable that the different varieties are so complete here.

SERVICE: The aforesaid service of the tea ceremony is free of charge. The other services are well-done and considerate.

53F, THE RITZ-CARLTON SHANGHAI, PUDONG, 8 CENTURY AVENUE TEL: 021-20201888-1768
地址：上海浦东陆家嘴世纪大道8号上海浦东丽思卡尔顿酒店53层

RESERVATIONS: Recommended
DRESS CODE: Smart casual
LUNCH HOURS: 11:30 am-14:00 pm
DINNER HOURS: 17:30 pm-22:00 pm
LAST ORDER DINNER: 22:00 pm
EMAIL: JinXuan@ritzcarlton.com

VEGETARIAN DISHES: 5-10
NO SMOKING SECTION: Yes
CAR VALET: Yes
CREDIT CARDS: AE, D, J, MC, UP, V
YEAR ESTABLISHED: 2010
PRICE: RMB 400/Person

JING'AN RESTAURANT

SETTING: The restaurant is dedicated to minimalistic cuisine with maximum taste, while guests also appreciate the beautiful scenery of JiangAn Park. In the night, with the subtle lighting giving the restaurant a pearly glow, guests can almost feel Zen flowing amongst them. The water lily placed tables is a delightful feature.

FOOD: The excellence of the JingAn restaurant is based on its fine selection of fresh ingredients and unique secret recipe. The restaurant has always strived to integrate taste and freshness. Dane Clouston, the young head chef from New Zealand, earned his fame young and has won many honors in the restaurant where he has ever worked. The menu of JingAn Restaurant is very distinctive. JingAn Hamburger, recommended for lunch, is made with prime, tender beef and handmade chili sauce that tastes divine. The thick cauliflower soup is fragrant and delicious. The two Italian dumplings are also the highlight. The braised silvery pout with smoked chili and green olives and the caramelized ox cheek and green tomatoes are both recommended as main dishes. Both dishes are expertly cooked and really show off the freshness of the ingredients and skills of the chefs. Also, the choice of side dishes and sweet desserts are varied and not to be missed.

SIGNATURE DISHES
> Crayfish with pork scratchings
> Potted prawns
> Foie gras with chocolate
> Caramelized ox cheek
> Cod fillet
> Pimento and green olives
> Wagyu beef striplion

WINE: The wine list, containing many vintages and single glass champagne, includes various old world wines from France, Germany and Spain and new world wines from Australia, USA and South Africa.

SERVICE: The well-trained waiters provide efficient and professional service.

2F, 1 CHANGDE ROAD, SHANGHAI **TEL:** 021-22166988
地址：上海常德路1号2楼

RESERVATIONS: Recommended
DRESS CODE: Smart casual
LUNCH HOURS: 11:30 am-14:30 pm
DINNER HOURS: 18:00 pm-22:00 pm
LAST ORDER DINNER: 22:00 pm
WEBSITE: www.jinganrestaurant.com

VEGETARIAN DISHES: 3-5
NO SMOKING SECTION: Yes
CAR VALET: Yes (06:30-23:00)
CREDIT CARDS: AE, D, J, MC, V
YEAR ESTABLISHED: 2009
PRICE: RMB 500/Person

JING CHI FANG RESTAURANT

🍴 9   🍴 9   🍷 9   🎀 9

SETTING: A folding screen and drapes divide the lobby into a luxurious and minimalistic space, which is full of the nostalgic sentiment of the Old Shanghai.

FOOD: Jing Chi Fang provides excellent shark's fin and abalone, and features delicious Cantonese cuisine. There are also some authentic Taiwanese dishes that the owner brought over from Taiwan. In its 7 years since opening for business Jing Chi Fang has maintained a very high standard. It follows the traditional cooking style of the imperial palace, which can take more than 40 hours of preparation and cooking, and therefore is a big hit with the celebrities and epicures of Shanghai who are attracted to the royal banquets. The specialties include shark's fin, abalone, bird's nest, fish maw and sea cucumber. All the ingredients, whether best King Shark's Fin or Clear Chicken Soup with Shark's Fin, are of the highest quality. Their texture and taste are all excellent. The lunch set meal is very substantial and you certainly get your money's worth. Other dishes include Pan-fried sliced silver cod, French goose liver, Wagyu Beef and Rice with Pork Shallot Sauce and steamed rice with salmon, among others. Don't forget to try the different Taiwan side dishes and pickled vegetables that perfectly compliment the main courses.

SIGNATURE DISHES
> Fried mushroom
> XO sauce/mullet roe/Taiwan sausage
> Peking imperial shark fin/ Braised abalone
> Fish maw with sea cucumber/ French style goose liver

WINE: There are many wines from France and New World, as well as Chinese rice wine and local yellow wine.

SERVICE: The reception is polite in all matters and the waiting staff are considerate and efficient.

2F, 298 WULUMUQI ROAD S., SHANGHAI **TEL:** 021-64457111
地址：上海乌鲁木齐南路298号2楼（近建国西路）

RESERVATIONS: Recommended	**VEGETARIAN DISHES:** 10+
DRESS CODE: Smart casual	**NO SMOKING SECTION:** Yes
LUNCH HOURS: 11:30 am-14:30 pm	**CAR VALET:** Yes (11:30-22:00)
DINNER HOURS: 17:30 pm-22:00 pm	**CREDIT CARDS:** AE, D, J, MC, UP, V
LAST ORDER DINNER: 21:00 pm	**YEAR ESTABLISHED:** 2003
WEBSITE: www.jingchifang.com	**PRICE:** RMB 400/Person

JW'S CALIFORNIA GRILL

🍴 8 🍴 9 🍷 8 ⋈ 9

SETTING: The ambience of JW's California Grill created by the warm red candles, tablecloths and red gauze curtains around the circular open kitchen settles diners right in.

FOOD: A playful menu offers a mouth-watering selection of red meats in different grades of superlative quality, all from Australia. The seasoned connoisseur will not be disappointed, and there are steaks for different budgets. Gippsland Fresh, with its organic cuts and Ranger Valley and Cargill Angus are becoming familiar breeds and locations to discerning diners in Shanghai and the cooking and presentation does justice to the quality. The flamboyant wagyu and fois gras beef burger is beautifully textured, the goose liver not overpowering, and enhanced with a thin layer of parmesan and light greens. Char-grilled sea bass with Mediterranean relish is rich with its butter-sauce and goes well with the slightly crunchy sautéed asparagus and hard-to-resist steak fries. The crisp thin skin of the potato is echoed on the sea bass crust, which comes topped with tomato, capers and a morsel of tasty micro-greens.The selection is tempting and could ideally be shared. It boasts a 'melt-in-the-mouth' warm chocolate mud cake with bitter chocolate sauce, baked on the spot.

SIGNATURE DISHES
> Beef carpaccio
> Prawn cocktail
> Caesar salad
> Ranger valley-wagyu
> T-bone steak
> Ranger valley-300days grain fed tenderloin

WINE: Excellent selection of old and new world wines, though the 'by the glass' selection is limited.

SERVICE: Considerate and informed service affords privacy and space for guests.

40F, 399 NANJING ROAD W., SHANGHAI **TEL:** 021-53594969-6455
地址： 上海南京西路399号JW万豪酒店40楼

RESERVATIONS: Recommended
DRESS CODE: Smart casual
LUNCH HOURS: 11:30 am-14:00 pm (Monday-Friday)
DINNER HOURS: 17:30 pm-22:30 pm
LAST ORDER DINNER: 22:25 pm
WEBSITE: No

VEGETARIAN DISHES: 10+
NO SMOKING SECTION: No
CAR VALET: No
CREDIT CARDS: AE, D, J, MC, UP, V
YEAR ESTABLISHED: 2003
PRICE: RMB 500/Person

KATHLEEN'S 5 ROOF TOP RESTAURANT

♨ 8   🍴 8   🍷 9   🎀 8

SETTING: The restaurant is surrounded by clear glass and guests will feel comfortable and enthralled by the myriad shinning lights.

FOOD: Kathleen's 5 is an old-style continental cuisine restaurant. Opening the menu, you may at first feel that the selection is not rich. It is unusual for a western restaurant to serve just 1 soup, 7-8 starter dishes, 7-8 main dishes, 5 side dishes and 6-7 desserts. But each dish is exquisite and of the highest quality.The first soup uses broccoli, strong cheese and almond; it has a wonderful, rich flavor. It is warming and really stimulates the appetite. There are a lot of vegetable dishes among the starters. Boiled eggplant wrapped with pancake is recommended. The vegetables are lightly sprinkled with olive oil. The hand-made pancake is crisp yet supple. It is a healthy and delicious dish. The main courses are all rich in flavor and delicious, and demonstrate the creativity of continental cuisine. The cod with seafood is very fresh. The fish is tender, cooked to perfection, and brimming with a fishy taste. Try it with sweet and sour sauce. There is a tough choice among meat lovers: Australia beef filet, beefsteak and mutton chop. All are highly recommended and delicious. The choice of desserts is not extensive, but all are delicious.

SIGNATURE DISHES
> Goose liver teerrine
> Marinated salmon
> Roasted codfish
> Chocolate fordant with Vanilla Ice cream
> Coconut mousse on peal pastry sable

WINE: The wine list is beautiful. Besides the excellent grape wine list, the distilled spirits are also recommended. The homemade carbonated fruit beverage are worth trying.

SERVICE: Waiters provide considerate service, and give good advice when guests order.

5F, 325 NANJING ROAD W., SHANGHAI **TEL:** 021-63272221
地址： 上海南京西路325号上海美术馆5楼

RESERVATIONS: Recommended
DRESS CODE: Smart casual
LUNCH HOURS: 10:30 am-14:30 pm (Monday-Friday)
DINNER HOURS: 17:30 pm-22:30 pm
LAST ORDER DINNER: 22:30 pm
WEBSITE: www.kathleens5.com

VEGETARIAN DISHES: 5-10
NO SMOKING SECTION: Yes
CAR VALET: No
CREDIT CARDS: AE, J, MC, V
YEAR ESTABLISHED: 2003
PRICE: RMB 350/Person

KOI JAPANESE RESTAURANT

♨ 8   🍴 8   🍷 8   🎀 8

SETTING: The high ceiling and the large open space all provide for a relaxing atmosphere, and thanks to the bright lights you'll even be able to actually see what you're eating!

FOOD: Koi's selection boasts all the classics of Japanese cuisine: from tempura to sushi and sashismi, from teppanyaki to sukiyaki ad shabu-shabu. Dinner courses are available, as well as a tantalizing eat-till-you-drop menu that is reasonably priced. For those who don't like spending time browsing menus, plenty of sets are on hand. From the specialty appetizers, definitely try the Wagyu beef tataki, lightly seared on the outside and rare in the inside, served in thin slices topped with daikon mash, fried garlic slices and chopped chives, and accompanied by tangy dices of jelly. Moving on to the main courses, ordering the sukiyaki will get you a dedicated waiter cooking right next to your table! You'll first get to taste the beef alone, slice by slice in sweet soy sauce, then with tofu and caramelized onions, and finally with veggies and udon noodles. For something less complicated, the sirloin and tenderloin is seared on the teppan to your desired texture, and served diced with a couple of classic dips. You can also choose between a standard Angus beef or the highly praised Wagyu variety, both imported from Australia.

SIGNATURE DISHES
> Wagyu tataki
> Foie gras saikyo
> Avocado salad
> Australian Wagyu beef tenderloin
> Gindara saikyo
> Australian Angus beef sukiyaki

WINE: Characterized by an impressive variety of drinks, ranging from liquors to fresh juices and all sorts of sake, while only a few options each are featured, they are all carefully selected rare labels. Wines are available too, though only by the glass.

SERVICE: Koi's staff try hard to please each and every diner, and will be ready to accommodate your special requests.

2F, 500 HENGFENG ROAD, SHANGHAI **TEL:** 021-52539999-6326
地址：上海恒丰路500号上海浦西洲际酒店主楼2楼

RESERVATIONS: Recommended
DRESS CODE: Smart casual
LUNCH HOURS: 11:30 am-14:30 pm
DINNER HOURS: 17:30 pm-22:00 pm
LAST ORDER DINNER: 21:55 pm
WEBSITE: www.intercontinental.com/shanghai-puxi

VEGETARIAN DISHES: 10+
NO SMOKING SECTION: Yes
CAR VALET: No
CREDIT CARDS: AE, J, MC, V
YEAR ESTABLISHED: 2009
PRICE: RMB 400/Person

KOREAN BARBECUE RESTAURANT

🍽7 🍴8 🍷8 🎀9

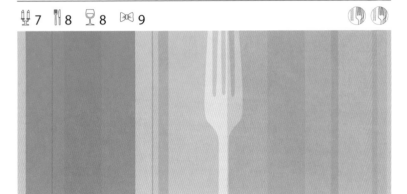

SETTING: The stone mill matching an N-shaped bridge and the silk flower tied to bamboo poles with hemp cord in this elegant setting embodies Zen.

FOOD: The appetizers consist of 6 dishes, and are changed regularly according to the different seasons, as is common is Korea. Of course, Korean cuisine is mostly barbecue-based dishes. In addition to barbeque, the other dishes are delicious. For example, fried vermicelli with mixed vegetable, seafood cakes and stewed oxtail in casserole is. The beef tastes excellent and is perfectly cooked and mixed with fresh and savory sauces. The mushroom and onion which are barbecued before the beef are sweet, and with the juices from the beef are truly delicious. Grilled streaky pork is a must order when we have Korean cuisine. The method of grilling in Korean Barbecue Restaurant is different from that of other restaurants and is served lightly seared. In addition, waitresses often help to cut the beef, which isn't fatty. Mixed with pieces of sauced cucumber and carrot, the fragrance of the beef and faint scent of the vegetables mix together and produces a wonderful taste. The soup with the stewed oxtail in casserole is creamy white and the sautéed oxtail is crispy and tasty. The Seafood cake is also recommended.

SIGNATURE DISHES
> Raw beef tartar
> Kimchi Pancake
> Marinated beef ribs barbecue
> Ox tail soup

WINE: Jinro rack and rice wine are sweet and pure. In addition, there are beers and ale that are imported from Korea. The grape juice is excellent.

SERVICE: Though the waitresses are few, they are very professional and attentive.

S205, 8 XINGYI ROAD, SHANGHAI **TEL:** 021-52081579/52081557
地址： 上海兴义路8号万都商城S205

RESERVATIONS: Necessary for Lunch
DRESS CODE: Smart casual
LUNCH HOURS: 11:30 am-14:00 pm
DINNER HOURS: 17:30 pm-22:00 pm
LAST ORDER DINNER: 22:00 pm
WEBSITE: No

VEGETARIAN DISHES: 5-10
NO SMOKING SECTION: Yes
CAR VALET: No
CREDIT CARDS: AE, D, J, MC, UP, V
YEAR ESTABLISHED: 1993
PRICE: RMB 200/Person

LAKE VIEW

♨ 9 🍴 8 🍷 8 🎀 9

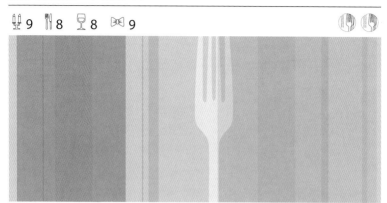

SETTING: Outside the restaurant are garden sculptures, and artificial beach and flowing water. Customers can walk and watch the stars and moon in this quite retreat away from the bustle of Shanghai. The dining room, with both ancient and modern styles, is the model for five-star hotels.

FOOD: A delicious dinner is one that touches on all the senses, and the food here strives to achieve this. Golden Streaky Pork, a cold dish, is cooked with selected streaky pork. The skin is crisp and the meat tender. It is said that the cooking process is very complicated. When the pork is medium cooked, the chef will cut many eyelets on the skin with bamboo sticks and season with spices, then leave it to air. Finally, the meat is oven roasted until the skin is crispy. Of the hot dishes, the turbot is very fresh and recommended. It is cooked with shredded green onion and soy sauce and the fish has a wonderful delicate flavor. The soup of the day is boiled with chops, clam and yam. The clams act as a detoxin, and the yam can improve a weak body and dissipate fatigue. The fragrant and creamy white soup is delicious and renews vigor. "One palm deciding heaven and earth" is the new specialty of Lake view, pettitoes braised with sticky rice. Red date braised with aloe is an excellent dessert.

SIGNATURE DISHES
> Barbecued pork with mustard
> Stir-fried diced beef with black truffle
> Braised pork feet filled with sticky rice and grains

WINE: The drinks are varied. Besides traditional Chinese spirits, yellow wine and wine, there are red wines from famous foreign chateaus. Moreover, tea, all kinds of soft drinks and fresh fruit juices are available.

SERVICE: Waitresses are informed, warm and considerate.

5F, 1288 LINYIN XIN ROAD, SHANGHAI **TEL:** 021-57799999-7766
地址： 上海松江区佘山林荫新路1288号世茂佘山艾美酒店5楼

RESERVATIONS: Recommended
DRESS CODE: Smart casual
LUNCH HOURS: 11:00 am-14:00 pm
DINNER HOURS: 17:30 pm-22:00 pm
LAST ORDER DINNER: 21:45 pm
EMAIL: lakeview@sheshan.lemeridien.com

VEGETARIAN DISHES: 10+
NO SMOKING SECTION: Yes
CAR VALET: Yes
CREDIT CARDS: MC, V
YEAR ESTABLISHED: 2005
PRICE: RMB 200/Person

LAO CHENG XING RESTAURANT

SETTING: The interior has a typical Chinese layout with a series of award-winning photos of the executive chef hanging on the walls.

FOOD: Several innovative local signature dishes are created in Lao Cheng Xing, attributable to the executive chef Sun Xing, such as Braised Pig Knuckle, Crystal Chicken with Little Chinese Greens and Fresh Crab Gnocchi. Braised Pig Knuckle, after being braised and simmered in soy sauce for quite a long time, it tastes sweet and fresh as, once the sugar is added, it shines red because of the soy sauce, an achievement that cannot be realized without authentic materials and superior culinary skills. Though unfatty, Crystal Chicken with Little Chinese Greens is still bursting with flavor. The little greens taste refreshing and delicious when dipped with the meat juice. Doubling as a main course and a soup, Fresh Crab Gnocchi uses gnocchi common in Northern rustic dishes and mixes it with ingredients like fresh crabs and tomatoes, which help redden the soup. The very first bite of the dish throws you into total bliss of the chewy gnocchi with a mouthful of light tomato and garlic sauce.

SIGNATURE DISHES
> Spicy smoked fish
> Steamed chicken
> Tossed crown daisy
> Stewed pork
> Dough drop with crab meat in soup
> Sauteed green cabbage

WINE: Lao Cheng Xing provides a wide collection of wines ranging from white spirits like Wuliangye Liquor, grape wine like Changyu, various Shao Xing Wine and beers, to all kinds of bottled drinks and teas.

SERVICE: Standing at the service counter next to customers, modest and honest waiters are ready to serve plates at any time.

399 FENGZHUANG ROAD N., SHANGHAI **TEL:** 021-69195577
地址：上海嘉定区丰庄北路399号

RESERVATIONS: Recommended
DRESS CODE: Smart Casual
LUNCH HOURS: 11:30 am-13:30 pm
DINNER HOURS: 17:00 pm-21:00 pm
LAST ORDER DINNER: 21:00 pm
EMAIL: xijiaowuhao@126.com

VEGETARIAN DISHES: 10+
NO SMOKING SECTION: Yes
CAR VALET: No
CREDIT CARDS: MC, V
YEAR ESTABLISHED: 2005
PRICE: RMB 100/Person

LAPIS SKY GARDEN

🍴 8   🍴 8   🍷 9   🎀 9

SETTING: Lapis Sky Garden restaurant lies surrounded by phoenix trees in the heart of the former French concession area. The restaurant has a Mediterranean style and a décor that brings you into a fusion of the 70's European culture , and a cozy and relaxed atmosphere.

FOOD: Lapis' menu is sorted by appetizers, soups and salads, mains and pasta/pizza, and has a set menu that offers great value for money. From the signature dishes, the hot spring egg is a Mediterranean re-invention of the Japanese Onsen-tamago, with its warm runny core on a bed of creamed baby spinach, and it goes very well with the crunchy focaccia bread it's served with. The foie gras terrine is excellent: creamy and smooth, intense but refined, it's best savored on toasted brioche with a dollop of rich fruit compote. Of the main courses, the spiced salmon is a generous chunk of tender seafood, served with a smooth pumpkin mash, couscous, and a little salad with zucchini julienne. For meat lovers, try the classic lamb chops, grilled to succulent perfection and served with mashed potatoes, grilled asparagus, and an intense plum and Port sauce. For the perfect end, try Lapis' lavish cheese-cake foam, flavored with lime and served in a glass topped with vanilla ice-cream and blueberry compote.

SIGNATURE DISHES
> Hot spring egg
> Seared bay scallops
> Foie gras terrine
> Seafood Bouillabaisse
> Grill beef tenderloin

WINE: A great venue for drinks at night, or to chill out in the afternoon, the list features a plethora sorts of options, ranging from cocktails and liquors to milk shakes and smoothies. Wines from all over the world are available too, from super chic to very affordable, with quite a few by the glass.

SERVICE: Staff is welcoming, friendly but smooth, and very accommodating.

7F, 10 BAOQING ROAD, SHANGHAI **TEL:** 021-64747979
地址： 上海宝庆路10号7楼

RESERVATIONS: Necessary for Dinner
DRESS CODE: Smart casual
LUNCH HOURS: 11:30 am-14:30 pm
DINNER HOURS: 18:00 pm-22:00 pm
LAST ORDER DINNER: 21:30 pm
WEBSITE: www.lapiscasahotel.net

VEGETARIAN DISHES: 1-2
NO SMOKING SECTION: Yes
CAR VALET: No
CREDIT CARDS: MC, V
YEAR ESTABLISHED: 2010
PRICE: RMB 300/Person

LEONARDO'S

♨ 9 ‖ 9 ♟ 9 🍴 9   (🖐)(🖐)(🖐)

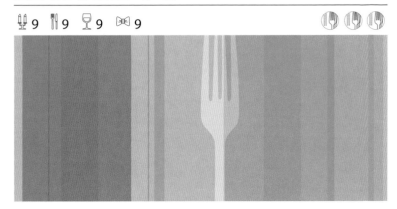

SETTING: Featuring elegant table settings with fresh flowers, the space between tables are more than enough to keep conversation private. Full wine list from all over the world, offer some half bottle wine as well. Careful service with good English.

FOOD: 6 different varieties of bread are offered before meal, served with balsamic vinegar and olive oil. A great traditional Mediterranean appetizer. Start with Spanish Iberico ham or Kuluga caviar. They can be ordered In three quantities. The Iberico ham is so tender and soft it melts in the month, the succulent meat meld mingling with the natural fatty sweetness. 30g is enough for 2 people. The hot starter foie gras wrapped in lettuce is light and delicious and, like all good foie gras, isn't oily. Vegetables are served on the side. Imported Angus rib eye steak Is lightly grilled to a perfect tenderness and comes with a side dish of onions, tomatoes and carrots and side sauce. Chili Lobster pasta is just a little spicy and wonderfully supple. The desert menu includes traditional Italian deserts and some other creative choices. The chocolate is outstanding.

SIGNATURE DISHES
> Steamed scallops
> Australian Wagyu beef carpaccio
> Seafood and rock lobster
> 450 day's grain fed Australian premium Wagyu beef striploin

---

WINE: Most wines are grouped by variety of grapes with a good balance between Old and New World and the selection ranges from drinks by the glass and half bottles to Reserves, Magnums, legendary chateaux and rare vintages.

SERVICE: The staff are extremely professional, kind and knowlegeable.

1F, 250 HUASHAN ROAD, SHANGHAI **TEL:** 021-62480000-1850
地址: 上海华山路250号上海希尔顿酒店1楼

RESERVATIONS: Recommended
DRESS CODE: Smart casual
LUNCH HOURS: No
DINNER HOURS: 18:00 pm-22:30 pm
LAST ORDER DINNER: 22:00 pm
WEBSITE: www.shanghai.hilton.com

VEGETARIAN DISHES: 1-2
NO SMOKING SECTION: Yes
CAR VALET: No
CREDIT CARDS: AE, D, J, MC, UP, V
YEAR ESTABLISHED: 1988
PRICE: RMB 400/Person

LOST HEAVEN ON THE BUND

 9 8 8 8

SETTING: The very dark environment with spot lights, the lacquer-red and mahogany interiors, and a painstaking attention to detail, from the signature stupa-like copper cloches to the tea pots to the fresh-flower decorations.

FOOD: From the cold starters, the eggplant with tofu salad is very refreshing, with hints of crunchy textures and mild chili. Another suggested snack, the Yunnan wild veggie cakes, are fun to eat and quickly disappear from the plate after a short brush with the fresh tomato dip they come with. The Burmese crab cakes are very tasty too, with their crisp skin, earthy filling, and green-and-yellow bell-pepper sauce. The steamed cod, a specialty from the Dai people, is simply a very good dish. Enjoy the tender meat and intriguing flavor of this fish, coated with seven types of veggies and herbs and steamed in banana leaves. Another local re-interpretation, simple scrambled eggs are turned into a special dish by the intensity of Yunnan's mushroom. As is typical of most Asian venues, the dessert list is particularly short. Nevertheless, try the soothing shaved ice with fresh fruits and tapioca "pearls", or why not, a simple, familiar ball of strawberry ice cream.

SIGNATURE DISHES

> Yunnan wild vegetable cakes
> Mandalay fish cakes
> Burmese lamb samosa
> Tibetan style grilled rack of lamb
> Spicy cod steamed in banana leaves

WINE: A complete list of wines and spirits, fine cocktails, fruit juices and wonderful Pu-erh teas, also available in intriguing mixes with Jasmine, lemon grass and many others.

SERVICE: Polite, available and attentive, everybody here is gorgeously dressed up in Yunnan's typical minority styles, adding a pleasant feeling of authenticity.

17 YAN'AN ROAD E., SHANGHAI **TEL:** 021-63300967
地址：上海延安东路17号

RESERVATIONS: Recommended
DRESS CODE: Smart casual
LUNCH HOURS: 11:30 am-14:00 pm
DINNER HOURS: 17:30 pm-24:00 pm
LAST ORDER DINNER: 22:30 pm
WEBSITE: www.lostheaven.com.cn

VEGETARIAN DISHES: 5-10
NO SMOKING SECTION: Yes
CAR VALET: No
CREDIT CARDS: AE, J, MC, V
YEAR ESTABLISHED: 2009
PRICE: RMB 150/Person

MADO IZAKAYA

🕯8 🍴8 🍷9 🎀9   🖐 🖐 🖐

SETTING: Mado Izakaya is located on the ground floor of the boutique hotel, with a sake jar and a wood partition at the entrance to separate the inside space from the outside. Decorated in a chic way, there are tatami seats and sashimi & sushi bar on the two sides of the corridor.

FOOD: The restaurant serves a rich and complete menu, basically covering all parts of the Japanese cuisine, while maintaining high quality. The expensive king crab dishes are handled properly, presenting fresh and sweet flavour in both sauce and stew. Today's choice is Assorted Sushi Platter, including white meat fish and red meat fish, as well as salmon roe sushi, octopus sushi and shrimp sushi. Different fishes show different flavours. The white meat fish tastes light and sweet, while the red meat fish tastes rich in oil. The octopus is chewy and the salmon roe is fresh and sweet. The shrimps are delicious too. The sushi rice shows great culinary skill in both handwork and seasoning. Neither too loose or too tight, the rice keeps shape when taken up by the chopsticks and falls apart in the mouth. Though the materials are not rare, the quality makes it a good dish. Another recommendation is the tenpura, especially the vegetables. Mado Izakaya is attractive in both the various choices and steady quality.

SIGNATURE DISHES
> King Crab Miso Pot
> Assorted Sushi Platter
> Beef Tofu Pot
> Carbon Roast Eel
> Mixed Tenpura Platter
> Inaniwa Udon Noodles

WINE: There are not many choices of sake and shochu, but they are all good ones. On the sake list there are mainly ginjo and daiginjo. There are also different wines and soft drinks, as well as two kinds of Japanese loose teas.

SERVICE: The restaurant provides warm and friendly service in an efficient and polite way.

1F, 740 HANKOU ROAD, SHANGHAI **TEL:** 021-60800745
地址：上海汉口路740号朗廷扬子精品酒店1楼

RESERVATIONS: Recommended
DRESS CODE: Smart casual
LUNCH HOURS: 11:30 am-14:30 pm
DINNER HOURS: 17:30 pm-22:30 pm
LAST ORDER DINNER: 22:00 pm
WEBSITE: www.langhamhotels.com

VEGETARIAN DISHES: 10+
NO SMOKING SECTION: Yes
CAR VALET: No
CREDIT CARDS: AE, D, J, MC, UP, V
YEAR ESTABLISHED: 2009
PRICE: RMB 200/Person

MAGGIE'S RESTAURANT

♟ 9 ᵀ¶ 9 ♟ 9 ⋈ 9   🖑 🖑 🖑

SETTING: A typical Spanish style building by the Xijiao Hotel, uniquely decorated and with no straight lines, produces an enjoyable visual effect. It is a typical Antoni Gaudi style. Series European furniture gives you a sense of Shanghai in the 1930s.

FOOD: The original dishes made of fresh seasonal ingredients are managed by Mr. Sun Zhaoguo, a veritable kitchen God. Chinese and western food are expertly incorporated. Each dish is a masterpiece. The signature dish sea slug rice with highland barley is very fragrant, and is soft, fresh and sticky. Mist iced abalone made of Australian fresh abalone produces mist after low temperature treatment and tastes delicious. Wine-preserved crab with tofu uses crab and shrimp meat made of seasonal female crab, live shrimp and the self-made flavoring, which is placed at the tofu base and covered with caviar; the taste delightfully lingers on the tongue. Please don't miss the autumn chrysanthemum with wine-preserved crab which uses stewed big female crab matching with aquavit, rice wine and shaddock flesh. It tastes perfect. Try their self-made baked buckwheat tea with enduring fragrance. A healthy drink "Wuliangye" boiled with five kinds of grain crops can invigorate the spleen and stomach.

SIGNATURE DISHES
> Pickled Cucumber
> Spicy smoked fish
> salted crispy-skin chicken
> Braised beef steak
> Roasted cod
> Stewed rice with sea cucumber and fish lips

WINE: Various Chinese distilled spirits and yellow rice wine of Jiangnan, including Chef Sun's private brew, west suburb's ten years special brewed rice wine. Various wines from the world are available here.

SERVICE: Waiters are considerate.

669 HONGGU ROAD, SHANGHAI **TEL:** 021-62957138/62957199
地址： 上海长宁区虹古路669号

RESERVATIONS: Recommended
DRESS CODE: Smart casual
LUNCH HOURS: 11:00 am-15:30 pm
DINNER HOURS: 16:30 pm-21:30 pm
LAST ORDER DINNER: 21:30 pm
WEBSITE: www.xjwh.com

VEGETARIAN DISHES: 10+
NO SMOKING SECTION: Yes
CAR VALET: Yes
CREDIT CARDS: AE, D, J, MC, V
YEAR ESTABLISHED: 2008
PRICE: RMB 400/Person

MAISON DE L'HUI AT SINAN

♨ 9 🍴 8 🍷 8 🎀 9

SETTING: The restaurant neighbors the residences of such celebrities and dignitaries as Sun Yat-sen, Zhou En-lai, Zhang Xueliang, Xue Dubi and Mei Lanfang, and transports guests a peaceful and comfortable place in which to enjoy the delicacies of the world.

FOOD: The restaurant features exquisite Shanghai private home cuisine. The special cold dishes are made up of Vegetarian Bean Curd Rolls, Smoked Fish and Jelly Fish with Golden Squash. The bean curd rolls are small and delicate with a refreshing taste. The smoked fish is sweet and not greasy. The jelly fish has a fine taste and is well complemented by the squash. The soup is Double-boiled Pigeon Sea Cucumber Soup with Monkey Head Mushroom with dried scallops and ham. The sea cucumber is tender and spicy. The double-boiled pigeon and monkey head mushroom are very sapid and nutritious. Braised Tofu with Hairy Crab Roe Cream is made with fresh crab meat and tofu, and well represents the crab culture of Jiangnan. It is also the seasonal dish of autumn. The vegetarian choice is Organic Green Peas Leaf with organic green peas in soup stock. Just boiled for a moment, it is very delicious and the soup has a very pure taste. Yellow Croacker AoZao Soup Noodles is the only soup available in Kunshan.

SIGNATURE DISHES
> Smoked fish fillet
> Vegetarian bean curd rolls
> Jelly fish with golden squash
> Pan-fried supreme beef
> Braised cod fish
> Pan-fried king prawn

WINE: Many kinds of good wines.

SERVICE: It offers formal hotel-style service with supreme soup to a high standard. Generally, the requirements of the guests are met. There is a also special parking service.

59 SINAN ROAD, SHANGHAI **TEL:** 400-820-2028
地址：上海思南路59号

RESERVATIONS: Recommended
DRESS CODE: Smart casual
LUNCH HOURS: 11:00 am-14:00 pm
DINNER HOURS: 17:00 pm-22:00 pm
LAST ORDER DINNER: 21:00 pm
WEBSITE: www.xnggroup.com

VEGETARIAN DISHES: 5-10
NO SMOKING SECTION: Yes
CAR VALET: Yes
CREDIT CARDS: AE, D, J, MC, UP, V
YEAR ESTABLISHED: 2010
PRICE: RMB 500/Person

MAISON POURCEL

 9   9   9   9

SETTING: Halls, rooms and balconies here not only bear a strong historical sense, but also reflect the quintessential elegance of French décor and architecture.

FOOD: Traditional French dishes with a pure taste. Carpaccio of pigs trotters, fresh salad of artichokes, prawn kebab served with Mediterranean vinaigrette. The heavily-seasoned fresh ingredients, thin slices of stuffed breads, the Carpaccio of pigs trotters cut into thin pieces; all of these rich these delicacies are utterly delicious and you will savor every succulent bite. Prawn kebabs beautifully complement the salad. Puree of butternut and chestnut with Boletus mushrooms, cracked hazelnut and bread with comte cheese. The puree of butternut and chestnut is very finely pureed and tastes divine. Boletus mushrooms are spread onto the puree, giving off an enticing aroma. This wonderful soup bears witness to the saying that 'the soup is not for drinking, but for eating'. Pan fried beef fillet on the bone, pan fried French duck liver, braised sliver beet and truffle and puffed potato gnocchi. The beef fillet is medium-rare, so it is very tender. The fried French duck liver is crispy outside and soft inside. If you still have an appetite, you can try the desserts, which are full of signature French artistry.

SIGNATURE DISHES
> led narides de Fore qnw de Cenand
> Cneeyfish tail salad
> Scallops in the sheel tapioca truffle
> Frogs prepcre as Gonjonettcs
> slow toasted codfish

WINE: Since the owner of the restaurant also runs a Jacques chateau, there is a rich collection of wines ranging from medium to top-grade red and white wines. There are also professional bartenders.

SERVICE: The service there is very satisfying and you will be given brief introductions. There are many guests, but the dishes are always served quickly.

---

35 SHANXI ROAD S., SHANGHAI **TEL:** 021-62879777
地址： 上海陕西南路35号楼（近长乐路）

RESERVATIONS: Necessary for Dinner
DRESS CODE: Smart casual
LUNCH HOURS: 11:30 am-14:30 pm
DINNER HOURS: 18:00 pm-22:30 pm
LAST ORDER DINNER: 22:30 pm
WEBSITE: www.maisonpourcel.com

VEGETARIAN DISHES: 1-2
NO SMOKING SECTION: Yes
CAR VALET: Yes
CREDIT CARDS: AE, D, J, MC, UP, V
YEAR ESTABLISHED: 2010
PRICE: RMB 1000/Person

MANCHURIA

SETTING: Floral cloth with a rural flavor covering dining chairs delivers a certain charm. Clever internal design provides a relatively private dining atmosphere for each table.

FOOD: Not a literal interpretation of its title 'Manchuria' mysteriously offers authentic Cantonese, not Northeastern cuisine. Guests should not miss the appetizer Yam in Blueberry Jam, a harmonious combination of yam and sour-sweet blueberry jam. Delicious crisp Black Fungus in vinegar is a new-creation and a healthy dish. Braised Small Yellow Croakers in Rice Wine Sauce shows-off excellent skill in dealing with rice wine whose fresh flavor is also good at working up an appetite. As for hot dishes, Stir Fried Sliced Conch with Tea Tree Mushroom and Green Pepper is remarkably tasty, the fresh and chewy sliced conch combining well with the strong aroma of tree mushrooms. White Jade Chicken Soup requires a highly skilled chef. The somewhat pedestrian turnip has a delicate flavor after seasoning with thick chicken stock. Stir-fried Crab Paste is not quite as good, though 'each to their own'. The menu of additional snacks provides many choices, among which, Walnut Cream and Shaddock Drink with Mango Juice and Milk deserve high praise.

SIGNATURE DISHES
> Daily Soups and Stew soup
> Sliced conch in a scent of abalone
> Stewed Tofu with prawns in abalone sauce
> Snow peas with minced prawns

WINE: There is a wide range of choice, including a selection of wines.

SERVICE: Waiters are warm and attentive.

3F-4F, BLDG 11-12, 889 JULU ROAD, SHANGHAI **TEL:** 021-64458082
地址：上海巨鹿路889号11-12幢3-4楼

RESERVATIONS: Recommended
DRESS CODE: Smart casual
LUNCH HOURS: 11:30 am-14:30 pm
DINNER HOURS: 17:30 pm-22:00 pm
LAST ORDER DINNER: 21:30 pm
WEBSITE: www.FCCshanghai.com

VEGETARIAN DISHES: 5-10
NO SMOKING SECTION: No
CAR VALET: No
CREDIT CARDS: AE, D, J, MC, UP, V
YEAR ESTABLISHED: 2009
PRICE: RMB 400/Person

MANDARIN PAVILION

🍽 8   🍴 8   🍷 8   🎀 8

SETTING: The elegance of Mandarin Pavilion is wholly demonstrated by the huge wooden screen engraved in the word "double blessing".

FOOD: As a signature dish of the cold dishes, Deep-fried Sliced Gluten with Peanuts, Day-lily, Fungi and Mushrooms is not to be missed as the gluten absorbs the vegetable juices after deep-frying and tastes salty yet sweet, delicious and nutritious when mixed with mushrooms with a wonderful mouthful of fragrance. Being a renowned Cantonese dish, Steamed Fresh Spotted Garoupa requires rigid mastering of the cooking time since spotted garoupa is pliable and tough with smooth skin and the dish fails if cooked improperly. The Steamed Fresh Spotted Garoupa served in Mandarin Pavilion is delicate, juicy and chewy. Dim sum in Mandarin Pavilion is fantastic, an unarguable fact that can be proved by the Steamed Buns which taste authentic, with the bigger ones being classified as Small Steamed Buns. Its skin is so thin that the swaying juice inside can be easily seen from outside.

SIGNATURE DISHES
> Marinatel Bencard
> Sauteed river shrimp
> Braised whole ablone in superior oyster sauce
> Live Australian lobster with cheese and butter
> Steamed spotted groupa

WINE: Mandarin Pavilion provides a rich collection of wines ranging from Moutai and Wuliangye Liquor to imported vintage wines.

SERVICE: The waiting staff are insufficient for the number of customers. Waiters often appear helpless even though they strive to maintain every table.

3F, 1225 NANJING ROAD W., SHANGHAI **TEL:** 021-62791888-5301
地址： 上海南京西路1225号3楼

RESERVATIONS: Recommended
DRESS CODE: Smart casual
LUNCH HOURS: 11:30 am-14:00 pm
DINNER HOURS: 17:30 pm-21:30 pm
LAST ORDER DINNER: 21:00 pm
WEBSITE: www.meritus-hotels.com

VEGETARIAN DISHES: 10+
NO SMOKING SECTION: Yes
CAR VALET: No
CREDIT CARDS: AE, D, J, MC, V
YEAR ESTABLISHED: 2004
PRICE: RMB 250/Person

MARDI GRAS

🕯9 🍴9 🍷9 🎀9   🖐 🖐 🖐

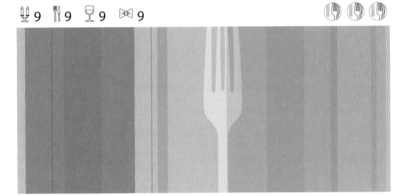

SETTING: An old cream color Spanish villa with a beautiful garden. Nice decoration, quiet and elegant surroundings with a colonial style interior.

FOOD: Start with the seared duck liver, the taste is similar to foie gras. It is cut in to large pieces and seared to a gentle crispiness, but remains tender inside. Caesar salad, with fresh vegetable, sliced avocado and bacon bits is devilishly delicious. However, the thick salad dressing is a little on the heavy side. Fortunately, you can ask for this to be served on the side. The recommended main course is Paella with whole grilled fish served on a big ceramic plate. Waiters will bring and prepare the dish, taking out the fish bones. The rice is a perfect al dente, with the slightest hint of an Asian flavor. As well as the whole fish, the rice is braised with yellow and red pepper. All In all a healthy dish. Another main course is the duck confit, which is not oily as braised duck can be. The meat is exceptionally flavored due to the marinating. Comes with a side dish of olive, potato and tomato.The deserts feature lemon tarte and cheese cake. The tarte is sweat and sour, and the cake creamy with a strong cheese flavor. All deserts are served with sliced fresh fruits. A nice French Asian fusion restaurant.

SIGNATURE DISHES
> Smoked salmon confit
> Onion gratin soup
> Ducker liver with port wine sauce
> Bouillabaisse
> Roasted codfish
> Beer braised veal cheek

WINE: The wine list is well balanced between old and new world and affordable to gorgeous prices.

SERVICE: The service is professional and friendly.

---

372 XINGGUO ROAD, SHANGHAI **TEL:** 021-62807598
地址： 上海兴国路372弄1号

RESERVATIONS: Recommended
DRESS CODE: Smart casual
LUNCH HOURS: 12:00 am-14:30 pm
DINNER HOURS: 18:00 pm-00:00 pm
LAST ORDER DINNER: 22:30 pm
EMAIL: khnemu321@hotmail.com

VEGETARIAN DISHES: 3-5
NO SMOKING SECTION: Yes
CAR VALET: No
CREDIT CARDS: MC, V
YEAR ESTABLISHED: 2009
PRICE: RMB 400/Person

MI TIERRA MEXICAN RESTAURANT & TACO BAR

8 8 8 8

SETTING: The dining area is set in an eclectic acienda Mexicana, with tables in a patio with an elegant, tall roof and glass ceiling. The dark wooden tables are decorated with Aztec calendar engravings.

FOOD: Mi Tierra's menu boasts a traditionally Mexican earthy selection. It features tantalizing appetizers good enough for just one or two, as well as large portions for as many as six. Opening with a classic, the guacamole is freshly made with quality avocado, with the pip for a dash of color, topped with sour cream, and served with crispy nachos and a few spicy dips. The beef coyotas, served as three cute sandwiches filled with plenty of succulent meat, while the tostada de carne asada is like a giant version of the coyotas, with a mountain of tender meat dressed with spices and fresh veggies, sitting on a single tortilla. From the main courses, the costilla de lechon is excellent: pork ribs slowly grilled, served in an elegantly carved pot, and drowned into plenty of green mole. The succulent meat, bursting with flavor, will literally melt in your mouth, with a delectably smooth cocoa aftertaste. Mi Tierra also provides home-delivery services, with a full range of dishes.

SIGNATURE DISHES
> Guacamole con Chips
> Beef Coyotas
> Chicken Flautas
> White Bicentenario Enchiladas
> Costilla de Lechon en Mole Verde

WINE: The list is simply a feast of Latino choices, from a range of Tequilas and Margaritas to the wines. Few options by the glass for the latter, but plenty of liquors, juices and soft drinks.

SERVICE: Mi Tierra's staff is very polite, and even the locals strive hard to communicate in Mexican to add to the overall atmosphere.

17 YONGJIA ROAD, SHANGHAI **TEL:** 021-54655837
地址： 上海永嘉路17号

RESERVATIONS: Recommended
DRESS CODE: Smart casual
LUNCH HOURS: 11:00 am-15:30 pm
DINNER HOURS: 17:00 pm-23:00 pm
LAST ORDER DINNER: 22:30 pm
WEBSITE: www.tierramex.com.cn

VEGETARIAN DISHES: 10+
NO SMOKING SECTION: Yes
CAR VALET: No
CREDIT CARDS: AE, J, MC, V
YEAR ESTABLISHED: 2010
PRICE: RMB 300/Person

M ON THE BUND

♔ 9   ▌9   ♀ 9   ▧ 9   ⦅♩⦆ ⦅♩⦆ ⦅♩⦆

SETTING: The dark wooden floor and the imposing bar counter are balanced out by the open terrace with stunning views over the Bund. Lights are also well dosed, to allow for romantic privacy while enjoying what you are eating.

FOOD: M's menu is surprisingly short for a Shanghai restaurant, but well balanced and selected with a mix of French, North African and international, and every diner can surely find at least a couple of tempting dishes to enjoy. From the starters, the tomato consommé may be a somewhat understated way to start, but its refreshing sour feel, and the touches of dill, all pair well with its soft crab meat. From the mains, the plump turbot fillet comes with crispy capers, colorful boiled veggies, and tangy grapefruit, which all provide for a continuous surprises of different textures and flavor combinations. On the lighter side, the fish in the Provencal stew is incredibly tender, and its buttery but light, intense but delicate sauce will surely force you to dip in more bread than you'd want! The dessert list is very large and absolutely tempting. If the abundant portions of the main courses left any space, definitely indulge yourself with M's lavish Grand Platter, accompanied perhaps with a special Sauternes or any other of the sweet wines suggested.

SIGNATURE DISHES
> Soft crab meat and fresh herbs in a tomato consommé
> Steak tartare
> A Turkish Mege
> M's crispy pig
> Salmon served in the Scandinavian style

WINE: The wine list is hugely comprehensive and reasonably priced.

SERVICE: Service gets close to impeccable at M on the Bund, from the phone reservation to the welcome at the reception desk, all the way to the runners in the hall. Abundant and good-mannered, even in the most crowded moment there will always be somebody ready to serve and coddle you.

7F, 20 GUANGDONG ROAD, SHANGHAI **TEL:** 021-63509988
地址：上海市外滩5号（广东路20号）7楼

RESERVATIONS: Necessary
DRESS CODE: Smart casual
LUNCH HOURS: 11:30 am-14:30 pm
DINNER HOURS: 18:00 pm-22:30 pm
LAST ORDER DINNER: 22:00 pm
WEBSITE: www.m-restaurantgroup.com

VEGETARIAN DISHES: 3-5
NO SMOKING SECTION: Yes
CAR VALET: Yes (18:00-22:30)
CREDIT CARDS: AE, D, J, MC, UP, V
YEAR ESTABLISHED: 1999
PRICE: RMB 400/Person

MOON'S STEAKHOUSE

 8   9   9   9

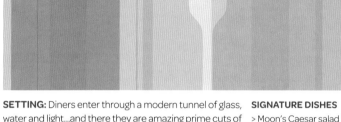

SETTING: Diners enter through a modern tunnel of glass, water and light...and there they are amazing prime cuts of the most appetizing beef maturing before your very eyes in a shiny display fridge.

FOOD: From the starters, Moon's Caesar salad is a modern interpretation of the classic American dish, with huge leaves layered into a small tower, evenly coated with the creamy dressing, and topped with crispy ham bits, large, thin cheese slices, and crunchy croutons.The hardest choice you'll be faced with is between the "standard", mouth-watering Australian Wagyu or Moon's signature meat, slowly dry-aged for 15 days before hitting the grill. Moon's gets quite picky on its cooking styles, with textures ranging from super-rare to the black-grilled "Chicago" style. If you are not eating alone, you can have your steak cut in half for sharing and cooked in two fashions, with two different sauces. We shared a mix of Premium dry-aged ribeye steak and Australian Wagyu striploin, of course cooked to perfection. While we appreciated the tenderness and delicate touch of the striploin, being hard-core meat lovers we did love the intense flavor of its dry-aged counterpart. And everything accompanied by a small mountain of crispy fries.

SIGNATURE DISHES
> Moon's Caesar salad
> Steak tartare
> Cappuccino mushroom soup
> Premium dry aged ribeye steak
> Australian Wagyu striploin
> Black cod "en papillote"

WINE: Featuring mainly vineries from the New World, though quite a few famous names appeared here and there, we found the prices to be very reasonable. An amazing selection of whiskey is also available, together with other liquors.

SERVICE: Gentle and smooth, knowledgeable and ready to be of help, the staff at Moon's really strives to make you feel at home.

1F, 1 YUYUAN ROAD, SHANGHAI **TEL:** 021-63365683
地址： 上海愚园路1号宏安瑞士大酒店1楼

RESERVATIONS: Recommended
DRESS CODE: Smart casual
LUNCH HOURS: 12:00 am-14:30 pm (Monday-Friday)
DINNER HOURS: 17:00 pm-24:00 pm
LAST ORDER DINNER: 23:00 pm
WEBSITE: www.moonsteakhouse.com

VEGETARIAN DISHES: 3-5
NO SMOKING SECTION: Yes
CAR VALET: No
CREDIT CARDS: AE, D, J, MC, V
YEAR ESTABLISHED: 2005
PRICE: RMB 400/Person

MR. & MRS. BUND-MODERN EATERY BY PAUL PAIRET

9 9 9 9

SETTING: This elegant and romantic restaurant is divided into several different dining areas. Ancient pendant lamps, red sofas, and stylish dining tables exert an alluring visual impact on guests.

FOOD: The restaurant menu, artfully depicted as an album of paintings, features an eclectic mix of international fare. The appetizer Tuna Mousse with sliced bread simply steals the show. The smooth and fragrant tuna melts in the mouth with the sliced bread, revealing a wonderful texture. There are many other appetizers for your choice, the oysters from Japan and the United States being a firm favorite, with two flavors that are well worth sampling. There are also Iberian prosciutto, sesame leaf salad, truffle and Paris mushroom and Parma cheeses on offer. The Main courses are varied and wonderful. Besides the Steamed Jumbo Tiger Prawn with Orange and the Boston Lobster, Grilled Bullfrog Leg a delicacy not to be missed. Together with Alliaceous caraway sauce and mild mashed potatoes the dish is an utter delight. Desserts are rich and indulgent, whether you choose French chocolate ice cream, Snow White Lady or Strawberry Cake you will have a perfect end to your meal.

SIGNATURE DISHES
> Foie gras light crumble
> Meuniere bread truffle original
> Picnic chicken ailloli
> Black cod in the bag pp
> Long short rib teriyaki PP(2pax)

WINE: There are more than 250 varieties of wine. Each table is given two wine cards, and customers can use one of the cards to sample wine at an automatic wine machine. The machine has three taps. Guests can then choose the wine they prefer.

SERVICE: With each dish served, waiters will patiently disclose the major ingredients and cooking process, and recommend the right wine.

6F, 18 ZHONGSHAN NO.1 ROAD E., SHANGHAI **TEL:** 021-63239898
地址：上海中山东一路18号6楼（外滩18号）

RESERVATIONS: Recommended
DRESS CODE: Smart casual
LUNCH HOURS: 11:30 am-14:00 pm (Mon-Fri)
DINNER HOURS: 18:30 pm-22:30 pm (Sun-Mon)
18:30 pm-04:00 am (Tue-Sat)
WEBSITE: www.mmbund.com

VEGETARIAN DISHES: 10+
NO SMOKING SECTION: Yes
CAR VALET: Yes
CREDIT CARDS: AE, MC, V
YEAR ESTABLISHED: 2009
PRICE: RMB 600/Person

NADAMAN

8 | 9 | 9 | 8

SETTING: Located on the second floor of Pudong Shangri-La, Nadaman is a chain restaurant of Nadaman Restaurant (a top-grade restaurant in Japan with a history of 180 years) in Shanghai. Adopting the same décor and design concepts as that of its headquarters, Nadaman features an affinity for natural water, stone and wood and creates an ambience of Zen.

FOOD: Honda Masami, a distinguished chef from Japan with 43 years of cooking experience who has won a number of awards during his 28 years of service in Nadaman, has headed Shanghai Nadaman's drive to successfully provide such exquisitely cooked dishes as top-level kaiseki, sushi, roasted dishes, tempura and fresh sashimi. Nadaman provides a wide array of menu choices, like the sushi set meal, seasonal kaiseki set meal, and Japanese cattle hot pot. With every dish being cooked innovatively by combining and complementing aspects such as color, fragrance, appearance and flavor, the cuisine leads gourmets to endless taste sensations. Tuna TORO and Japanese Cattle Hot Pot are highly recommended.

SIGNATURE DISHES
> Daily chef's assortment of appetizers
> Steamed egg custard mix with paste foie gras
> Deluxe assortment of sushi
> Teriyaki Hokkaido kink fish
> Onigara-yaki boiled lobster

WINE: Top-grade sakes can be seen on the wine list, particularly when there are sake promotions. Iichiko and plum wines of all kinds are available.

SERVICE: Waiters here are modest and professional in general. However, there is a definite sense of being haughty to Chinese while courteous to Japanese.

2F, 33 FUCHENG ROAD, SHANGHAI **TEL:** 021-68828888-260
地址： 上海浦东富城路33号上海浦东香格里拉大酒店紫金楼2层

RESERVATIONS: Recommended
DRESS CODE: Smart casual
LUNCH HOURS: 12:00 am-14:30 pm
DINNER HOURS: 18:00 pm-22:30 pm
LAST ORDER DINNER: 22:15 pm
WEBSITE: www.shangri-la.com

VEGETARIAN DISHES: 10+
NO SMOKING SECTION: Yes
CAR VALET: Yes (7:00-23:30)
CREDIT CARDS: AE, D, J, MC, UP, V
YEAR ESTABLISHED: 2005
PRICE: RMB 600/Person

NEW HEIGHTS

♨ 8   🍴 8   🍷 8   🎀 8

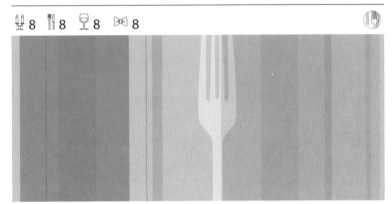

SETTING: The dark wooden-plank floor and low ceiling are balanced out by natural light on two sides and mesmerizing views over the Bund and across the Huangpu river.

FOOD: The menu therefore boasts plenty of starters, salads, side dishes and desserts. Southeast as well as vegetarian delicacies are available too, and well characterize the fusion theme of this venue. And at lunchtime, a special set of 2 dishes of your choice is also available for just 148+ RMB.Starting on an Oriental food, the salmon and seaweed terrine has a cute pinkish note to it, and is smooth with a crunchy broccoli silhouette as its centerpiece. Best enjoyed with its wasabi mayonnaise and crispy salad. The red snapper is tenderly pan-fried, plump and juicy, and topped with plenty of colorful seaweed, and rests on a sweet bed of apple-curry sauce and red peppers.To close with finesse, try the apple crumble: served in a white ramequin to preserve its warmth; it will tantalize you layer after layer with its different textures, and please your palate with its intense yet delicate nuances of cinnamon. Melt into it while digging into the vanilla ice-cream and biting on the crunchy apple crisp that comes with it.

SIGNATURE DISHES
> Crispy tiger prawn rolled
> Minute marinated king fish
> Pear salad with blue cheese and pecan nuts
> Veal tenderloin
> Roasted lamb saddle
> Roasted half lobster

WINE: As opposed to most of the Bund's establishments, the carte of wines is not offering only expensive champagnes and unreachable chateaux; quite the opposite, indeed, as the list features mainly New World choices.

SERVICE: Professional and friendly, from the phone reservation all the way to the runners in the hall. Abundant and quite good-mannered.

7F, 3 ZHONG SHANG NO.1 ROAD E., SHANGHAI **TEL:** 021-63210909
地址：上海中山东一路3号7楼

RESERVATIONS: Recommended
DRESS CODE: Smart casual
LUNCH HOURS: 11:30 am-14:30 pm
DINNER HOURS: 18:00 pm-23:00 pm (Fri-Sat)
LAST ORDER DINNER: 22:00 pm
WEBSITE: www.threeonthebund.com

VEGETARIAN DISHES: 3-5
NO SMOKING SECTION: Yes
CAR VALET: Yes
CREDIT CARDS: AE, D, J, MC, V
YEAR ESTABLISHED: 2008
PRICE: RMB 400/Person

NINA SPICY CUISINE

🍴 8   🍽 8   🍷 8   🎀 9

SETTING: You'll find large, comfortable seats and cozy, romantic lighting. With a plush atmosphere and tranquil melodies, it's a restaurant of fine, personalized calm.

FOOD: Authentic Sichuan cuisine is hot on the menu. Sliced beef and ox tongue in chili sauce has heaps of ox head skin and tastes delightfully crispy, with quite a bang. The beautiful Xishi's corn, a round two-layer dish made of corn and mashed green soy bean, is light and refreshing after some of the spicier dishes. The hot dishes are also exceptional. The irresistibly tasty bullfrog is cooked to order, so the meat is delectably tender; besides the cayenne pepper, the seasoning uses red and green pepper, with the key lying in the sauté spices and red oil. Prawns with Green Mustard use wasabi and are supple to the bite but don't stick to the teeth. Connoisseur's favorite Pork Steak is four steamed ribs wrapped with paper to preserve the moisture and really bring out the flavor, then fried covered with breadcrumbs. They're only RMB 68 Yuan, and well worth it. Flash-Fried Broad Beans taste are very crisp, and have a flavor of green prickly ash (from which Sichuan pepper is made). Stir-Fried Fat Beef with hot green pepper is cooked on a stone plate, and is also bursting with green prickly ash.

SIGNATURE DISHES

> The beauty Xishi's corn
> Sliced beef and ox tongue in chilli sauce
> Tasty chicken cooked in a pot
> Stewed the Yangtze River fish
> Irresistable tasty bullfrog
> Prawn with green mustard

WINE: Offers a wide choice of wines of low, intermediate, and high grades. The wine list is wine-bottle-shaped, which is very novel. The featured black tartary buckwheat tea of the Restaurant is very popular among guests.

SERVICE: Waiters offer a relatively standard service. They answer all questions with a smile.

1F, 227 HUANGPI ROAD N., SHANGHAI **TEL:** 021-63758598
地址： 上海黄陂北路227号中区广场1楼

RESERVATIONS: Recommended
DRESS CODE: Smart casual
LUNCH HOURS: 11:00 am-14:00 pm
DINNER HOURS: 17:00 pm-22:00 pm
LAST ORDER DINNER: 21:30 pm
WEBSITE: www.ninaspicy.com

VEGETARIAN DISHES: 10+
NO SMOKING SECTION: Yes
CAR VALET: No
CREDIT CARDS: MC, V
YEAR ESTABLISHED: 2005
PRICE: RMB 100/Person

NOBLE HOUSE RESTAURANT

♟ 9 ❚❙ 9 ♟ 9 ⋈ 9   (Ⅱ) (Ⅱ) (Ⅱ)

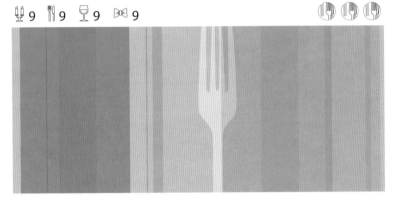

SETTING: The Restaurant is located at the fashionable, recently reconstructed club house of the famous Dr. Shen's old residence built in 1885 beside the busy Century Road. The green space along the road and the garden of the club house boasts a quiet dining area. Guests will experience the old Shanghai.

FOOD: The restaurant specializes in classic Shanghai and Guangdong Cuisines, such as sea cucumber with shark fin, abalone and crab. The starter dishes are tasty and refreshing. The skin of salted chicken Noble House style is crisp and the meat is tender. The chicken is all locally sourced. Deep-fried baby yellow croaker (frog) is a good cold dish. They are cooked well and preserve the natural flavor. The signature dish superior braised shark's fin with crab meat and roe is a delicacy of the restaurant and is also a seasonal dish. It tastes fantastic and it is just the right amount. Crab with fresh shark's fin and sticky rice, sautéed crab roe in pumpkin, crab cream and vinegar crab are all good choices. The snacks include is pan-fried dumplings filled with crab meat. They are fried well and are neither oily nor fatty but very delicious.

SIGNATURE DISHES
> Deep-fried baby yellow croaker
> Salted chicken Noble House style
> Superior braised shark's fin with crab meat and roe
> Sautéed crab meat and roe

WINE: Features high grade rice wines and spirits and grape wines from the new world. Small and large Chateau Lafites bottles are offered.

SERVICE: It can provide hotel level service. All waiters are hardworking and considerate.

679 SHANGCHENG ROAD, SHANGHAI **TEL:** 021-58793179
地址： 上海浦东新区商城路679号

RESERVATIONS: Necessary for Dinner
DRESS CODE: Smart casual
LUNCH HOURS: 11:00 am-14:00 pm
DINNER HOURS: 17:00 pm-22:00 pm
LAST ORDER DINNER: 21:30 pm
WEBSITE: www. noblehouserestaurant.cn

VEGETARIAN DISHES: 10+
NO SMOKING SECTION: Yes
CAR VALET: Yes
CREDIT CARDS: AE, D, J, MC, V
YEAR ESTABLISHED: 2003
PRICE: RMB 500-800/Person

NOBLE SEAFOOD RESTAURANT

 9   9   9   9

SETTING: Designed by world famous architect Leoh Ming Pei, Noble (Pudong) delivers an 18th Century European palace atmosphere.

FOOD: The restaurant features high-end Cantonese cuisine and seafood. The taste of caviar, which is among the top three delicacies in the world, is exercised to the full. French Caviar, a special of Noble is a premier art. The taste of Oyster in Red caviar, and Shrimp In Caviar with Yellow Mustard is unforgettable. As for the main courses, Japanese roasted beef with Italian Fried Vegetable uses extremely tender beef. What's more, special sauce is absorbed into every particle of each slice of beef. Tea-flavored Beef, a cold dish among Noble specials is stewed in black tea, boasting the aroma of black tea and beef and works well as an appetizer. Drunken Chicken with Rice Wine is cooked with home-raised chicken and superior rice wine. With bones removed, it has smooth skin and tender meat, giving out a strong pleasing aroma. Stewed Assorted Seafood and Fowls (Fotiaoqiang), Noble's trump card made with a secret recipe, is a superior soup stewed for several hours with abalone, ginseng, shark fin, fish maw, premier scallop and Jinhua Ham. The soup is thick in flavor with a pleasing aroma.

SIGNATURE DISHES
>Soft Pan-fried goose's liver
> Braised sea cucumber in brown sauce
> Squilla with spicy salt

WINE: Lots of choices, including traditional spirits, rice wine and Chinese wine, as well as wine from famous international wineries.

SERVICE: Service personnel are considerate and polite. Guests feel well looked after.

1600 CENTURY AVENUE, SHANGHAI **TEL:** 021-58207777
地址：上海市浦东世纪大道1600号（浦电路交界）

RESERVATIONS: Recommended
DRESS CODE: Smart casual
LUNCH HOURS: 11:30 am-14:30 pm
DINNER HOURS: 17:30 pm-22:00 pm
LAST ORDER DINNER: 22:00 pm
WEBSITE: www.shnoble.com

VEGETARIAN DISHES: 10+
NO SMOKING SECTION: Yes
CAR VALET: No
CREDIT CARDS: AE, D, J, MC, UP, V
YEAR ESTABLISHED: 2006
PRICE: RMB 500/Person

NOBLE SEAFOOD RESTAURANT

♟9 ᵼᵼ9 ♟9 ⋈9

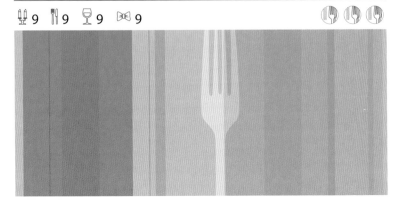

SETTING: The decoration, in a luxury palace design and Shanghai style, is magnificent, and the fantastic artworks reveal the true luxury of Minghao.

FOOD: Minghao is committed to popularizing innovative Cantonese cuisine. In addition to having an experienced Guangdong chef, there are a number of chefs specializing in Western cuisine. Stewed sea cucumber, one of the specialties of Minghao, can't but have a delightful taste. The greasy, fragrant and thick sea cucumber lingers on the palate. Its characteristics are that the normally dry sea cucumber is suffused with juice. With added deep fried shredded green onion and shrimps, the sea cucumber tastes even more delicious. The most innovative feature is that dishes are arranged in the form of a Chinese painting: one distant and the other close; one white and the other is black, which makes the dish profound. Minghao Noble Shrimps (also known as the Mantis Shrimps) are twice as large as the more common variety. Not only is their meat plump but the added pepper salt is delicious. Stewed Shark's Fin in Brown Sauce, one of the specialties, comes in many styles. All the dishes are cooked with broth on a low heat, so each one has thick soup and strong taste.

SIGNATURE DISHES
> Superior Braised Shark's Fin With Crab Meat And Roe
> Braised Live Australian Abalone In Chicken Soup

WINE: There are many beverage choices. Not only traditional alcohol, yellow wine and Chinese wine but also wine from famous overseas chateaus is served here.

SERVICE: The waiters here are thoughtful and urbane. The service is standard from ordering to serving. The service quality can be up to that of star-rated hotels.

3883 HONGMEI ROAD N., SHANGHAI **TEL:** 021-62625555
地址： 上海长宁区虹梅北路3883号

RESERVATIONS: Recommended
DRESS CODE: Smart casual
LUNCH HOURS: 11:00 am-14:00 pm
DINNER HOURS: 16:00 pm-23:30 pm
LAST ORDER DINNER: 23:00 pm
WEBSITE: www.shnoble.com

VEGETARIAN DISHES: 10+
NO SMOKING SECTION: No
CAR VALET: Yes
CREDIT CARDS: AE, D, J, MC, V
YEAR ESTABLISHED: 2002
PRICE: RMB 500/Person

PALLADIO

🍴 8   🍴 9   🍷 9   🎀 9   (👐) (👐) (👐)

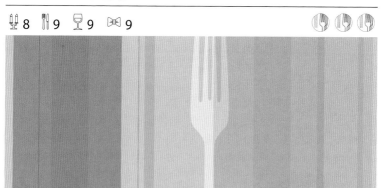

SETTING: Being dignified and elegant, with soft mood lighting and mild music, this Italian restaurant is quite suitable for lovers or gatherings of friends.

FOOD: If the ever-updating menu in Palladio appears to be overwhelming, why not make a lazy choice and order a set meal? Even separate orders ranging from appetizers to grape wines can be matched perfectly with the help of waiters or chefs who always love to help. Despite the fact that the dishes provided in the restaurant differs from that in Italy, Palladio still succeeds in making all its dishes taste authentic, and can be recognized as the best in Shanghai. Frozen Corn Soup with Crab Meat Salad and Potato Sherbet, an original dish that is in the shape of a flower basket with vegetables forming a circle, egg crisp cake as the handle and freshly sweet crab meat stuffing inside, and is embellished with dill, basil and celery leaves, tastes quite unique with the potato sherbet cast upon it having a special, slightly spicy flavor. Banana Scallops and Goose Liver are of sufficient quantity, with the goose liver melting in the mouth instantly and tasting fatty yet not greasy, with the scallops tasting freshly sweet. As to dessert, the first recommendation is Tiramisu, which is of fine quality, delicate style and wonderful flavor.

SIGNATURE DISHES

> Parmesan Cheese cream brucee
> Foie Gras Terrine
> Linguine with clams & eucchini
> Two ways of cod
> Striocoin grilced

WINE: Palladio provides a rich collection of wines including expensive wines from Italy and France together with vintage wines.

SERVICE: Waiters here have a good attitude and are hospitable when inquiring about dishes.

1F, 1376NANJING ROAD W., SHANGHAI **TEL:** 021-62797188
地址： 上海南京西路1376号上海商城1楼

RESERVATIONS: Recommended
DRESS CODE: Smart casual
LUNCH HOURS: 11:30 am-14:30 pm
DINNER HOURS: 17:30 pm-22:30 pm
LAST ORDER DINNER: 22:30 pm
WEBSITE: www.ritzcarlton.com

VEGETARIAN DISHES: 3-5
NO SMOKING SECTION: Yes
CAR VALET: No
CREDIT CARDS: AE, D, J, MC, V
YEAR ESTABLISHED: 1998
PRICE: RMB 400/Person

PARADISE GARDEN

🍴 8   🍴 8   🍷 9   🍽 9

SETTING: The restaurant combines Chinese and post-modern styles, with harmonious red and golden colours, creating a great dining atmosphere.

FOOD: The Paradise Garden embodies a modern fusion dining concept, offering classic Shanghai and Cantonese cuisine, and select delicacies from Jiangsu, Cantonese dim sum and Northern cuisine. The cold dishes come as a platter. Pan Fired local Pomfret in Brown Sauce has a wonderfully fragrant sauce and the fish is very succulent. The Marinated Pumpkin with Caramel is stewed before being sprinkled with caramel on the pumpkin strips. With the marinated Yellow Squash with Seaweed in Vinegar is heavily marinated and crispy. The unique and delicious Pan Fried Fillet of Wayu Beef with Black Fungus in Red Wine Sauce is sprayed with red wine and sprinkled with black fungus on the fried Wayu beef, which leaves it very tender and with a delightful fragrance and taste of red wine. Morel and Deep-sea Conch Stew is both delicious and healthy. Deep Fried Glutinous Dumplings with Fruits are unique, with papaya, and well worth a try. Also, the sweetened Almond Ice Cream is rich in the flavors of Beijing.

SIGNATURE DISHES
> Pan fired pomfret
> Sauteed River shrimps
> House Specialty Juicy Steamed Pork Dumplings
> Pan Fried Fillet of Wayu Beef with Black Fungus in Red Wine Sauce

WINE: Both France for Old World and Australia for New World provide vintage wines. Imported wines include XO and Brando Super Red Bordeaux, which is the house wine.

SERVICE: Paradise Garden provides sure and steady hotel-style service. The waiters are always ready to help. Waiters offer napkin-cushioned plates for customers to put their phones on, which is a nice touch.

6F, 88 CENTURY BOULEVARD, SHANGHAI **TEL:** 021-50477773
地址： 上海浦东世纪大道88号金茂大厦裙房6层

RESERVATIONS: Recommended
DRESS CODE: Smart casual
LUNCH HOURS: 11:00 am-16:00 pm
DINNER HOURS: 17:30 pm-23:00 pm
LAST ORDER DINNER: 22:45 pm
WEBSITE: www.Jade388.com

VEGETARIAN DISHES: 10+
NO SMOKING SECTION: Yes
CAR VALET: Yes
CREDIT CARDS: AE, D, J, MC, V
YEAR ESTABLISHED: 2005
PRICE: RMB 300/Person

PELHAM'S

🍴 9　🍴 9　🍷 9　🎴 9

🖐 🖐 🖐

SETTING: Located at No.2 on the Bund, the Waldorf Astoria Club occupies the same spot as the former Shanghai Club, which was an exclusive club originally built in 1910. Today this neo-classic architectural gem has been meticulously restored with the assistance of archival photographs and historic records.

FOOD: New York cuisine is typically innovative and devilishly indulgent. The waiters serve champagne and a snack of fresh Citrus Cured Salmon Toro and sweet eggplant with miso before the meal. Pelham's offers cold and hot starters for your choice, the tender Slow Braised Octopus with Italian bread salad and olive and vanilla salad being the stand out option, served with a matching US Chardonnay. The prime hot starter dish is Crisp Pork Belly with potato mash beneath two portions of streaky pork and apple sauce. The streaky pork is more tender and crisp than Chinese styled streaky pork. The main course of Olive Oil Poached Halibut is served with a green lemon sauce that goes great when dipped in bread. Another main dish is Wagyu NY Strip, using the finest Australian Wagyu Beef. It is served with beetroot, Garbanzo Bean and Garbanzo bean sauce. The dessert of chocolate cake and Bailey ice cream is a super finish to the meal.

SIGNATURE DISHES
> Wagyu Steak Tartare "a la Reuben"
> Slow Braised Octopus
> Lamb with "Moroccan Flavors"

WINE: Middle and high grade wines of both the old and new worlds are offered. The wines can be matched to dishes by sommelier.

SERVICE: The waiters are warm-hearted and considerate. The waiters possess a wide knowledge of the food and beverages.

NO.2 ZHONG SHAN DONG YI ROAD, SHANGHAI TEL: 021-63229988
地址： 上海中山东一路2号上海外滩华尔道夫酒店1楼

RESERVATIONS: Necessary for Dinner
DRESS CODE: Smart casual
LUNCH HOURS: 11:30 am-14:30 pm
DINNER HOURS: 18:00 pm-23:00 pm
LAST ORDER DINNER: 22:45 pm
WEBSITE: www.waldorfastoriashanghai.com

VEGETARIAN DISHES: 1-2
NO SMOKING SECTION: Yes
CAR VALET: No
CREDIT CARDS: AE, D, J, MC, UP, V
YEAR ESTABLISHED: 2010
PRICE: RMB 800/Person

PIN CHUAN

♨8 🍴8 🍷8 🎀8   🖐🖐

SETTING: This charming restaurant at Plaza 66 instantly sows a seed of warm comfort in your mind, and once you delve into the spicy dishes that seed of contentment takes root and gently sprouts.

FOOD: First, let's talk about the signature dish of the restaurant, Braised Abalone with Rice Cakes. Rice Cakes famous from big streets to small alleys as a delicacy that is thick, heavy and glutinous. The sauce and seasonings are spicy and crisp, which creates produces a growing feeling of warmth in your mouth. But the highlight of the dish lies in the abalone, which, after being halved and cooked in a heavy sauce and seasonings tastes, is swollen with sweet flavors. Totally wonderful! Green Crab and Bean Curd Soup boasts a rich texture, while the cucumber and apricot mushroom offer an exquisite counterbalance of flavor to the green crab and bean curd. The green crab mixed with egg yolk is sweet and tender, while the bean curd, not cooked in the style of Benbang cuisine, offsets the strong fishy smell and tastes wonderful, without diminishing the green crab. The Shredded Beef with Chillies & Onions in Oil with Hot Stones well deserves a mention. The beef is flash-fried in the glass bowl with very hot oil, brilliantly unleashing an array of flavors.

SIGNATURE DISHES
> Belly pork slices
> Mouth watering chicken
> Traditional Sichuan cold cuts
> Shredded beef with chilies & onions with hot stone
> Cod fish (sour soup style)
> Baby Tiger Prawns with Chillies

WINE: The restaurant has a complete range of alcohols and yellow wines, and grape wine is abundant. The tea selection is also excellent.

SERVICE: The service here is warm and considerate. Waiters serve you promptly and with a smile, and maintain a good distance that makes you feel more relaxed and comfortable.

5F, 1266 NANJING ROAD W., SHANGHAI **TEL:** 021-62888897
地址： 上海静安区南京西路1266号恒隆广场5楼

RESERVATIONS: Recommended
DRESS CODE: Smart casual
LUNCH HOURS: 10:00 am-17:30 pm
DINNER HOURS: 17:30 pm-22:00 pm
LAST ORDER DINNER: 21:30 pm
WEBSITE: www.pinchuan-china.com

VEGETARIAN DISHES: 10+
NO SMOKING SECTION: Yes
CAR VALET: Yes
CREDIT CARDS: AE, D, J, MC, UP, V
YEAR ESTABLISHED: 2010
PRICE: RMB 150/Person

PREGO ITALIAN RESTAURANT

♨ 8   🍴 9   🍷 9   🎀 9

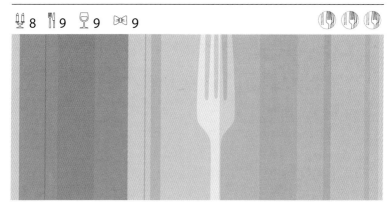

SETTING: The fine-dining touch is mellowed by the casual atmosphere, but the long aisle-space occupied by the restaurant still offers plenty of private alcoves for romantic evenings.

FOOD: A starter for absolute beginners as well as the seasoned diner, the abundant Antipasto Prego is an amazing concoction of bite portions for all palates, ranging from seafood to meat, veggies and cheese. If you'd rather stick to seafood, try the soup; mildly intense and generously topped with shrimps and clams alike. Prego's pasta menu features plenty of classics as well as original recipes, but it also leaves free flow to one's fantasy with its separate lists of pasta shapes and sauces, to be paired according to one's caprice. Back to seafood and from the main courses, the mixed grill is simply amazing, featuring all of sea's best including half lobster, tuna, salmon, sword fish and others, paired with colorful veggies and baked potatoes, and served with a pesto-oil dressing. Most important, definitely leave some space for dessert! The choice ranges from modern, melt-in-the-mouth creations to Prego's classic Tiramisu; and to finish in grandeur, do not forget the classic Espresso, perhaps "cut" with a dash of Italian grappa.

SIGNATURE DISHES
> Tangy crab meat
> Insalata Caprese
> Affettati Misti
> Pappardelle all herbs
> T-bone steak
> Sea bass fillet

WINE: Its choices are well selected, covering a bit of the whole world. Definitely worth noting is the large selections of champagnes and wines by the glass, as well as the "degustation" set.

SERVICE: The staff here definitely puts you at ease and makes you feel at home with their very sociable attitude. Never be afraid to ask for the extra mile at Prego!

2F, 88 HENAN ROAD M., SHANGHAI **TEL:** 021-63351888-7360
地址：上海河南中路88号威斯汀大饭店2楼

RESERVATIONS: Recommended
DRESS CODE: Smart casual
LUNCH HOURS: 11:00 am-14:30 pm
DINNER HOURS: 18:00 pm-22:30 pm
LAST ORDER DINNER: 22:20 pm
WEBSITE: www.westin.com/shanghai

VEGETARIAN DISHES: 5-10
NO SMOKING SECTION: Yes
CAR VALET: No
CREDIT CARDS: AE, D, J, MC, UP, V
YEAR ESTABLISHED: 2002
PRICE: RMB 350/Person

RESTAURANT MARTIN

♨ 9 🍴 9 🍷 9 🎀 9

SETTING: Found at the French styled 1920s building in Xujiahui Park, the Baidai Gramophone Company now resonates with the vibrant tunes and tastes of Flamenca. The dining atmosphere is comfortable and chic.

FOOD: Martin Berasategui, the famous three-star Michelin chef hailing from Spain, is renowned as a creator of astonishing taste, color and fragrance. As one of the prominent attractions in San Sebastián, Spain, he incorporates a sense of aesthetics into the culinary art, and has widely influenced world cuisine. Martin uses a huge varierty ingredients to create beautiful colors and luxurious tastes. His colorful creation of dishes, like vivid fireworks, fascinates and entices guests. Warm poached egg is the best appetizer and a must try, but make sure not to miss the succulent Iberian Ham. The meat is a dazzling red with a beautiful marble pattern and tastes wonderful with a lingering, divine fragrance. Roast suckling pig and Spanish seafood paella are main course signature dishes and should not be missed. The skin is crisp and the meat tender with a full, rich flavor.

SIGNATURE DISHES

> Peach gazpacho with tomato bread and Iberian ham
> Iberian ham
> Spanish seafood paella
> Roasted suckling pig
> Spanish red head prawn

WINE: The wine list is very rich and features high quality Spanish vintages.

SERVICE: Very professional waiters are keen and efficient. They are warm-hearted and polite.

811 HENGSHAN ROAD, SHANGHAI **TEL:** 021-64316639

地址： 上海衡山路811号，靠近余庆路（徐家汇公园内）

RESERVATIONS: Recommended
DRESS CODE: Smart casual
LUNCH HOURS: 11:30 am-14:30 pm
DINNER HOURS: 18:30 pm-22:30 pm
LAST ORDER DINNER: 22:30 pm
WEBSITE: www.restaurantmartin.com.cn

VEGETARIAN DISHES: 5-10
NO SMOKING SECTION: Yes
CAR VALET: Yes
CREDIT CARDS: AE, D, J, MC, UP, V
YEAR ESTABLISHED: 2009
PRICE: RMB 500/Person

ROOSEVELT PRIME STEAKHOUSE

🍴 9   🍴 9   🍷 9   🎀 9

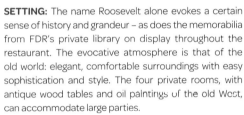

SETTING: The name Roosevelt alone evokes a certain sense of history and grandeur – as does the memorabilia from FDR's private library on display throughout the restaurant. The evocative atmosphere is that of the old world: elegant, comfortable surroundings with easy sophistication and style. The four private rooms, with antique wood tables and oil paintings of the old West, can accommodate large parties.

FOOD: Roosevelt serves classic, yet first-rate, steakhouse steaks – big, thick cuts that are at least 16 ozs (448g). Diners can choose carious cuts from tender filet mignon, flavorful New York Strip, marbled bone-in ribeye or a real and sublime Prime and aged Porterhouse. For lighter fare, the kitchen also serves many steakhouse favorites such as grilled salmon steaks, juicy roast chicken, or whole roasted sea bass. Pair that with any of the creative starters, such as the Tuna Tartar, or the classic Caesar Salad prepared fresh at the tableside. And if you somehow still find room, and you know you'll want to when you see the selection, finish with one of Roosevelt's homemade desserts. This is honest, delicious dining with superior ingredients you won't find anywhere else in China.

SIGNATURE DISHES
> Caesar Salad
> Tuna Tartar
> Shrimp Two Way
> Bone – In Ribeye
> Bone – In Filet
> Porterhouse

WINE: The backlit bar serves some of the best martinis in town, along with a wide selection of single malt scotches, cognacs and ports, and the wine list features both Old World gems and California cult wines found nowhere else in China.

SERVICE: Staff are friendly, have genuine smiles, and are at the ready to accommodate requests.

160 TAIYUAN ROAD, SHANGHAI **TEL:** 021-64338240
地址： 上海太原路160号

RESERVATIONS: Necessary
DRESS CODE: Smart casual
LUNCH HOURS: No
DINNER HOURS: 17:30 pm-23:00 pm
LAST ORDER DINNER: 22:30 pm
WEBSITE: www.rooseveltsteakhouse.com

VEGETARIAN DISHES: 1-2
NO SMOKING SECTION: Yes
CAR VALET: No
CREDIT CARDS: AE, D, J, MC, V
YEAR ESTABLISHED: 2007
PRICE: RMB 500/Person

SAM'S RESTAURANT

8   8   8   8

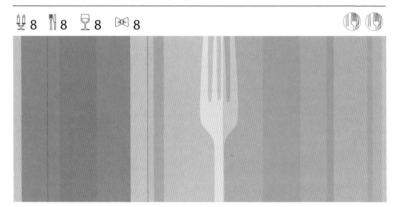

SETTING: Among the four or five restaurants along North Chaling Road, you will catch sight of a restaurant veritably glowing in lush green, instantly making you feel cool on a hot summer day.

FOOD: The restaurant specializes in local cuisine, while it also has a wonderful selection of Guangdong cuisine. Shoulder of Pork in Jelly, similar to Salt Peter Pork, is succulent, though the jelly is limited. Bitter Melon & Pear topped with Blueberry is a famous seasonal dish with blueberry sauce that eases the bitterness of the melon and adds sweetness. It also has small pear blocks that are the main ingredient of the dish. Stir Fried Kidney with Black Pepper is juicy and tender and the pepper increases the fragrance of the dish. In the hot dishes, Panfried Pomfret with Honey Sauce is aromatic and delicious and enhanced by lightly frying it. After being diced, cooked and arranged in the shape of a fish, the dish looks very becomes appetizing. Beef Short Rib with Black Pepper tastes fresh and is delicious when mixed with the black pepper. The courses are all of the highest quality. Braised Sea Cucumber with Spring Onion is the signature dish of the restaurant and a must try.

SIGNATURE DISHES
> Shoulder of Pork in Jelly
> Panfried Pomfret
> Bitter Melon & Pear top with Blueberry
> stir Fried kidney
> Beef Short Rib
> Braised Sea Cucumber

WINE: The restaurant stocks a wide variety of wine and the owner specializes in Italian wines of varying quality and all of good value for money.

SERVICE: The service is thoughtful and efficient.

10 CHALING ROAD N., SHANGHAI **TEL:** 021-64047300
地址：上海茶陵北路10号

RESERVATIONS: Recommended
DRESS CODE: Smart casual
LUNCH HOURS: 11:00 am-14:00 pm
DINNER HOURS: 17:00 pm-22:00 pm
LAST ORDER DINNER: 22:00 pm
EMAIL: liangxuan9@gmail.com

VEGETARIAN DISHES: 10+
NO SMOKING SECTION: Yes
CAR VALET: No
CREDIT CARDS: AE, D, J, MC, V
YEAR ESTABLISHED: 2007
PRICE: RMB 100/Person

SAZANKA TEPPANYAKI

🍴 9 🍴 9 🍷 8 🎀 9

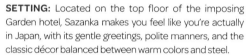

SETTING: Located on the top floor of the imposing Garden hotel, Sazanka makes you feel like you're actually in Japan, with its gentle greetings, polite manners, and the classic décor balanced between warm colors and steel.

FOOD: Sazanka's menu is classic, with a-la-carte choices of meat, seafood, and veggies, and plenty of set menus from 498 to over 2,000 RMB per head. The set-menus mainly have different combinations of either meat or seafood or both, and various origins including Australia and, of course, Japan. Try the highly-prized matsutake mushrooms when in season. Attention to detail is paramount, and your teppan's chef will work on one ingredient at a time, with dedicated sauces paired to perfection to ensure each side is well colored, and each piece tastefully arranged, and surprising you occasionally with a sudden "flambé!" of scorching, fragrant flames. Definitely try the Wagyu beef – either fillet or sirloin according to whether you prefer amazing tenderness or a more intense flavor – seared to perfection and great savored straight or in your favorite dip. The beef consommé with truffle bits is amazing too, with its beautiful cognac color and intense aroma.

SIGNATURE DISHES
> Sauteed goose liver
> Sashimi plate
> Original consommé
> Wagyu beef filet or sirloin
> Fresh Australian abalone
> Lobster

WINE: Hosting by a wide range of vineries and sophisticated vintages, with reds mainly from France's most famous chateaux, the list is a little paradise for wine lovers.

SERVICE: Extremely attentive while non intrusive, with literally plenty of staff attending to each diner.

33F, 58 MAOMING ROAD S., SHANGHAI **TEL:** 021-64151111-5211
地址： 上海茂名南路58号花园饭店33楼

RESERVATIONS: Recommended
DRESS CODE: Smart casual
LUNCH HOURS: 11:30 am-14:30 pm
DINNER HOURS: 17:30 pm-22:30 pm
LAST ORDER DINNER: 22:30 pm
WEBSITE: www.gardenhotelshanghai.com

VEGETARIAN DISHES: 5-10
NO SMOKING SECTION: Yes
CAR VALET: No
CREDIT CARDS: AE, D, J, MC, UP, V
YEAR ESTABLISHED: 1990
PRICE: RMB 500/Person

SCENA

🕯8 🍴9 🍷9 🎀9

SETTING: A vast, high-ceilinged dining room of creams and shining beige hues, with a open show kitchen and jaw-dropping views of the Pearl Tower, Lujiazui and the Bund.

FOOD: Traditional Italian dishes, ranging from pizzas to seafood and steaks, made with outstandingly fresh ingredients. The kitchen produces each dish flawlessly, from preparation to plating. The smoked scallop with tomato caviar features three scallops with a seared outside surrounding a barely cooked, beautifully tender interior. They're utterly delectable on a small bed of fragrant fennel and celeriac. Angus beef tenderloin carpaccio comes in a pungent, delicious dressing of lemon olive oil with smoked salt. The wild mushroom and asparagus risotto is terrific—cooked to a creamy luscious texture in the way risotto was meant to be, but so rarely is; it's unctuous and loaded with fresh mushrooms and truffle oil galore. A sprinkling of micro sprouts add a bright subtle freshness. The angus beef tenderloin is a generous portion cooked to your own idea of perfection, with a luxurious foie gras sauce and tender potato slices.

SIGNATURE DISHES
> Vitello Tonnato
> Beef tenderloin carpaceio
> Smoked scallops
> Pumpkin panzotti pasta
> Pan froed turbot
> Slow roasted pork belly

WINE: Travel the globe on this wine list of New and Old labels in a range of vintages, all organized by taste such as "deliciously fruity white" or "bold and juicy red".

SERVICE: The Ritz-Carlton service is renowned the world over, for good reason. Staff are knowledgeable, smiling and unfailingly polite, making every guest feel like a VIP.

52F, THE RITZ-CARLTON SHANGHAI, PUDONG, 8 CENTURY AVENUE **TEL:** 021-20201888-1758
地址： 上海浦东陆家嘴世纪大道8号上海浦东丽思卡尔顿酒店52层

RESERVATIONS: Recommended
DRESS CODE: Smart casual
LUNCH HOURS: 11:30 am-14:30 pm
DINNER HOURS: 17:30 pm-22:30 pm
LAST ORDER DINNER: 22:30 pm
WEBSITE: www.ritzcarlton.com/shanghaipudong

VEGETARIAN DISHES: 3-5
NO SMOKING SECTION: Yes
CAR VALET: Yes
CREDIT CARDS: AE, D, J, MC, V
YEAR ESTABLISHED: 2010
PRICE: RMB 400/Person

SCENERY BUILDING

🍴8 🍴9 🍷8 🎀8

SETTING: Scenery Building's classical Chinese architectural style and the beautiful natural environment truly bring out the best in each other. It is definitely one of the best venues for family or business banquets in Shanghai, all while enjoying the stunning scenery of the Royal Garden, and getting close to nature on the terrace.

FOOD: The Scenery Building specializes in hosting luxury banquets. The fantastic menu is designed by the Executive chef, Mr. Huang, and his inspired "A-team" and dazzles the most discerning of connoisseurs. But never fear, it's still possible for non-connoisseurs to dine in luxury at a reasonable price here. And there's no need to bring the whole family or a horde of friends for banquets. By integrating the essence of different cuisines, the restaurant creates a contemporary fusion of delicacies that climbs to new heights of culinary excellence for Hong Qiao State Guest Hotel's signature gastronomic artistry. Of the many superb dishes available, the pièces de résistance include the braised shark's fin in superior sauce, braised beef ribs with spices, double boiled local chicken with truffle in soup and braised yellow croaker with garlic.

SIGNATURE DISHES

> Braised shark's fin in superior sauce
> Braised beef ribs with spices
> Double boiled local chicken with truffle in soup
> Braised yellow croaker with garlic

WINE: It features a complete wine list ranging from domestic spirits and international wines, to various soft drinks and juices.

SERVICE: It is convenient for reservation and the staff is considerae and always ready to offer some good suggestions.

1591 HONGQIAO ROAD, SHANGHAI **TEL:** 021-62198855-5379
地址：上海虹桥路1591号（上海虹桥迎宾馆）

RESERVATIONS: Necessary
DRESS CODE: Smart casual
LUNCH HOURS: 11:30 am-14:00 pm
DINNER HOURS: 17:30 pm-22:00 pm
LAST ORDER DINNER: 22:00 pm
WEBSITE: www.hqstateguesthotel.com

VEGETARIAN DISHES: 10+
NO SMOKING SECTION: Yes
CAR VALET: No
CREDIT CARDS: J, MC, V
YEAR ESTABLISHED: 2005
PRICE: RMB 400/Person

SHENG HUI TANG

♟ 9   🍴 8   🍷 8   ﷽ 8

SETTING: Famous for its elegance and magnificence, and located in the Intercontinental Hotel in World Expo Village, Sheng Hui Tang boats a marvelous collection of ceramic murals "Tao Meng Shang Qing" in the form of four stereoscopic and plump terrines.

FOOD: While renowned for Cantonese cuisine, some Shanghai dishes are also offered, such as Deep-fried Fish in Sweet Soy Sauce, a nice sweet and tender appetizer that is flash fried in hot oil. Famous for its broad range of ingredients, Cantonese cuisine devotes itself to freshness, tenderness, delicacy and smoothness, aspects embodied by the Baked Codfish in Mushroom Sauce. The deep-sea codfish is vibrantly nutritious and distinctly tender, it's swimming in subtle flavors of the fish and mushrooms, and is of the highest quality. For soups, Shark Fin Soup, after being stewed for a long time, leads one to endless aftertastes of deliciousness. Dim sum is also a must in Cantonese cuisine and a random selection of any dim sum at Sheng Hui Tang will never disappoint.

SIGNATURE DISHES
> Marinated fish fillet "Shanghai" style
> Braised shark's fin with crab meat
> Baked cod fish with mushroom sauce

WINE: Sheng Hui Tang has a rich collection of wines, teas, coffees and mixed drinks.

SERVICE: The service reflects the excellent location. Waiters wear constant smiles when ushering customers in, serving teas and dishes and cleaning, and provide prompt answers. The service is quite considerate.

2F, 1188 XUEYE ROAD, SHANGHAI **TEL:** 021-38581188-5218
地址： 上海浦东新区雪野路1188号世博洲际酒店2楼（南码头渡口）

RESERVATIONS: Recommended
DRESS CODE: Smart casual
LUNCH HOURS: 11:30 am-14:30 pm
DINNER HOURS: 17:30 pm-21:30 pm
LAST ORDER DINNER: 21:00 pm
WEBSITE: www. intercontinental.com

VEGETARIAN DISHES: 10+
NO SMOKING SECTION: Yes
CAR VALET: Yes
CREDIT CARDS: AE, J, MC, UP, V
YEAR ESTABLISHED: 2010
PRICE: RMB 250-350/Person

SHINTARO

🍷 8   🍴 9   🍷 9   🎀 9

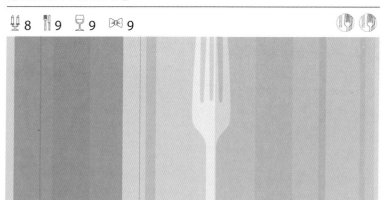

SETTING: The soft lighting and ample space between tables ensures a more intimate dining experience. The restaurant features 43 seats in total and a private Tatami room for 8.

FOOD: The open kitchen at Shintaro provides all kinds of fresh and authentic Sashimi, Sushi, wheaten dishes and elegant Japanese Cuisine. All Japanese Cuisine and Sashimi dishes are fresh and cooked with flair using fresh, local ingredients by expert and talented chefs. The specialties include: Chili tuna, Australia Wagyu beef and Hot Plate Seafood hors d'oeuvres platter. The price of the set meal has risen this year: a hotplate set costs RMB 688, and you should expect a 15% service fee. The buffet dinner is a cheaper option, but lacks the lobster and Wagyu beef. We therefore chose a separate order. The Chili tuna and tenderloin with sauce is slightly cool so it melts in the mouth. The lobster in Hot Plate Seafood hors d'oeuvres platter is sweet and fresh. The meat is healthy, low fat and high protein. The lobster has a unique flavor of heat and fragrance after baking on the hot plate. The traditional Roast Beef with Teriyaki Sauce and the Grilled Codfish (specialties of Shintaro) and Australia Wagyu beef should not be missed.

SIGNATURE DISHES
> Spicy tuna tartare
> Thin yellow tail
> Fresh Canadian oysters
> Misa cod fish
> Teppayaki AUS kabe beed
> Teppayaki seafood platten

WINE: There is an abundance of wine, more than maybe any other restaurant. You can of course also find a wide range kinds of Sakes, as well as fresh juices and soft drinks.

SERVICE: The smiling waitresses provide charming and affectionate service.

500 WEIHAI ROAD, SHANGHAI **TEL:** 021-62568888-1290
地址： 上海威海路500号

RESERVATIONS: Recommended
DRESS CODE: Smart casual
LUNCH HOURS: No
DINNER HOURS: 17:00 pm-22:00 pm
LAST ORDER DINNER: 21:55 pm
WEBSITE: www.fourseasons.com/shanghai

VEGETARIAN DISHES: 3-5
NO SMOKING SECTION: Yes
CAR VALET: Yes
CREDIT CARDS: AE, D, J, MC, UP, V
YEAR ESTABLISHED: 2002
PRICE: RMB 500/Person

SHINTORI NULL-2

♨ 8   🍴 9   🍷 9   🎀 9   🖐 🖐 🖐

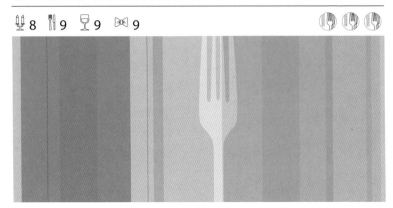

SETTING: A winding path leads to a nicely secluded scene. Slim bamboo graces the winding path. An Indoor open kitchen, transparent elevator for serving dishes and a long slate Sushi plate reveal the post-modern Zen of the restaurant.

FOOD: The dishes here are innovations of well known Japanese cuisines. Rock salad is the featured started dish: fresh vegetables and lemon slices are the main ingredients. The flavors are rich and the ingredients fresh. The dish is prepared by the table, which is a nice feature. Fresh fried bean curd roll is delicious and well worth trying. The Live sashimi and various types of sushi use fresh ingredients and the dishes are appetizingly placed. The boiled goose liver with radish is one of the signature cuisines. The radish is boiled until it becomes soft. The goose liver is fried first and then boiled with soy sauce. Because of the perfect degree of cooking, the goose liver is very tender and the radish balances its fatness. The Sukiyaki Beef is good selection for warming you up on a cold evening. The Shaoshao desert is the recommended choice, which is cooked by incorporating cheese cake, Sesame tofu, red bean cake and chocolate cake.

SIGNATURE DISHES
> Rocking salad
> Crab meat and tomato salad
> Foie gras cooked with radish
> Selection of sushi
> Black sesame ice cream and white sesame seed pudding
> Deep-fried tofu skin roll

WINE: There are various styles of middle and high grade sakes and grape wines.

SERVICE: The well-trained waiters can provide guests with considerable service.

803 JULU ROAD, SHANGHAI **TEL:** 021-54045252
地址：上海巨鹿路803号

RESERVATIONS: Recommended
DRESS CODE: Smart casual
LUNCH HOURS: 11:30 am-14:00 pm (only Sat and Sun)
DINNER HOURS: 17:30 pm-23:00 pm
LAST ORDER DINNER: 22:30 pm
WEBSITE: www.shintori.com.tw

VEGETARIAN DISHES: 5-10
NO SMOKING SECTION: No
CAR VALET: No
CREDIT CARDS: AE, D, J, MC, UP, V
YEAR ESTABLISHED: 2002
PRICE: RMB 400/Person

SICHUAN COURT

🍴 9 🍴 8 🍷 9 🎀 9   (🖐) (🖐) (🖐)

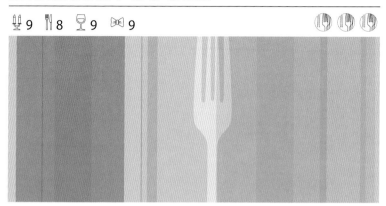

SETTING: The restaurant is very stylish and elegant, and customers can gaze at the beautiful scenery of Shanghai.

FOOD: The restaurant is furnished with vintage dinnerware that is customized to improve Sichuan cuisine. The appetizer of Sichuan treasure box includes five cold appetizers: Dengying shredded beef, Steamed Chicken with Chili Sauce, cucumber, smoked fish and dried bean curd. The quantity is more than sufficient for two or three people. The well-known representative of Sichuan cuisine is shredded pork with garlic sauce, in which the pork is shredded by creative chefs into prawns. Fish Fillets in Hot Chili Oil is not covered with Chili oil, but lightly seared in chilli broadbean paste. The boneless Mussels are smooth and slick, waft with the fragrance of Chili and bean paste, and are not greasy. Smoked Duck is expertly matched with sticky rice cake and fish-flavored sauce. The smoked duck is fresh and delicious and melts in the mouth. The sour, hot and sweet flavour made by pickled pepper and fresh ginger, together with fragrant sticky rice cake, is a perfect blend. Other specialties include Dry-Braised Minced Mandarin Fish, Sautéed Shrimp with Nuts and Chilli, Walnut Mud, Almond bean curd and Sichuan style noodles with pepper sauce.

SIGNATURE DISHES
> Sichuan treasure box
> Sliced beef and ox tongue
> Chilied almond jelly
> Fish filets in hot chili oil
> Poached sliced beef in hot chili oil
> Fried shrimps in spicy sauce

WINE: There are many red wines, white wine, champagne, draft beer and liqueurs. Red and white wine from Australia and France is also sold by the goblet; if the wine bottle is opened, the wine will be sold on the same day.

SERVICE: Although the waiters are few, their service is excellent. The interval of serving dishes is just perfect and guests feel at home.

39F, 250 HUASHAN ROAD, SHANGHAI **TEL:** 021-62480000-1890
地址：上海华山路250号希尔顿酒店39楼

RESERVATIONS: Recommended
DRESS CODE: Smart casual
LUNCH HOURS: 11:30 am-14:00 pm (Mon-Fri)
DINNER HOURS: 18:00 pm-22:00 pm (Mon-Fri)
LAST ORDER DINNER: 22:00 pm
WEBSITE: www.shanghai.hilton.com

VEGETARIAN DISHES: 10+
NO SMOKING SECTION: Yes
CAR VALET: Yes
CREDIT CARDS: AE, MC, UP, V
YEAR ESTABLISHED: 1988
PRICE: RMB 300-400/Person

SIMPLY THAI

🕯8 🍴9 🍷8 🎀8   👐 👐

SETTING: Intricately carved dark-red wood decorations catch the eye and balance the basic table settings, and the bountiful tropical Thai flowers add a touch of color and life.

FOOD: The menu uses only quality ingredients, and is an entertaining mix of specials, classics, and a few original dishes. Many dishes come in bite portions, ideal for sharing. Among the suggestions, the lemon grass chicken skewers are incredibly juicy and succulent, with a crispy skin served with oranges and a sweet-and-sour sauce. Also, the chicken bits wrapped and cooked in Pandan leaves are both delicate and intense, while Rice paper rolls with shrimps are also delicious. One cannot go for Thai food and forget curry. The house's green curry is another great dish, filled with crunchy veggies and topped with your favorite meat, is Simply Thai's perfect answer to diners' dream of a balanced dish that is spicy but not overwhelming, mild but not bland, flavorful but elegant. To close on a sweet note, the sago coconut pudding melts in your mouth; and for something juicer, try the Siam ruby.

SIGNATURE DISHES
> Green papaya salad
> Spring Rolls
> Tom Yum seafood soup
> Green curry (chicken)
> Thai fried noodles with shrimps
> Steamed Mandarin fish

WINE: The wine list here gathers a bit of everything from all main producing regions, China included, though it falls short on wines by the glass.

SERVICE: Staff at Simply is as it can be expected at a Thai venue: friendly, big genuine smiles, and ready to accommodate diners' requests.

---

159 MADANG ROAD, SHANGHAI **TEL:** 400 880 7729
地址： 上海马当路159号（近兴业路）

RESERVATIONS: Recommended
DRESS CODE: Smart casual
LUNCH HOURS: 11:00 am-18:00 pm
DINNER HOURS: 18:00 pm-24:00 pm (Sun-Thu)
LAST ORDER DINNER: 22:30 pm
WEBSITE: www.simplythai-sh.com

VEGETARIAN DISHES: 3-5
NO SMOKING SECTION: Yes
CAR VALET: No
CREDIT CARDS: AE, D, J, MC, UP, V
YEAR ESTABLISHED: 2001
PRICE: RMB 200/Person

SINCERE RESTAURANT

🍴 8　🍴 9　🍷 8　🎀 9

🖐 🖐 🖐

SETTING: A spacious dining hall with large and small private rooms offers guests a pleasant and comfortable dining environment.

FOOD: This seasonal restaurant uses only the best of ingredients, and even produces many of its own. As such, it guarantees most of its own ingredients are pesticide and growth hormone free. The vegetables are seasonal so the quantity is limited, so the restaurant has established its own cold warehouse and transport team to ensure access to ingredients. One of its signature dishes, Vegetarian Duck (tofu), can be ordered at any time. The outside tofu skin is crisp and delicious and the vegetables are very fresh. The steamed Hakka style eggplant with sauce is also well worth sampling. And for the ladies, the Sweet Potato Salad with Walnuts can is said to enhance beauty. The rare Jinhua pig is the signature dish of the restaurant. Nearly all tables order the Jiangnan style Braised Pork Belly made with black pig, pickled egg and sliced bean curd or the equally delicious fried Jinhua pig. The former dish is fatty but not oily and the thin meat is flowing with juices. The latter dish offers guests the original flavor of the pork, but with added succulence.

SIGNATURE DISHES
> Deep-fried long-tailed anchovy
> Walnut and yam salad
> Crispy pork ribs
> Deep sea premium dried male fish maw
> Sautéed sea whelk with ginger

WINE: It offers all kinds of domestic high grade distilled spirits and new and Old World wines. Various kinds of seasonal fruit and vegetable wines are served.

SERVICE: It provides guests with warm-hearted service and sufficient private space.

1726 HUAIHAI ROAD M., SHANGHAI **TEL:** 021-64332882
地址：上海淮海中路1726号

RESERVATIONS: Necessary for Dinner
DRESS CODE: Smart casual
LUNCH HOURS: 11:00 am-14:00 pm
DINNER HOURS: 17:00 pm-22:00 pm
LAST ORDER DINNER: 21:00 pm
WEBSITE: No

VEGETARIAN DISHES: 5-10
NO SMOKING SECTION: Yes
CAR VALET: Yes
CREDIT CARDS: J, MC, UP, V
YEAR ESTABLISHED: 2007
PRICE: RMB 400/Person

SIR ELLY'S

🕯9 🍴9 🍷9 🎀9

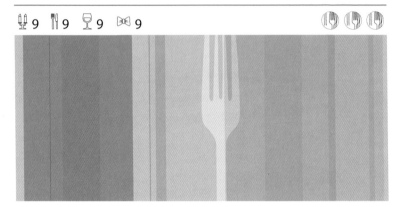

SETTING: Named after the founder of The Peninsula Hotels' parent company, this stately and modern dining room provides much sought after tranquility in Shanghai.

FOOD: With a line-up of fresh appetizer creations, the Macaroons with foie gras torchon, pickled cherry, and arugula stand out, a luxurious blending of savory and sweet sumptuousness. The generous portion of liver is literally sandwiched by the macaroons. Confronted by so many opulent choices for main courses, it's hard to decide between the land and sea dishes. Wagyu Beef and Pork Belly stampeded off the page of terrestrial offerings while Lobster and Octopus surfaced above the other aquatic selections. We took the plunge and got the Octopus and Lobster. Lightly grilled and well seasoned Octopus makes this dish an exotic delight. The accompanying pig ear may pleasantly surprise you with its unexpected texture. The lobster plays a more subdued tone, swimming in a light cornucopia of citrus flavors with lemongrass and turmeric froth. Once again, sugar complements salt through a bed of banana-vanilla polenta underneath. For dessert, the Noir rounds out the experience handsomely, presenting the faithful duo of chocolate mousse and ice cream.

SIGNATURE DISHES
> Foie Gras
> Tuna
> Gillardeau Oyster
> Wagyu Beef
> Maine Lobster
> Duck Breast

WINE: An assotment of high quality wines are available.

SERVICE: Attentive but discreet wait staff with a good command of English makes the dining experience seemingly effortless.

13F, 32 ZHONGSHAN NO.1 ROAD E., SHANGHAI **TEL:** 021-23272888-6756
地址：上海中山东一路32号半岛酒店13楼

RESERVATIONS: Recommended
DRESS CODE: Smart casual
LUNCH HOURS: 12:00 am-14:30 pm
DINNER HOURS: 18:00 pm-22:30 pm
LAST ORDER DINNER: 22:30 pm
WEBSITE: www.peninsula.com

VEGETARIAN DISHES: 10+
NO SMOKING SECTION: Yes
CAR VALET: Yes
CREDIT CARDS: AE, D, J, MC, UP, V
YEAR ESTABLISHED: 2009
PRICE: RMB 500/Person

STEAK HOUSE

⌇ 8   ⫙ 9   ☲ 9   ⋈ 9

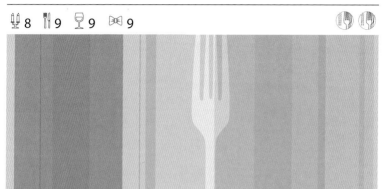

SETTING: The prominent open kitchen in the centre of the House boasts a skylight ceiling window, bathing the area in warm sunshine, while the dinnerware is composed of French cutlery.

FOOD: Sampling an authentic American food experience starts with a fine appetizer. Goose liver with apple jam or prawn with potato horseradish juice are excellent choices. As to the main courses, dishes cooked with beef and seafood serve as good options. For steak lovers, having a steak is something that requires substantial considerations: first and foremost, the steak must be of fine qualify and be produced by a renowned country such as Brazil, Australia or North America; in addition, the cooking time must be perfect to match your preferred steak style, medium rare being the perfect choice to bring out the steaks tenderness. A wise suggestion is that you choose the super-lean roasted American superfine sirloin, roasted American loin or roasted American T-bone loin. An important difference from other steak houses is that the House boats steak that is roasted on an open fire. The dining experience can be brought to a perfect, indulgent conclusion by a strawberry cheese cake with cream or vanilla-flavor ice cream.

SIGNATURE DISHES
> Grilled shrimp cocktail
> Crab cake corn crusted
> Oyster Rockefeller
> Australian Grain Fed Lamb T-Bone 400g
> Barramundi 250g (Main-Ocean)

WINE: About a hundred brands of wine are available, twenty of which are of the highest grade. Imported wine and various drinks are provided as well.

SERVICE: The service here is good. You will feel at home when the waiter and waitress introduce to you the distinct features of every main course recommend to you to the degree to which a particular the steak should be cooked.

500 WEIHAI ROAD, SHANGHAI **TEL:** 021-62568888-1270
地址： 上海威海路500号

RESERVATIONS: Recommended
DRESS CODE: Smart casual
LUNCH HOURS: No
DINNER HOURS: 17:00 pm-22:00 pm (Tue-Sat)
LAST ORDER DINNER: 22:00 pm
WEBSITE: www.fourseasons.com/shanghai

VEGETARIAN DISHES: 10+
NO SMOKING SECTION: Yes
CAR VALET: Yes
CREDIT CARDS: AE, D, J, MC, UP, V
YEAR ESTABLISHED: 2002
PRICE: RMB 500/Person

SUMMER PAVILION

♨ 8 🍴 9 🍷 9 🎀 9

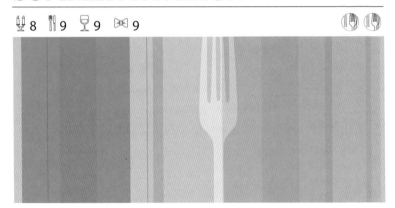

SETTING: The Summer Pavilion boasts an elegant ambience, with exquisite lotuses and lotus leaves painted on the light golden columns in the hall and Chinese landscapes painted on the ceiling.

FOOD: A plate of cashews is provided before the main courses, which are crisp and savoury. The cold Roast Suckling Pig is a recommended cold dish. Sliced into thin pieces, this dish is not greasy it but very juicy. One of the signature dishes, named Fried Spring Chicken, is a Cantonese delicacy. With crispy skin and tender meat, it is a must have for any banquet. The Fried Spring Chicken in the Summer Pavilion is unique for its crispy outer skin, golden colour, fragrant aroma and delicious taste, and is than in many other restaurants. The Bamboo and Wild Mushroom Soup, delicious and good for the health, is especially favoured in autumn. Various mushrooms such as nameko, coprinus mushroom, straw mushroom and abalone mushroom are added to the soup stock and then boiled. It is highly nutritious. The dim sum, made of shrimp, is fabulous and well worth trying. Varieties include Deep-fried Prawn topped with Mustard and Shrimp and Pea Shoot Dumpling. This dim sum will leave you with an unforgettable memory of the unique mixed flavour of meat and cream.

SIGNATURE DISHES
> Maronated Goose liver in sake
> Roasted crispy Sucklong Pig
> Stir-fried Prrawns
> Nuts and Tomato in wasali sauce
> Braised Codfish shallots
> Pan-fried Groose liver

WINE: Summer Pavilion is extraordinary as it provides a great variety of wines, allowing customers to choose from over 100 varieties.

SERVICE: Waiters wear smiles from beginning to end. Being observant and quick, they will figure out a customer's needs the moment they make a tiny movement.

1F, 1376 NANJING ROAD W., SHANGHAI **TEL:** 021-62798888-4770
地址：上海南京西路1376号波特曼大酒店1楼

RESERVATIONS: Recommended
DRESS CODE: Smart casual
LUNCH HOURS: 11:30 am-14:30 pm
DINNER HOURS: 17:30 pm-22:30 pm
LAST ORDER DINNER: 21:00 pm
EMAIL: terrence.yin@ritzcarlton.com

VEGETARIAN DISHES: 10+
NO SMOKING SECTION: Yes
CAR VALET: No
CREDIT CARDS: AE, D, J, MC, UP, V
YEAR ESTABLISHED: 2007
PRICE: RMB 400/Person

T8 RESTAURANT & BAR

 8   9   9   7

SETTING: T8 embraces an antique Eurasian style of decoration; graceful black wood carvings with luxurious curtains and distinct rooms separated by screens echo the traditional Shanghai style, making people comfortable and relaxed.

FOOD: Many say that T8 is one of the best places to enjoy European cuisine in Shanghai, giving nearly full marks when evaluating the restaurant. The cuisine, cooked using the best sauces, has attracted many overseas travelers and distinguished personages in Shanghai and famous gastronomes. In T8, you can mix fragrant foods with excellent wines that complement the sauces made by chef, which is why the restaurant is full of customers night after night and thus you must make a reservation. The restaurant provides many daily dishes, the appetizers of which include Crab Meat Soup, Minor Decoction of Bupleurum with Spanish ham and or French goose liver. Among the main courses, the lobster, beef of Japanese cattle, toasted weever with scallop are all famous and excellent choices. For dessert, you may choose various ice creams, chocolate desserts or a Cheese platter to wrap up the dinner.

SIGNATURE DISHES
> Tataki of sesame crusted tuna
> Seared foie gras
> Pickled and grilled zucchini
> Australian wagyu beef
> Boston lobster
> Miso poached black cod fish

WINE: The bar serves a rich and colorful list of cocktails, numerous French wines and New World wines.

SERVICE: Service here is professional and considerate. However, it is a pity that waiters treat customers from China and those from foreign countries in different ways, such as serving foreign customers with great respect and serving Chinese customers with prejudice.

NO.8 NORTH OF XINTIANDI PLAZA, 181 TAICANG ROAD, SHANGHAI **TEL:** 021-63558999
地址： 上海太仓路181弄新天地北里8号

RESERVATIONS: Recommended
DRESS CODE: Smart casual
LUNCH HOURS: 11:30 am-14:30 pm (Mon No)
DINNER HOURS: 18:00 pm-23:30 pm
LAST ORDER DINNER: 22:30 pm
WEBSITE: www.t8shanghai.com

VEGETARIAN DISHES: 3-5
NO SMOKING SECTION: Yes
CAR VALET: No
CREDIT CARDS: AE, D, J, MC, UP, V
YEAR ESTABLISHED: 2001
PRICE: RMB 400/Person

TABLE NO.1

♨ 7 🍴 9 🍷 9 🎀 8   🖐 🖐 🖐

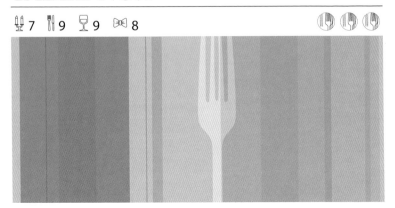

SETTING: The Table No.1 uses a simplest decoration style and boasts traditional European cooking techniques with a modern twist.

FOOD: The restaurant is managed by Mr. Jason Atherton, a famous three-star Michelin chef. He has worked in such famous foreign restaurants as Gordon Ramsay, Ferran Adria and Marco Pierre White. He has now left Ramsay Empire and his position as head chef of Maze and opened his first restaurant in Asia. Although Mr. Atherton is not in every day, Mr. Scott Melvin, his old colleague at Maze acts as the executive chef of the restaurant. In order to guarantee the excellence of ingredients, Mr. Jason only gets them from the local area. The appetizers can serve many persons and are well cooked with fresh ingredients. Crab Bisque is innovative and the taste is wonderful. The starter dishes include clam with chorizo, tuna matched with Tata sauce and sesame, local shrimps boiled on a low heat and dried scallop with mashed spinach are all worth mentioning. The main courses of flatfish and cuttlefish with organic rice are excellent choices. The pork with mashed beetroot is also one of the featured dishes and it is crisp on the outside and tender inside. The sweet desserts are all worthy of praise.

SIGNATURE DISHES

> Tuna tarte ponzu dressing
> Racor clams, chorizo, corriander
> Ceviche of scallop, gazpaclto
> Sole, cuttlefish, ink rice, garlic
> Suckling pig, beefroot, tetrvres

WINE: Features many vintage wines from the new and old world. Various cocktails are also available.

SERVICE: All waiters can speak English fluently and they provide good service.

1-3 MAOJIAYUAN ROAD, SHANGHAI **TEL:** 021-60802918
地址：上海毛家园路1-3号

RESERVATIONS: Recommended
DRESS CODE: Smart casual
LUNCH HOURS: 12:00 am-14:30 pm
DINNER HOURS: 18:00 pm-22:30 pm
LAST ORDER DINNER: 22:30 pm
WEBSITE: www.tableno-1.com

VEGETARIAN DISHES: 3-5
NO SMOKING SECTION: Yes
CAR VALET: No
CREDIT CARDS: AE, D, J, MC, UP, V
YEAR ESTABLISHED: 2010
PRICE: RMB 400/Person

T'ANG COURT

🍷 9　🍴 9　🍷 8　🎀 9　　　　🖐 🖐 🖐

SETTING: The surroundings of this Michelin 2-stared restaurant are quiet, tasteful and comfortable. The private rooms and private spaces in the lobby are suitable for both business dinners and friends or family.

FOOD: The first dish worthy of recommendation is the award-winning Stir-Fried Fresh Lobster with Spring Onion, Red Onion and Shallots. There's also a choice of Australian lobsters, a cheaper option, baby lobsters, and lobster noodles with soup, which complements the baby lobsters perfectly and is well worth trying. Epicures often frequent T'ang Court for the Stir-Fried Fresh Lobster with Spring Onion, Red Onion and Shallots: it's a deservedly renowned choice. Pan-Fried Salmon Lillet with Taro Puffs is prepared with preserved bean curd and is an unforgettable visual and gustatory experience. In addition, Sautéed Prawns and Crab Roe, Crispy Salty Chicken and Sautéed Scallops with Asparagus are unique and delicious. Cantonese seafood like Steamed Soon Hock Fish with Spring Onion and Ginger has a beautiful and vitalizing dressed squid. Of special mention is the Guangzhou-style dessert and barbecued set meals. All the dim sums are very beautifully presented and bursting with flavor.

SIGNATURE DISHES
> "Tang court" combination
> BBQ combination
> Chilled shredded abalone, cuttle fish and packing with fresh fruits
> Stir-fried fresh lobster
> Sautéed prawns and crab roe

WINE: There is no lack of vintage wines in both the Chinese and Western styles. Be aware that there is a corkage fee of RMB 100 for your own wine.

SERVICE: The service here is up to the standard of a five–star hotel. The waiters are cordial and polite.

2F, 740 HANKOU ROAD, SHANGHAI **TEL:** 021-60800733
地址：上海汉口路740号朗廷扬子精品酒店2楼

RESERVATIONS: Recommended
DRESS CODE: Smart casual
LUNCH HOURS: 11:30 am-14:30 pm
DINNER HOURS: 17:30 pm-22:30 pm
LAST ORDER DINNER: 22:10 pm
WEBSITE: www.langhamhotels.com

VEGETARIAN DISHES: 10+
NO SMOKING SECTION: Yes
CAR VALET: No
CREDIT CARDS: AE, D, J, MC, UP, V
YEAR ESTABLISHED: 2009
PRICE: RMB 300-400/Person

THAI GALLERY

🕯8　🍴8　🍷8　🎀9

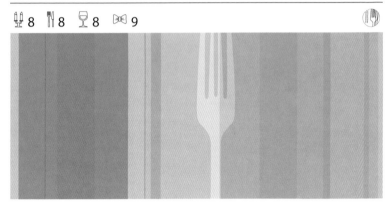

SETTING: This stunning multi-level space is filled with contemporary artworks and South East Asian décor.

FOOD: The kitchen employs a rich variety of authentic Thai spices and ingredients, which is sadly a rarity in Shanghai. Go for the appetizer platter, beautifully presented, to enjoy a selection of these excellent tidbits, from shrimp spring rolls to the aromatic and spicy tender fish cakes. Green papaya salad is a masterful, complex dish with ripe cherry tomatoes, green beans, dried baby shrimps and, of course, papaya slivers in a stimulating, sour spicy dressing; the roasted peanuts add a satisfying crunch. The pumpkin soup with fresh shrimp may be the best dish on the menu—rich with lemongrass and creamy with coconut, this soup is so delicious, you may just want to bathe in it. Curries in red, yellow and green flavors can be cooked with your choice of meats. The green curry with shrimp is a delicious combination; the fat shrimp are very fresh and perfectly cooked. Yellow curry crab is an impressive dish—a giant crab with plenty of tender meat served bathing in a slightly sweet and spicy thick curry which goes great over rice. The unique taro custard dessert is made up of a mildly sweet spongy texture cake, which has a tender moist bite.

SIGNATURE DISHES
> Golden fried prawn cake
> Green papaya salad
> Wok fried crab in yellow curry sauce
> Steamed fish of the day
> Deep fried chicken wrapped with pandan leaves

WINE: A solid selection of affordable reds and whites and some tasty tropical cocktails like the sweet, fragrant Coconut Republic.

SERVICE: A friendly, smoothly managed team of helpful staff who all know the menu very well, and also speak good English.

127-1 DATIAN ROAD, SHANGHAI **TEL:** 021-62179797
地址：上海静安区大田路127－1号（近北京西路）

RESERVATIONS: Recommended
DRESS CODE: Smart casual
LUNCH HOURS: 11:00 am-14:30 pm
DINNER HOURS: 17:30 pm-00:00 pm
LAST ORDER DINNER: 22:30 pm
WEBSITE: No

VEGETARIAN DISHES: 5-10
NO SMOKING SECTION: Yes
CAR VALET: No
CREDIT CARDS: AE, D, J, MC, UP, V
YEAR ESTABLISHED: 2004
PRICE: RMB 200/Person

THE CHINOISE STORY

🍴8 🍴9 🍷8 🎀9

SETTING: Decorative and distinctive lighting and a beautiful aquarium at the entrance of Le Chinoise Storie create an ambience of elegance and mystery and are major attractions, as well as the exceptional cuisine of course.

FOOD: For appetizers, Le Chinoise Storie Five Flavors, a dish made up of five classic cold dishes, is a wonderful mix of flavors: it includes Smoked Bean Curd with Seasonal Vegetables, Pumpkin Yam, Jellyfish in Black Vinegar and Turnip, Crisp Barbecued Pork and Diced Beef Fillet with Orange. Seafood is definitely top drawer, with Grilled Codfish with Honey utterly superlative and refreshingly novel. Being a very special dish, Lobster Trilogy is a must have. Half small lobsters are cooked in salty egg yolk, mustard and sautés creating a splendid blend of textures; the lobster flesh is carefully scraped out making it easier to eat. The restaurant also offers novel Shanghai dishes that retain their history, such as the handmade Steamed Crab Meat with Minced Pork Balls, a greatly loved traditional Shanghai dish that is delightfully juicy. The dining experience can be excellently rounded off with Double-Boiled Superior Bird's Nest with Almond Juice and Myricaceae Nectar Ice-cream.

SIGNATURE DISHES
> Sliced roasted puck
> Tuna corn roll
> Shanghai style root tuck
> Braised shark's fin in chicken stock
> Lobster in 3 ways
> Australia Waygu with foregras

WINE: Le Chinoise Storie has a series of wines, mainly wines from New World like Australia, and vintage wines from France.

SERVICE: Waiters have smiles on their faces from beginning to end and are ready to cater to customers' requirements.

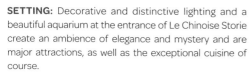

1F, NORTH BUILDING, 59 MAOMING ROAD S., SHANGHAI **TEL:** 021-64451717
地址： 上海茂名南路59号锦江饭店北楼1楼

RESERVATIONS: Recommended	**VEGETARIAN DISHES:** 10+
DRESS CODE: Smart casual	**NO SMOKING SECTION:** Yes
LUNCH HOURS: 11:30 am-15:00 pm	**CAR VALET:** No
DINNER HOURS: 17:30 pm-23:00 pm	**CREDIT CARDS:** AE, D, J, MC, V
LAST ORDER DINNER: 22:30 pm	**YEAR ESTABLISHED:** 2006
WEBSITE: www.tunglok.com	**PRICE:** RMB 300-500/Person

THE DOOR RESTAURANT & BAR

♟9 🍴9 🍷9 🎀9   ✋ ✋ ✋

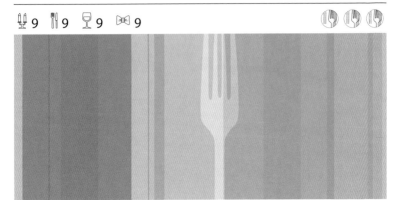

SETTING: Walking into the Door Restaurant & Bar, you seem to enter a museum. The designer isolated such a big space into various private spaces with wooden doors. The designer took such unrelated things as Decree, Buddha statue, and opium bed and integrated them into a harmonious whole.

FOOD: The owner is also the boss of the best Kaiseki Cuisine of the capital city. The chef of the Door Restaurant & Bar is a Japanese master and he excels good at elaborate French cuisine. The starter dishes consist of crab salad, spring roll with snails and steamed live oysters with curry paste. The common features of French cuisine, such as snail and oysters, are used innovatively here and you will be pleasantly surprised by the food on offer. Beef soup with tomato possesses a delicious flavor. Buckwheat noodle with dry mashed abalone is the highlight of the whole set meal. The dry mashed abalone is very fresh and it is very refreshing. The beef are the signature dishes of the restaurant and is best with Bordeaux red wine sauce and onion sauce in a Russian Style. The superior Japanese beef is cooked to perfection. The assorted desserts are all delicious and the perfect end to the meal.

SIGNATURE DISHES
> Wagu beef

WINE: The wine list is rich. Famous cocktails are also offered.

SERVICE: The waiters provide a good service and there is a pleasant Japanese foreman.

4F, 1468 HONGQIAO ROAD, SHANGHAI **TEL:** 021-62953737
地址：上海虹桥路1468号4楼

RESERVATIONS: Recommended
DRESS CODE: Smart casual
LUNCH HOURS: 11:30 am-14:00 pm
DINNER HOURS: 18:30 pm-21:00 pm
LAST ORDER DINNER: 21:00 pm
EMAIL: annieweiqingwang@hotmail.com

VEGETARIAN DISHES: No
NO SMOKING SECTION: Yes
CAR VALET: Yes
CREDIT CARDS: AE, MC, V
YEAR ESTABLISHED: 2001
PRICE: RMB 1200/Person

THE GRILL

♟ 8 🍴 8 🍷 9 🎔 9

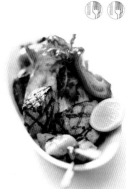

SETTING: There are four restaurants on the 56th floor, with each situated in its own corner. Window seats are very popular, and usually must be booked in advance.

FOOD: In an open kitchen, five or six chefs display their masterful skills. There's a large seafood bar nestled around the open kitchen, which houses a vast, tantalizing array of international seafood. Appetizers are "seafood on ice", and includes crab, shrimp and oysters, among others. Of course, all are very fresh and high quality. After sampling the appetizers, you simply must try with the "lobster bisque", a very hot soup with a light, delicate yet savory flavor. Other starters such as the Raw Oysters and Seared Foie Gras are very popular among guests. The Grill is in an American Style, with plenty of meat dishes such as Australian "Wagyu Beef", which is served in satisfyingly large portions. Other Aussie steaks and mix grilled meat are on offer. The juicy, flavorsome and tender meat is cooked with just salt and pepper, allowing the natural flavors to come through. Boston and Australian lobster can also be ordered, whole or half. All kind of grilled fish, like Norwegian salmon, are grilled to a light crispness. This is a great venue to sample international fare from all over the world in a single venue.

SIGNATURE DISHES

> ON 56 seafood on ice
> North American oysters
> Caesar salad
> On 56 combination grill
> Australian "Wagyu" beaf
> Half organic spit roasted chicken

WINE: A rich selection of red wines to match meat and white wines to match seafood.

SERVICE: Good service. The staff are warm.

56F, GRAND HYATT SHANGHAI, 88 CENTURY ANVENUE, SHANGHAI **TEL:** 021-50491234
地址：上海市浦东新区世纪大道88号金茂君悦大酒店56楼

RESERVATIONS: Recommended
DRESS CODE: Smart casual
LUNCH HOURS: No
DINNER HOURS: 17:30 pm-22:30 pm(Sunday to Thursday)
LAST ORDER DINNER: 22:30 pm(Sunday to Thursday)
WEBSITE: www.shanghai.grand.hyatt.com

VEGETARIAN DISHES: No
NO SMOKING SECTION: Yes
CAR VALET: No
CREDIT CARDS: AE, J, MC, V
YEAR ESTABLISHED: 1999
PRICE: RMB 400/Person

THE HOUSE OF ROOSEVELT

🍷 9 🍴 9 🍷 9 🎀 8   (🍴) (🍴) (🍴)

SETTING: Opening its doors in mid 2010, the grand House of Roosevelt is probably the largest of all the Bund's venues. There's a stark contrast between the traditional old-manor exterior and the minimalist-modern atmosphere inside.

FOOD: The menu at Roosevelt is a great touch, looking like an old newspaper, with different sections for each floor. You can order whatever you like, though dishes coming from other floors may take a bit longer. On top of the a-la-carte selection, plenty of suggested combinations are available too, including tasting plates for wines and champagnes, tapas sets, an amazing lunch set for 98++ RMB and a dinner set priced at 158+RMB. From the appetizers, the beef carpaccio with toasted focaccia is beautifully plated, and comes with tasty olives, capers and crunchy pickles. The caviar and shrimp is bright and colorful; a delightful concoction of textures and flavors, with a nice touch of quail eggs and endives. The Boston clam chowder is also a must try. From the mains, the veal ossobuco is a rich French interpretation of the classic Milanese dish, topped with lashings of gravy and served on a delicious potato mash and crunchy pea pods. If you've got only a little space left for desserts, try the trio plate.

SIGNATURE DISHES
> Bone marrow
> Duck rillette with croutons
> Baby leaf salad
> Wagyu bite size steak
> Grilled Boston lobster
> Crispy duck breast with foie gras, fig and pumpkin puree

WINE: The wine list boasts plenty of choices, probably the best in all of Shanghai, with thousands of choices, and it's quite relieving for novices (and the lazy diner) to know that a condensed selection is provided too, with suggestions from the maitre-d'.

SERVICE: The staff is helpful and caring, sincerely concerned, prompt and smooth.

2F, 27 ZHONGSHAN NO.1 ROAD E., SHANGHAI **TEL:** 021-23220800
地址： 上海中山东一路27号2楼

RESERVATIONS: Recommended
DRESS CODE: Smart casual
LUNCH HOURS: 11:30 am-14:30 pm
DINNER HOURS: 18:00 pm-23:00 am
LAST ORDER DINNER: 22:30 pm
WEBSITE: www.rooseveltchina.com

VEGETARIAN DISHES: 3-5
NO SMOKING SECTION: Yes
CAR VALET: Yes
CREDIT CARDS: AE, D, J, MC, UP, V
YEAR ESTABLISHED: 2010
PRICE: RMB 400/Person

THE MARKET

🍴 8   🍴 8   🍷 7   🎀 8

SETTING: With a modern, welcoming feel to it, the dining room is bright and spacious, and the table setting Spartan yet refined.

FOOD: The venue offers a-la-carte or buffet style dining in a fusion of Asian-Western typical of hotels in this area of the world. Wandering around the colorful food displays is lots of fun, and the buffet sets provide for extremely affordable deals too. Don't forget to indulge in the various dips and toppings provided at almost every station. The cheese-and-snacks station offers fare from many countries, as well as smoked fish, cold cuts and slowly cooked foie gras. What's more, from raw oysters and clams to boiled shrimps, there's plenty of choice for the seafood lovers. Hot mains feature both meat and seafood delicacies. A luxurious salad bar is also available, including plenty of ready preparations to tantalize the lazier guests. Asian-food lovers can feast on the stir-fried entrees, or order fresh noodles from the live station. Another live station churns out hot pasta dishes. There's also a roast section for something earthier. There are literally dozens of desserts to choose from, but don't forget to dip the home-made marshmallows under the chocolate fountain!

SIGNATURE DISHES
> Smoked chicken orange salad
> Slow cooked goose liver
> Chicken rice
> Roasted pork belly
> Stewed seafood ragout

WINE: The drink list is full of choices from liquors and soft drinks, but quite short on the wines. The buffet set includes free-flow juices.

SERVICE: The staff at the Market is very welcoming and friendly, including some very smart and proactive people. Good English is spoken too.

1F, 388 DADUKE ROAD, SHANGHAI **TEL:** 021-60958888-7023
地址： 上海大渡河路388号（云岭东路路口）国盛中心国丰酒店1楼

RESERVATIONS: Recommended
DRESS CODE: Smart casual
LUNCH HOURS: 12:00 am-15:00 pm
DINNER HOURS: 18:00 pm-22:00 pm
LAST ORDER DINNER: 22:00 pm
WEBSITE: www.guoman.com

VEGETARIAN DISHES: 3-5
NO SMOKING SECTION: Yes
CAR VALET: No
CREDIT CARDS: AE, D, J, MC, UP, V
YEAR ESTABLISHED: 2010
PRICE: RMB 350/Person

THE STRIP PRIME STEAKHOUSE SHANGHAI

🍽 8   🍴 9   🍷 9   ✉ 8   🖐 🖐 🖐

SETTING: The Strip – Prime Steakhouse combines two levels of dining experience unlike any other venue in Shanghai. Both levels offer panoramic city views of the magnificent Shanghai skyline.

FOOD: The 7th floor space is dedicated to fine dining with detailed Michelin level experience. Along with the finest cuts of Prime imported steaks, the cuisine is highly refined with elegant tableside service. Dishes like Black Truffle Slow Poached Peach-fed Whole Chicken and Lacquer Black Hills Pork Belly' Mahjong' Style will grace the menu with modern interpretations based on refined French techniques. This fine dining room will seats 78 persons and also feature the finest cigar lounge in Shanghai. The 6th level is more casual and called the Lounge & Terrace. This area can seat more than 120 and is aimed at noshing and cocktailing for the young and hip. The menu on this level will feature an array of dishes dressed for sharing. This menu was culled, redefined and focused from the finest of the 14 restaurants owned and operated by Mr. Chen. Dishes include Stone Roasted Hamachi Collar, Sizzling Spicy Black Bean & Infused Pesto Oil and Angus Steak Tartar, Smoke Egg Sabayon, Capers, Toasted Pine Nuts.

SIGNATURE DISHES
> Ahi Tuna Tartar Poke Style
> Hand Chopped Burger 'Supreme' Black Truffle, Foie Gras, & Quail Egg
> 'Prime' Cut Steak Tartar
> Stone Roasted Angus (CAB) or PRIME Steaks

WINE: The Strip also features 2 bars with a featured outdoor glamour bar. We offer more than 20 signature cocktails with an extensive list of rare Scotches and Bourbons.

SERVICE: Considerate and hospitable service is provided for guests.

6-7F, 282 HUAIHAI ROAD M., SHANGHAI **TEL:** 021-60919893
地址： 上海淮海中路282号香港广场北楼6-7楼

RESERVATIONS: Recommended
DRESS CODE: Smart Formal
LUNCH HOURS: 11:30 am-14:30 pm
DINNER HOURS: 18:00 pm-22:30 pm
LAST ORDER DINNER: 22:30 pm
WEBSITE: www.thestripshanghai.com

VEGETARIAN DISHES: 10+
NO SMOKING SECTION: Yes
CAR VALET: No
CREDIT CARDS: AE, D, J, MC, UP, V
YEAR ESTABLISHED: 2010
PRICE: RMB 400/Person

VA BENE

🍷 8 🍴 9 🍷 9 🎀 9   👏 👏 👏

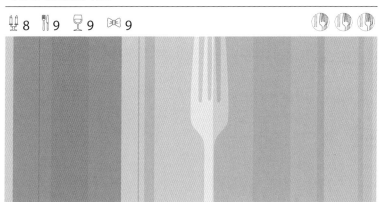

SETTING: Its dim lights, the soft jazz music, its brown-yellow interiors, the wooden flooring and linen-dressed tables all welcome you into a proper fine-dining setting.

FOOD: The menu features quite a wide selection covering the whole of Italy from North to South, presented in very classic styles as well as fancy, modern versions. Among the latter, the eggplant "Parmigiana" comes as a beautiful re-interpretation of this very Mediterranean dish, with an flavorful eggplant mash and fragrant tomato sauce accompanied by a crispy croquette hiding a surprising core of cheese fondue.There are also a couple of tasting menus, whose smaller portions allow sampling of more varieties while maintaining one's budget.From the mains, the sliced sea bass is another tasteful creation of colors and textures, with its soft meat in a crispy coat of olives and artichokes, and its incredibly smooth potato mash paired with crunchy veggies sticks. For something more hearty, try any of the meat dishes. The massive, fragrant Milanese, for example, or the ossobuco, with its melt-in-the-mouth tenderness and surprisingly delicate taste.The dessert list leans heavily on the indulgent side, featuring tantalizing proposals such as a chocolate sphere with hot chocolate fondue or a Valrhona molten chocolate gateaux.

SIGNATURE DISHES
> Not mentioned

WINE: A very complete and extensive list covering both Old and New world and even China, with a deep focus on Italy's best. Wines are orderly arranged by origin country, then grape variety and vintage, ranging in bouquet, body and prices from common to very rare.

SERVICE: The staff is cordially pleasant, and works hard to keep pace with this venue's steady inflow of guests.

BUILDING 7, NORTH BLOCK XINTIANDI, 181 TAI CANG ROAD, SHANGHAI **TEL:** 021-63112211
地址： 上海太仓路181弄新天地北里7号楼（近马当路）

RESERVATIONS: Necessary
DRESS CODE: Smart casual
LUNCH HOURS: 11:30 am-14:30 pm
DINNER HOURS: 18:00 pm-22:30 pm
LAST ORDER DINNER: 22:30 pm
WEBSITE: www.vabeneshanghai.com

VEGETARIAN DISHES: 3-5
NO SMOKING SECTION: No
CAR VALET: No
CREDIT CARDS: AE, D, J, MC, UP, V
YEAR ESTABLISHED: 2001
PRICE: RMB 400/Person

VILLAGE GUEST HOUSE

♔ 8   🍴 8   🍷 8   ⍟ 8

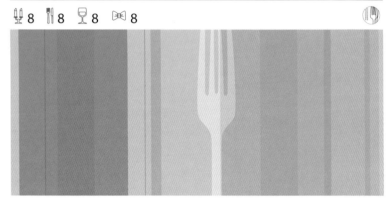

SETTING: With a graceful courtyard, millstone, stone channel, tables and benches and waterscape the restaurant is relaxing and a wonderful place to walk and dine.

FOOD: Village Guest House specializes in Guizhou style dishes, which is not overly spicy. The so-called Guizhou cuisine of Shanghai caters to the taste of Shanghainese. We order Multi-flavor Peanuts and Dry Wild Mushrooms, which is made up of wild mushrooms from Fanjing Mountain and dried by chilli oil on a slow fire. The wild mushroom is spicy and fragrant. Among the hot dishes, Pearl Abalone with Pickle is outstanding, which is sauted with fresh abalone and home-made pickle. WuJiang Fish in Sour Soup is made with wild Wujiang fish, which is fresh and tender and is boiled in the natural plant sour soup, and is a healthy option. Special Steamed Chicken can be described as "Steaming" chicken, and is pickled with special spices. Then, the chicken is steamed so that it is tender and fragrant, and the soup tastes delicious with its original flavor. The potato cake is highly recommended. Firstly, the potato is steamed and mashed, then salt, pepper and other seasonings are added. It is then friend to a delicious, gentle crispness.

SIGNATURE DISHES
> Tofu dumplings
> Wujiang fish in sour soup
> Home-made pickles

WINE: Guizhou is the home of Maotai, with a variety of Maotai spirits, yellow wines and grape wines for the customers to choose.

SERVICE: While the service is considerate, it is often done without smile, probably because the staff are very busy.

525 HONGZHONG ROAD, SHANGHAI **TEL:** 021-64019777
地址： 上海虹中路525号

RESERVATIONS: Necessary for Dinner
DRESS CODE: Smart casual
LUNCH HOURS: 11:30 am-14:00 pm
DINNER HOURS: 17:00 pm-22:00 pm
LAST ORDER DINNER: 22:00 pm
WEBSITE: www.qianxiangge.com

VEGETARIAN DISHES: 10+
NO SMOKING SECTION: Yes
CAR VALET: No
CREDIT CARDS: J, MC, UP, V
YEAR ESTABLISHED: 2004
PRICE: RMB 120/Person

VUE RESTAURANT

 9   9   9   9

SETTING: One side of the covered corridor to the restaurant on the 30th floor of Hyatt on the Bund has a vast array of beautiful crystal artworks and the other side features the beautiful scenery of both banks of the Pujiang River. The restaurant is designed with a private home concept, which is divided into different areas such as a study, living room, kitchen etc.

FOOD: It boasts authentic European cuisine. It is another western restaurant managed by Mr. Zhou Hongbin, who is very popular in China at present and has the title of Kitchen God, which is loved by Chinese and foreign epicures. Each dish is made of best ingredients and the food is all wonderful. The on-the-spot cooking stage is gives you a chance to appreciate the chef's exquisite cooking skills. Taste the beef tart, Boston lobster bisque, exquisite boiled cornmeal mash with eggs and truffle and fragrant Spanish ham stored in 36 months. Do not miss the Angus steak with sauce or the fried fat liver with tender inside and seared outside. The bread is excellent and the desserts have a wide selection, including Curaçao French pancakes. Do not miss the Sunday champagne brunch, which features oysters, lobster and Alaska's big crab.

SIGNATURE DISHES
> Beef steak tartar
> Goose liver terrine
> Caesar salad
> Steak au poivre
> Tiger prawns, pernod, bell poppers, zucchini
> Seabass, pan-fried

WINE: The wine collection is very rich with over 300 kinds of vintage wines from all over the world.

SERVICE: Waiters are very professional and they can politely communicate and interact with guests.

30F, 199 HUANGPU ROAD, SHANGHAI **TEL:** 021-63931234-6328
地址： 上海黄浦路199号外滩茂悦大酒店西楼30楼

RESERVATIONS: Recommended
DRESS CODE: Smart casual
LUNCH HOURS: No
DINNER HOURS: 18:00 pm-23:00 pm
LAST ORDER DINNER: 22:30 pm
WEBSITE: www.shanghai.bund.hyatt.com

VEGETARIAN DISHES: 5-10
NO SMOKING SECTION: Yes
CAR VALET: No
CREDIT CARDS: AE, D, J, MC, UP, V
YEAR ESTABLISHED: 2007
PRICE: RMB 600/Person

WAN HAO RESTAURANT

♨ 8　🍴 8　🍷 9　🎀 9

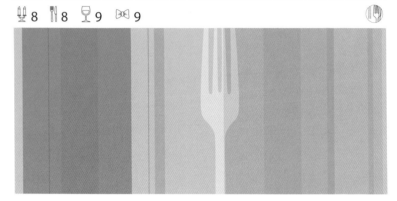

SETTING: The dinning environment is reasonably comfortable.

FOOD: The restaurant mainly features Cantonese Cuisine, along with a splash of Shanghai and Sichuan dishes. The cold dishes are fresh and delicate, and worthy of the five-star hotel. Marinated salty duck is bland at first, but is infused with freshness and a subtle taste of wild pepper. Sliced pork with cucumber and minced garlic has a gentle flavor as the minced garlic is not too strong. The hot dishes are wonderful, the Pan-fried beef ribs with soy sauce is succulent and tender and the meat is of good quality. Another favorite is braised Japanese bean curd with golden mushrooms and conpoy, which has a complementary taste of different seasonings. Conpoy and Bean Curd are braised together, but the flavors retain their distinctive character. In addition, the cabbage reduces greasiness. The soup is Double-boiled mushrooms soup with fish maw and Chinese cabbage. The fish maw is braised on a low heat so that the fish maw melts into the soup. The restaurant boasts a wonderful variety of Dim sum, the most popular being Hong Kong style Wonton noodle soup. The Wonton is fresh shrimp meat. "Sichuan" dan dan noodles are spicy, yet not stifling.

SIGNATURE DISHES
> Marinated salty duck
> Crystal cod fish jelly
> Smoked preserved egg yolk with caviar
> Pan-fried beef ribs
> Braised Japanese bean curd conpoy

WINE: Drinks are plentiful and varied and the restaurant has an extensive list of Old and New World wines. There is also no lack of high-middle and high-end spirits and yellow wine.

SERVICE: The service here is up to the hotel standard. Waiters devote themselves to their tasks while maintain a helpful attitude and are well informed.

39F, 399 NANJING ROAD W., SHANGHAI **TEL:** 021-53594969-6436
地址： 上海南京西路399号39楼

RESERVATIONS: Recommended
DRESS CODE: Smart casual
LUNCH HOURS: 11:30 am-14:30 pm
DINNER HOURS: 17:30 pm-22:30 pm
LAST ORDER DINNER: 22:25 pm
WEBSITE: No

VEGETARIAN DISHES: 10+
NO SMOKING SECTION: Yes
CAR VALET: No
CREDIT CARDS: AE, D, J, MC, V
YEAR ESTABLISHED: 2002
PRICE: RMB 150-300/Person

WAN LI RESTAURANT

🍴 8   🍴 8   🍷 8   🎀 9

SETTING: There is a wonderful old rattan chair with a silk cloth back cushion and the tables are separated by screens, which offer elegance and privacy.

FOOD: Specializing in Cantonese cuisine and some Shanghai dishes, the best cold dish is without doubt the Marinated Jellyfish in Shallot Oil. The jellyfish is crisp, tender and fresh, and wafts with the bountiful fragrance of shallots. The dish Tea Tree Mushroom is unique and a must try. The tea tree mushroom, covered with sauce and wrapped with rice flour, is fried until light yellow; it tastes divine and is best when dipped in the specially-made chili sauce. One of the signature hot dishes is Soon Hock Fish in Oil. The Soon Hock Fish gets this name as it looks similar to the soon hock. The meat is rich and smooth and thankfully it has few bones. It's also delicious steamed. As the restaurant focuses on Cantonese cuisine, do not miss the snacks, such as shrimp dumplings, which are plump and have a lively flavor. The pan fried tofu skin is crisp; the outside skin is fried to a golden yellow and the tender, crystal large shrimp inside tastes delicious when dipped in vinegar. As for the desserts, chrysanthemum sago ice cream, which is made with chrysanthemum tea, is highly recommended.

SIGNATURE DISHES
> Marinated black fungus with chill
> Jelly fish with spring onion
> Barbecued meat combination
> Sauteed shrimp balls with vegetables

WINE: The wine list is rich with vintage wines imported from various countries and home-made distilled spirits and rice wine.

SERVICE: The well trained waiters are keen and efficient.

2F, 100 CHANGLIU ROAD, SHANGHAI **TEL:** 021-38714888
地址：上海浦东新区长柳路（联洋新社区）100号2楼

RESERVATIONS: Recommended
DRESS CODE: Smart casual
LUNCH HOURS: 11:00 am-14:30 pm
DINNER HOURS: 17:00 pm-22:00 pm
LAST ORDER DINNER: 22:00 pm
WEBSITE: www.renaissancepudong.com

VEGETARIAN DISHES: 10+
NO SMOKING SECTION: Yes
CAR VALET: No
CREDIT CARDS: AE, D, J, MC, UP, V
YEAR ESTABLISHED: 2003
PRICE: RMB 150-200/Person

WHAMPOA CLUB

♟ 9 🍴 9 🍷 9 🎀 9   🖐 🖐 🖐

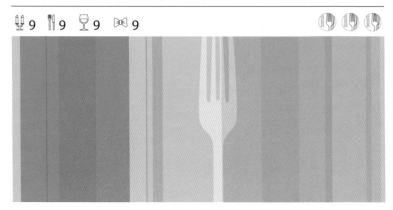

SETTING: The big crystal chandelier inside the restaurant and the outstanding wall decorations are very luxurious. Palace lanterns and the chair backs with dragon-carved patterns in the private rooms imply the high status of the diners.

FOOD: The emphasis for a restaurant must always be on taste. If its dishes are merely common it is doubtful that guests will return. Whampoa Club focuses on taste and preparation. Smoked fish (herring) of old Shanghai is one of the specialties of the restaurant, which offers guests the real taste of Old Shanghai. It is a slightly sweet and very refreshing. The crispy eel of Wuxi has crisp meat and sweet gravy. It is a good starter dish. Deep-Fried Prawn topped with mustard uses big prawn and it is worth trying. The two tastes only act to enhance the flavor of the other. The Chinese dish sticky rice with goose liver, chicken heart and dates is cooked in a western style. It melts in the mouth. The red dates are very tasty for they absorb the fragrance of the sticky rice. If you want to taste the real style of Shanghai cuisine, the traditional Shanghai dishes such as Crab Powder Ball, Boiled Dried Bean Curd and Stir-fried Rice Cake are served here. In addition, the restaurant also provides set meals of RMB 288 per person.

SIGNATURE DISHES
> Sugar-cured flutinous red dates with cinnamon apple and seared goose liver
> Old-fashioned Shanghainese smoked fish
> Deep-fried crispy eel strips. Wuxi style

WINE: Various kinds of wines are served here.

SERVICE: Waiters of high quality serve water and tea considerately.

5F, 3 ZHONGSHAN NO.1 ROAD E., SHANGHAI **TEL:** 021-63213737
地址： 上海中山东一路3号5楼

RESERVATIONS: Recommended
DRESS CODE: Smart casual
LUNCH HOURS: 11:30 am-14:30 pm
DINNER HOURS: 17:30 pm-22:00 pm
LAST ORDER DINNER: 22:00 pm
WEBSITE: www.threeonthebund.com

VEGETARIAN DISHES: 5-10
NO SMOKING SECTION: Yes
CAR VALET: Yes
CREDIT CARDS: AE, D, J, MC, UP, V
YEAR ESTABLISHED: 2009
PRICE: RMB 500/Person

WINE BAR & GRILL

🍴 8   🍴 8   🍷 9   🎀 9   🥄🥄

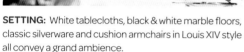

SETTING: White tablecloths, black & white marble floors, classic silverware and cushion armchairs in Louis XIV style all convey a grand ambience.

FOOD: Wine & Bar Grill's menu has a very helpful layout, offering suggestions by the chef, and is arranged by tapas and salads for light lunches and snacks, and a few choices of meats and fish broiled on the spot. From crunchy bread baskets to the many choices of side dishes, the attention to detail is quite pleasant. Start the dinner with the house's artistic amuse-bouche, and venture on with the delectable foie gras 3 variations, which come beautifully presented as a melt-in-the-mouth mousse on fine jelly, a diced terrine filled with crunchy dry fruits resting on a bed of sweet bell pepper ratatouille, and a pan fried with special wine sauce. Fresh off the grill, the 200 day grain-fed Wagyu beef is a rich, full flavorful rib eye seared to perfection; savor it with any of the many sauces and two side dishes of your choice. The desserts list is short but excellent. The luscious strawberry tiramisu` steals the show, artistically served as a four-variations arrangement featuring a mousse with insert, jelly, crispy macarons, and rich vanilla ice cream drowned under strawberry sauce.

SIGNATURE DISHES
> Goose liver
> Caesar salad
> French onion soup
> Rib eye steak
> Sirloin steak
> Norway salmon steak

WINE: Being also a wine bar and set within a hotel, the restaurant's list is extremely varied and complete, ranging from rare champagnes to freshly squeezed juice, liquors, soft drinks, cocktails and teas.

SERVICE: The staff is nice and polite and ready to accommodate the diners' requests.

3F, 1225 NANJING ROAD W., SHANGHAI **TEL:** 021-62791888-5306
地址：上海南京西路1225号3楼

RESERVATIONS: Necessary for Lunch
DRESS CODE: Smart casual
LUNCH HOURS: No
DINNER HOURS: 17:30 pm-22:00 pm
LAST ORDER DINNER: 21:30 pm
WEBSITE: www.meritus-hotels.com

VEGETARIAN DISHES: 3-5
NO SMOKING SECTION: Yes
CAR VALET: No
CREDIT CARDS: AE, D, J, MC, UP, V
YEAR ESTABLISHED: 2004
PRICE: RMB 400/Person

XINDALU-CHINA KITCHEN

♨ 8   🍴 9   🍷 9   🍽 9   🍴 🍴 🍴

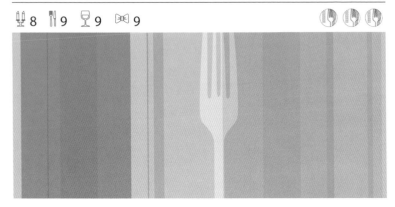

SETTING: It may be the most authentic Chinese Kitchen in Shanghai. The elegant ingredients and seasonings are a part of the decoration and originality of the restaurant. The decoration is luxurious and avant-garde. While having dinner, customers can watch the rotating duck in the traditional Beijing stone furnace and the chefs at work.

FOOD: If you are a roast duck fan, this restaurant is an excellent choice for it provides the some of the best authentic Beijing Duck roasted in traditional fruit tree wood. It takes considerable time to roast the duck in this way so you should order one hour ahead of time, but it is well worth the wait. Under the auspices of the famous chef Ken Jin, who is well-known in China, all the dishes here are elegant and delicious. Worth mentioning is the fried shrimps with Longjing tea and jasmine tea smoked fish. Pot Sticker features enticing colors, aromatic smell and a distinctive shape. Crab Powder Ball, cod fish in clay pot, Beggars Chicken (Baked Chicken), Wuliangye Pea Greens, Mushroom as well as seasonal vegetables, such as saury in Spring and live fresh water crab in autumn, can satisfy every customer. If you want to show off Chinese cuisine to a foreign friend, being them here.

SIGNATURE DISHES

> Smoked carp fillet
> Zhenjiang pork mushroom jelly, ginger vinegar
> Crispy fried fresh water shrimps, shaoxing wine
> Old fashioned peking duck from wood-fried oven

WINE: Many knds of beverages are availble including Chinese Chinese spirits and wine.

SERVICE: The service level here is professional and moderate, which is similar to that of the Hyatt Hotel.

1F, EAST TOWER, 199 HUANGPU ROAD, SHANGHAI **TEL:** 021-63931234-6318
地址： 上海黄浦路199号外滩茂悦大酒店东楼1楼

RESERVATIONS: Recommended
DRESS CODE: Smart casual
LUNCH HOURS: 11:30 am-14:30 pm
DINNER HOURS: 17:30 pm-23:00 pm
LAST ORDER DINNER: 22:30 pm
WEBSITE: www.shanghai.bund.hyatt.com

VEGETARIAN DISHES: 10+
NO SMOKING SECTION: Yes
CAR VALET: No
CREDIT CARDS: AE, D, J, MC, UP, V
YEAR ESTABLISHED: 2007
PRICE: RMB 400/Person

X-SENSATION

🍴 8   🍴 8   🍷 9   🎀 9

SETTING: The Revolving Restaurant on the 46th floor of the Jinjiang Oriental gives guests the feeling of floating above all the cares of the world as they gaze at the beautiful, wondrous scenery through 2 meter high French windows.

SIGNATURE DISHES
> Stir-fried Calamari
> Pan-fried foie gras
> Roasted veal loin
> Pan-fried codfish

FOOD: The restaurant is famous for its outstanding sea food, but offers excellent dishes besides. The sea food, such as salmon, Tuna and arctic surf clam, are all exceptionally fresh, especially the salmon. Staff are assigned specially for slicing, so no need to worry about running out. The vast array of sea food also includes sweet shrimps, Mantis shrimp, King crab and small lobsters. There's also a selection of sushi of eel, roe, among others, on offer, each being utterly delicious and fresh. Besides the seafood, the restaurant boats ten hot dishes, including roasted mutton chop, fried steak, fried goose liver, chicken shashlik and various western style vegetables. Still hungry? The fried goose liver on the Zero menu is well worth sampling. It melts in the mouth and is very popular among guests. The western snacks are also a must try. Although the choice is limited, all are delicious, especially the coffee flan. Don't forget the ice cream.

WINE: On normal days, a free drink with the supper may be supplied. There are also many wines with an additional charge. Coffee, mixed drinks and fresh fruit juices are also available.

SERVICE: Waiters with kind smiles provide sound service. Dinner plates are changed timely.

46F, 889 YANGGAO ROAD S., SHANGHAI **TEL:** 021-50504888-74602
地址： 上海浦东新区杨高南路889号东锦江大酒店46楼

RESERVATIONS: Recommended
DRESS CODE: Smart casual
LUNCH HOURS: No
DINNER HOURS: 18:00 pm-22:00 pm
LAST ORDER DINNER: 22:00 pm
WEBSITE: www.shanghaijjorientalhotel.com

VEGETARIAN DISHES: 10+
NO SMOKING SECTION: Yes
CAR VALET: No
CREDIT CARDS: AE, D, J, MC, UP, V
YEAR ESTABLISHED: 2002
PRICE: RMB 198+/Person

YAMAZATO

🍴 8 🍴 9 🍷 8 🎀 9

SETTING: Located on the second floor of Okura Garden Hotel Shanghai, YAMAZATO boasts an elegant ambience created by the authentic Japanese-style wooden décor and design. All private rooms are named after flowers and trees. In front of the bar counter, the Japanese sushi master from the headquarters in Okura presents live shows for guests.

FOOD: As well as being one of the seven restaurants in mainland Japan and abroad that are part of the Japan Okura Group, YAMAZATO is also one of the earliest and most authentic high-end Japanese restaurants in Shanghai. Specializing in Kansai cooking and using only fresh seasonal ingredients, YAMAZATO effortlessly provides a feast for all the senses, by placing colorful, fresh fish in exquisite tableware. Dishes are cooked with wonderful, rare skill. Delicate sushi made on the spot can be ordered a-la-carte. What is not to be missed are the Tuna TORO, Sushi, Sashimi, top-grade Japanese Black Cattle Hot Pot and Tricholoma Matsutake in autumn, which is a firm favorite in Shanghai.

SIGNATURE DISHES
> Today's cold 5 kind of appetizer
> Vegetable salad
> Assorted raw fish
> Special beef steak toubanyaki
> Special sushi set
> Assorted tempura

WINE: A rich collection of Japanese sakes, iichiko and plum wine complemented by grape wines and Chinese white spirits.

SERVICE: Well-trained waiters in kimono provide hospitable and impeccable service.

2F, 58 MAOMING ROAD S., SHANGHAI **TEL:** 021-64151111-5216
地址： 上海茂名南路58号花园饭店2楼

RESERVATIONS: Recommended
DRESS CODE: Smart casual
LUNCH HOURS: 11:30 am-14:30 pm
DINNER HOURS: 17:30 pm-22:30 pm
LAST ORDER DINNER: 22:30 pm
WEBSITE: www.gardenhotelshanghai.com

VEGETARIAN DISHES: 3-5
NO SMOKING SECTION: Yes
CAR VALET: Yes
CREDIT CARDS: AE, D, J, MC, UP, V
YEAR ESTABLISHED: 1990
PRICE: RMB 500/Person

YÈ SHANGHAI

🕯8 🍴8 🍷8 🎀8

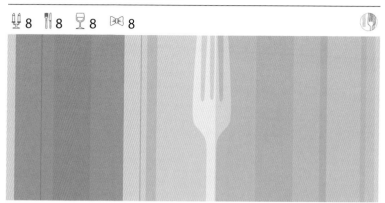

SETTING: The nostalgic surroundings and comfortable dining environment are the perfect location for sampling classical dishes.

FOOD: The cold dish Potpourri of Eighteen Vegetables isn't a tiger dish like with other restaurants. It is made from clean and tender cucumber, lettuce, carrot and other vegetables, so it looks very appetizing and healthy, but it also has a pleasant crispy character. Huadiao wine marinated "drunken" chicken has a vibrant bouquet to match the fresh and tender chicken. The hot dishes here are also excellent. The minced chicken with pine nuts in Sautéed minced chicken and the nuts served with sesame pastry pockets are fine examples of Huaiyang cuisine. The preparation technique is so good that the chicken is minced unbelievably well. The pine nuts in it are very delicate but bursting with flavor. Minced chicken and pine nuts with sesame seed cake is delicious and filling. The river shrimps are not large, but the meat is juicy and delicious. The soup here is also good. Double-Boiled Truffle Soup with Chicken and Conch as well as Dried Scallop, Clams and Pork Soup are both wonderful. The ingredients of Double-boiled Truffle Soup with Chicken and Conch are enchanting and its pure taste is clearly nourishing.

SIGNATURE DISHES

> Potpourri of eighteen vegetables
> Huadiao wine marinated "drunken" chicken
> Sea cucumber with wild sauce
> Sauteed river shrimps

WINE: There are all kinds of wine from the Old and New World, plus Chinese spirits and yellow wine as well as homemade yellow wine.

SERVICE: The service is up to standard. The waiters here are diligent and answer questions promptly.

BUILDING 6, XINTIANDI SQUARE, 338 HUANGPI ROAD S., SHANGHAI **TEL:** 021-63112323

地址： 上海黄陂南路338号新天地广场6号楼

RESERVATIONS: Recommended
DRESS CODE: Smart casual
LUNCH HOURS: 11:30 am-14:30 pm
DINNER HOURS: 17:30 pm-22:30 pm
LAST ORDER DINNER: 22:00 pm
WEBSITE: www.elite-concepts.com

VEGETARIAN DISHES: 10+
NO SMOKING SECTION: Yes
CAR VALET: No
CREDIT CARDS: AE, D, J, MC, UP, V
YEAR ESTABLISHED: 2001
PRICE: RMB 300/Person

YI LONG COURT

🍴 9   🍴 9   🍷 9   🎀 8   👐 👐 👐

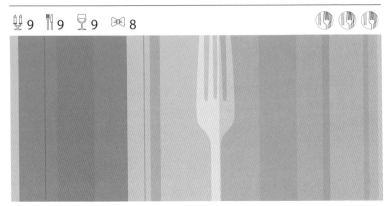

SETTING: Peach wooden floors, fireplace, upholstery sofa, big windows, exquisite porcelains and drinking vessels with Peninsula logo make the experience seem like a manor house in the old times. It has a exalted, glorious palatial style in which to enjoy exquisite food.

FOOD: The menu of Yi Long Court Restaurant has many beautiful things: the seasonal kitchen selection includes various cuisines of southern and northern regions of China, the exquisite home-made dishes that making you feel at ease, the set meals for two persons the exquisite maigre selection for vegetarians. Each of them is magnificent and difficult to resist. Chef Deng's Cantonese cuisine is exquisite and excellent. Braised crab with Chinese vermicelli is a great choice. The Chinese vermicelli is dried, and then the crab meat is added, together with paste and sauce. The process is complex and the resulting taste is very fragrant and delicious. The fresh abalone with plant worm soup, authentic mushroom with soy bean sauce, shark'fin dumpling stuffed soup cooked with an ancient method, the high-grade scalded beef, Beijing roast duck with an outer golden crisp coat covering the tender meat as well as the dessert of sesame pudding created by the Peninsula Shanghai are all difficult to forget.

SIGNATURE DISHES
> Sliced jellyfish
> Pan-fried bean curd sheet rolled with assorted fungus
> Marinated peppers with thousand years egg
> Diced beef with sliced garlic in honey sauce

WINE: The tea stage is a specially and the collection of tea and wine on the tea and wine lists are very rich, including Chinese distilled spirits, local rice wine, wine, champagne as well as various vintage wines of the old and new world.

SERVICE: The waiters can speak Chinese and English fluently. They look kind and warm but inattentive.

32 ZHONGSHAN NO.1 ROAD E., SHANGHAI **TEL:** 021-23276742
地址： 上海中山东一路32号

RESERVATIONS: Recommended
DRESS CODE: Smart casual
LUNCH HOURS: 11:30 am-14:30 pm
DINNER HOURS: 18:00 pm-22:30 pm
LAST ORDER DINNER: 22:30 pm
WEBSITE: www.peninsula.com

VEGETARIAN DISHES: 10+
NO SMOKING SECTION: Yes
CAR VALET: Yes
CREDIT CARDS: AE, D, J, MC, UP, V
YEAR ESTABLISHED: 2009
PRICE: RMB 500/Person

YIN CHU XUAN

🍴8 🍴8 🍷8 🎀8

SETTING: The simple yet magnificent interior decoration of the restaurant, together with background music, conveys a distinctly Chinese character.

FOOD: The restaurant serves two major varieties of cuisine, namely Cantonese and Sichuan. The cold dish Jellyfish has a mild but moreish flavor, while the Duck Tongue is somewhat plain. However, the Salted Peanuts boast a strong, vibrant flavor. The hot dishes, such as Stir-Fried Scallops with broccoli, are unique and wonderful. The fresh, plump and delicate American scallops are very fragrant, and the broccoli is light yet crisp. The Simmered Codfish is crisp and tender, and with its bitter melon, is harmonious in its five flavors (sweet, sour, bitter, pungent, and salty). The sautéed shrimp is a reinvention of the classic Cantonese shrimp and the Corn Juice poured over the dish is delicious. Also, the Asparagus with Shrimps is well worth trying. Iceberg lettuce, a fried lettuce in Cantonese style, holds a perfect color, aroma, taste and appearance. The Guangzhou rice is also very moist as it has added broth. The Dim sum specialty Shrimp Dumpling has large and succulent shrimps. Dessert Mango sago is refreshing and not too sweet.

SIGNATURE DISHES
> Jellyfish
> Bonbon Chicken in Sichuan Style
> Cantonese BBQ plate
> Braised shark's fin
> Stirfried scallp
> Simmered codfish

WINE: Mid-range wine from New and Old World are available, and yellow wine is abundant.

SERVICE: The hotel service here is considerate.

2F, 388 DADUHE ROAD, SHANGHAI **TEL:** 021-60958888-7086
地址： 上海大渡河路388号，云岭东路口国盛中心国丰酒店2楼

RESERVATIONS: Recommended
DRESS CODE: Smart casual
LUNCH HOURS: 11:30 am-14:30 pm
DINNER HOURS: 17:30 pm-22:30 pm
LAST ORDER DINNER: 22:00 pm
WEBSITE: www.guoman.com

VEGETARIAN DISHES: 10+
NO SMOKING SECTION: Yes
CAR VALET: No
CREDIT CARDS: AE, D, J, MC, UP, V
YEAR ESTABLISHED: 2010
PRICE: RMB 300/Person

YU SHANGHAI

♨8　♨8　♆8　♣8　◉

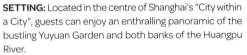

SETTING: Located in the centre of Shanghai's "City within a City", guests can enjoy an enthralling panoramic of the bustling Yuyuan Garden and both banks of the Huangpu River.

FOOD: The dishes are mostly Cantonese cuisine mixed with some local and Sichuan choices. The favorite appetizer is Fried Bean Curd Roll Stuffed with Carrot and Mushroom, or "ringing bell", which is lightly fried and crispy. Fresh Mixed Vegetable Roll with Five Treasure Sauce is a sweet vegetable roll covered with a delightfully tangy salad dressing. The specialty hot dish, Braised Fish Head Soup 'Canton' style, is a head of spotted silver carp steamed in an airtight casserole dish with a onion and garlic. It has many delicate flavors and is utterly delicious. Soup of Stewed Sharks Fin with Chicken is a rich combination of thick chicken soup and shark fin stewed with chicken fat and winter melon. Hangu Lamb Breast Pot is crisp and nutritious, and comes with preserved bean curd juice and chili sauce for dipping. Cantonese style Stir-fried Assorted Shrimp Flatcake has strips of shrimp, snow peas, carrots, water chestnuts and Chinese broccoli that are stir fried together and releases off an enticing aroma.

SIGNATURE DISHES
> Braised fish head soup
> Sweet and sour pork
> Stir-fried diced beef
> Marinated egg
> Braised squids
> Fresh mixed vegetable roll with treasure sauce

WINE: All kinds of wines of varying quality from the old and the new world are available. They also have a complete list of Chinese white wine and millet wine.

SERVICE: The waiters and waitresses are passionate and considerate. They are equipped with a complete, professional knowledge.

3F, 69 JIUXIAOCHANG ROAD, SHANGHAI **TEL:** 021-63283886
地址： 上海城隍庙豫园旧校场路69号悦宾楼3楼

RESERVATIONS: Recommended
DRESS CODE: Smart casual
LUNCH HOURS: 11:00 am-14:00 pm
DINNER HOURS: 18:00 pm-22:00 pm
LAST ORDER DINNER: 22:00 pm
WEBSITE: www.yushanghai.com

VEGETARIAN DISHES: 10+
NO SMOKING SECTION: Yes
CAR VALET: No
CREDIT CARDS: AE, D, J, MC, V
YEAR ESTABLISHED: 2010
PRICE: RMB 100-200/Person

YU TING CHINESE RESTAURANT

♟ 8 🍴 8 🍷 8 ⋈ 9   🤚 🤚

SETTING: The walls are decorated with golden calligraphic works and paintings of Shanghai life, which gives the restaurant tremendous vigor.

FOOD: The chefs in Yu Ting specialize in bringing the characteristics of the ingredients into play and expertly control the preparation. The cold dish Chilled Chicken in Yellow Wine Sauce is a delicacy from Shanghai prepared with wine. The dish is cooked with boneless chicken thighs and features bright colors and a bountiful aroma. It is fresh and succulent. Assorted Barbecue Platter from the Cantonese cuisine has barbecued pork and roasted goose, among others. Its ingredients are very fresh. The bright red barbecued pork seems to melt in the mouth. The dish looks oily but it is just very juicy. The meat is extraordinarily tender and will melt like butter in the mouth, while the flavor is full of natural goodness. The skin, meat, bone of roasted goose comes in one piece. The dish is rich in gravy, and features a mellow taste, crispy skin, tender meat and is aromatic. Deep Fried Prawns are first de-shelled, then wrapped with thin noodles and finally fried in the pan until golden brown. The meat of the big, fresh prawns is slightly sweet and chewy. It is a must-try specialty.

SIGNATURE DISHES
> Drunken Chicken
> Crispy Hei zhong Groose
> chilled coconut pudding and papaya
> Deep fried prawn roll with kataifi
> Sauteed shredded beef

WINE: It provides a wide variety of beverage services and soft drink choices.

SERVICE: The waiters are attentive, courteous and responsive.

535 PUDONG AVENUE, SHANGHAI **TEL:** 021-38789888-6350
地址： 上海浦东新区浦东大道535号

RESERVATIONS: Recommended
DRESS CODE: Smart casual
LUNCH HOURS: 11:00 am-14:30 pm
DINNER HOURS: 17:30 pm-22:00 pm
LAST ORDER DINNER: 21:45 pm
WEBSITE: www.etonhotelshanghai.cn

VEGETARIAN DISHES: 10+
NO SMOKING SECTION: Yes
CAR VALET: Yes
CREDIT CARDS: AE, D, J, MC, UP, V
YEAR ESTABLISHED: 2007
PRICE: RMB 250/Person

28 HUBIN ROAD

8   9   9   8

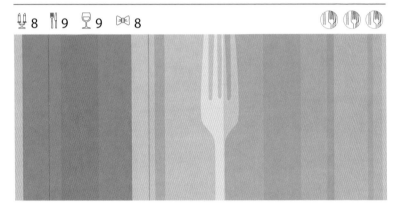

SETTING: When entering into the Hubin 28 Chinese themed restaurant, a huge carriage stands before you. This carriage, with a history of more than 100 years, is from Henan Province and full of the traditional Shaoxing wine jars. In under a minute, the sincere and warm atmosphere is peppered with the zealous welcome of the hosts.

FOOD: The characteristic dishes of Hangzhou cuisine, such as fried shrimp with Longjing tea and Beggar's chicken, can be found in the menu. Excellent ingredients, expert skills and enticing decoration are the main characteristics here. The special recommendations on the menu are all the seasonal dishes. One is Braised Qiantang River Crucian Carp in Folk Style. The fresh wild crucian carp is soaked with nourishing fish soup that is boiled for a long time and covered with soft glutinous rich cake, and the carp is tender and rich. Another recommended dish is Flavor Curry Crab: fat crabs with thick curry sauce that has a hot yet delicate flavor that is simply mouthwatering. The Beef Rib with Chili: tender beef with cattle bone juice, decorated with full and delicious chestnuts is bursting with tender and fragrant flavors. The ingredients embrace the flavors of the world, the special ingredients cooked by the master chefs of the Hyatt Regency creating the most delicious food.

SIGNATURE DISHES
> Double-boiled lamb
> Steamed shrimp and scallop
> Stir-fried shrimps
> Braised Qiantang river crucian carp with rice cake and brown sauce
> Braised Angus beef rib

WINE: In Hubin 28, there are more than 2,000 bottles of excellent wines from Australia and Chile, being a walk-in cellar which owns the most wines in Hangzhou.

SERVICE: Zealous and considerate service can meet the requirements of the customers. They happily recommend dishes and beverages to the customers.

1F, 28 HUBIN ROAD, HANGZHOU **TEL:** 0571-87791234
地址：杭州市湖滨路28号1楼

RESERVATIONS: Recommended
DRESS CODE: Smart casual
LUNCH HOURS: 11:30 am-14:30 pm
DINNER HOURS: 17:00 pm-21:30 pm
LAST ORDER DINNER: 21:00 pm
WEBSITE: www.hangzhou.regency.hyatt.cn

VEGETARIAN DISHES: 5-10
NO SMOKING SECTION: Yes
CAR VALET: Yes
CREDIT CARDS: AE, D, J, MC, V
YEAR ESTABLISHED: 2005
PRICE: RMB 500/Person

BAI YUN

🕯 9　🍴 8　🍷 9　🎀 9

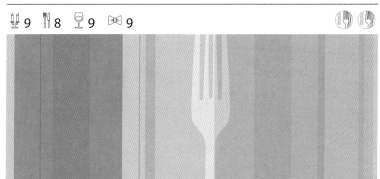

SETTING: Nestled amongst the wetlands, the restaurant, on the side of Xixi Banyan Tree Manor, has swimming fish, flying birds, and flourishing grasses and trees. Streams flow across bridges among elegant buildings. The exterior, with white wall and black tile, is stylish and peaceful. The interior, with its delicate design, uses cloud shaped shades as lighting and dark wood as seats.

FOOD: It is based on classical Hangzhou cuisine and Cantonese cuisine. Taking advantage of the fine weather and setting, all ingredients are sourced from the wetland. Steaming the wild wetland baby mandarin fish in an ancient style is a healthy and delicate dish. The mandarin, the specialty of the wetland, is fresh and tender in texture, smooth and light in palate, and not greasy. Steamed together with ham and mushroom serves to make the flavor richer. Dongpo Pork, the classic famous dish of Hangzhou, is well worth recommending. Using top-grade golden medal pork, it is stewed with ten-year Xieheng Diaohuang wine. With thin skin, tender meat, and an attractive brown-red color, it is mellow in flavor but abundant in juice.

SIGNATURE DISHES
> Glazed fish with sweet soya sauce
> Sweet scented lotus roots,glutinous rice
> Banyan tree combination
> Banyan tree fo-tiao-qiang
> Dong-po pork

WINE: A rich wine list, which gathers fine wines from Australia and France, among others. In addition, the excellent Dragon Well green tea is offered.

SERVICE: Waiters are all friendly, thoughtful and professional.

2 WESTBROOK RESORT ,ZIJINGANG RD. HANGZHOU,ZHEJIANG **TEL:** 0571-85860000
地址： 杭州市紫金港路，西溪天堂国际旅游综合体2号

RESERVATIONS: Necessary for Dinner
DRESS CODE: Smart casual
LUNCH HOURS: 12:00 am-14:00 pm
DINNER HOURS: 18:00 pm-23:00 pm
LAST ORDER DINNER: 22:30 pm
WEBSITE: www.banyantree.com

VEGETARIAN DISHES: 10+
NO SMOKING SECTION: Yes
CAR VALET: Yes
CREDIT CARDS: AE, D, J, MC, UP, V
YEAR ESTABLISHED: 2010
PRICE: RMB 350/Person

D'CAFÉ

🍽 8   9   🍷 9   🎎 9

SETTING: Covering an area of 1,200 square meters, D'café Cafeteria is counted among the top hotel cafeterias. Served on 88-meter ultra-long buffet tables, the dinners are divided into five distinctive areas, namely, seafood, Asian cuisine, Japanese sashimi sushi, Italian food and desserts, totaling some 300 dishes and 40 desserts.

FOOD: As the largest among the five, the Asian cuisine area boasts the widest variety of dishes, mainly serving Chinese cuisine as well as Singaporean, Thai and Malaysian dishes. Among them, the traditional Chinese cuisine includes braised Dongpo pork and old duck soup; Macao roast and Cantonese roast meat. The authentic flavors of Southeast Asia include curry dishes and Tom Yam Kong soup. The seafood area is the most strongly recommended one, which not only provides a rich choice of dishes, but also serves you with rare seafood, such as big green arowana and the opened whole oyster. Most impressive is the goose liver bread. The red wine-fried goose liver lies on a small piece of tender and crispy bread, which can instantly melt in the mouth, and is possibly the most delicious goose liver ever. In the dessert area, a charming chocolate fountain will tempt your taste buds to the limit.

SIGNATURE DISHES
> Fresh Seafood
> Australian Living Oyster
> French- Style Goose Liver
> Carrot Cured in Vinegar
> Sauced Cucumber
> Fried Green Broad Bean

WINE: It offers a wide choice of wines, including yellow rice wine, white spirits, red wine and beers, as well as a variety of whiskies, brandies, gins, vodkas and tequilas.

SERVICE: With excellent five-star service, waiters are warm and considerate, always serving with a smile. They work hard and serve you well, and can even help you fetch the dishes you need. Their service deserves 15% service charge.

1F, 120 SHUGUANG ROAD, HANGZHOU **TEL:** 0571-87998833
地址：杭州市西湖区曙光路120号黄龙饭店1楼

RESERVATIONS: Recommended
DRESS CODE: Smart casual
LUNCH HOURS: 11:30 am-15:00 pm
DINNER HOURS: 17:30 pm-22:00 pm
LAST ORDER DINNER: 21:45 pm
WEBSITE: www.dragon-hotel.com

VEGETARIAN DISHES: 5-10
NO SMOKING SECTION: Yes
CAR VALET: Yes
CREDIT CARDS: AE, MC, V
YEAR ESTABLISHED: 2009
PRICE: RMB 350/Person

GRAND DRAGON

🍽 9 🍴 9 🍷 9 🎀 9   👍 👍 👍

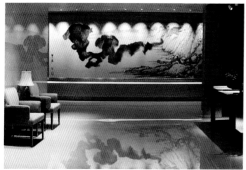

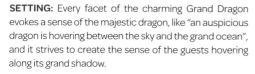

SETTING: Every facet of the charming Grand Dragon evokes a sense of the majestic dragon, like "an auspicious dragon is hovering between the sky and the grand ocean", and it strives to create the sense of the guests hovering along its grand shadow.

FOOD: The Grand Dragon is a magnificent venue, and its renowned chefs Liang Zigeng and Ye Baorong being the connoisseurs of its rich and exceptional Chinese cuisine, gifting the Grand Dragon with an indisputable guarantee of supreme quality. The Grand Dragon insists on using authentic local ingredients and cooking flair to preserve its innovative Hangzhou delicacies and Cantonese cuisines. Some of the outstanding dishes include Hangzhou-style Smoked Fish, Quick-fried Eel Back with Prawns and the The Kung Fu Shark Fin, which is prepared with mother chicken soup and stewed on a low heat for 24 hours, creating an intense fusion of flavors. There's also a wonderful array of dim sum. Also, the Sweet-scented Osmanthus Shrimp Meat comes highly recommended, a dish that uses shrimp meat bathed with seasonal, sweet-scented osmanthus and tastes of supple fragrant sweetness.

SIGNATURE DISHES
> New fashion smoked fish
> Chilled goose liver
> Chilled drunken chicken
> Braised 'Jin Shan Gou' shark's fin with crab meat
> Slow-cooked pointed-sea cucumber

WINE: The restaurant has a rich collection of wines, including various grape wines, white spirits and Shao Xing wines.

SERVICE: Waiters are of fine temperament and respectful attitudes, with high proficiency. The service level parallels with that of Western restaurants despite the fact that this is a Chinese restaurant.

1F, 120 SHUGUANG ROAD, HANGZHOU **TEL:** 0571-87998833
地址： 杭州市西湖区曙光路120号黄龙饭店1楼

RESERVATIONS: Recommended
DRESS CODE: Smart casual
LUNCH HOURS: 11:30 am-14:30 pm
DINNER HOURS: 17:30 pm-21:30 pm
LAST ORDER DINNER: 21:20 pm
WEBSITE: www.dragon-hotel.com

VEGETARIAN DISHES: 10+
NO SMOKING SECTION: Yes
CAR VALET: Yes
CREDIT CARDS: AE, D, J, MC, V
YEAR ESTABLISHED: 2010
PRICE: RMB 350/Person

JADE GARDEN

🍽8 🍴8 🍷8 🎀9

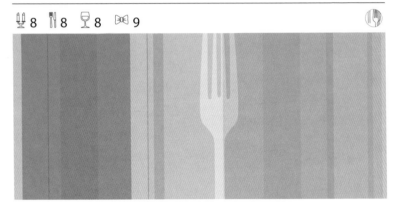

SETTING: Outside the windows you can watch the breeze playing amongst the trees and the bright moon, while the lights indoors are pearlescent and glowing. Lacking luxurious accessories or vulgar and gaudy decorations, Jade features a noble and elegant style.

FOOD: The most well-known principle of the restaurant is "large numbers of ingredients have been collected, but after sorting, only the perfect few will remain". One of the most popular dishes is Three Shreds --- it's the simplest dish but overflowing with the chef's skills. Following the old Shanghai recipe from the 1970s, with shiitake mushrooms on the bottom, the shredded ham, shredded chicken breast and shredded bamboo shoots are added and the soup is poured over. Every succulent piece of the dish is filled with deliciousness. Te flavor brings the kind of freshness that Shanghainese call: "the freshness is popping the eyebrows off". Sautéed River Shrimp is one of the famous old Shanghai dishes. The sparkling shrimp is like beauty personified. They are carefully prepared so there is no sand, and taste wonderfully juicy and succulent. The green beans shine with a fresh, vibrant color.

SIGNATURE DISHES
> Traditional Braised Shredded Mushroom,Ham & Chicken
> Steamed Reeves Shad with Noodles Nest(House Special)
> Sliced Ham with Honey Sauce
> Vietnamese Style Grainy Beef

WINE: A rich collection of different kinds of wines, Chinese spirits, rice wines and beers are offered.

SERVICE: Waiters are nice, hospitable and well-trained. They can explain each dish in detail. Since the kitchen was a little busy that day, the dishes were not served quickly. The waiter observed this and offered to ask the kitchen to speed up which was considerate.

6F, 701 FUCHUN ROAD, HANGZHOU **TEL:** 0571-89705570
地址： 杭州江干区富春路701号万象城6楼

RESERVATIONS: Recommended
DRESS CODE: Smart casual
LUNCH HOURS: 11:00 am-14:00 pm
DINNER HOURS: 17:00 pm-21:00 pm
LAST ORDER DINNER: 21:00 pm
WEBSITE: www.dianping.com/search/category/3/10/r61

VEGETARIAN DISHES: 10+
NO SMOKING SECTION: No
CAR VALET: Yes
CREDIT CARDS: J, UP, V
YEAR ESTABLISHED: 2010
PRICE: RMB 200/Person

NUMBER EIGHT DOWNING STREET

🍴 9   🍴 9   🍷 9   🎀 9

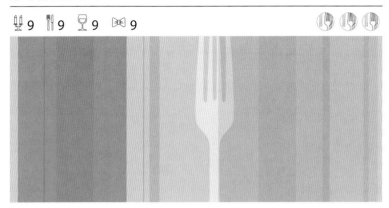

SETTING: It took two and a half years to decorate No. 8 Downing Street, where each rooms has a distinct design style that ranges from the Danube to Washington and from Milan to New York.

FOOD: Braised imperial bird's nest with eagle's brain is said to nourish the men's brains, while Braised imperial bird's nest with Japanese tomatoes is not only delicious but can also make women more beautiful. Mr. Shen Hongfei, a famous food critic, strongly recommends the Cod Cream, which is cooked with cod fat made from cod weighing over 4kg and local soy sauce from Zhoushan. Seasonal organic vegetables soaked in the water from Tiger Spring are distinctive; the slight, natural smell of earth is covered by seasonings. It is said that the vegetables change with the seasons, so every season there are new delicious dishes. Chinese giant salamander in strong soup is an excellent dish. The giant salamander here are not those that are protected but those that are farmed. Although it is not wild, the strong soup is rich in nourishment. The milky soup is stewed slowly with dozens of ingredients for more than ten hours, and it is one of the most popular dishes. The customized Hangzhou-style Noodles with Vegetable is transported by air and served in limited quantities.

SIGNATURE DISHES
> Touf
>Steamed crab with rice wine
>Jiangnan beef
>Oyster

WINE: Wine here is abundant. Red wine from different countries and Chinese famous spirits are available in all varieties.

SERVICE: The waiters here are thoughtful and respectful. Moreover, there is a Vip Account employee from Shanghai Yongfoo Elite who has won individual medals of Five Star Diamond Awards.

1 HANLIN STREET, HANGZHOU **TEL:** 0571-87290999
地址： 杭州市上城区翰林街1号

RESERVATIONS: Recommended
DRESS CODE: Smart casual
LUNCH HOURS: 11:30 am-14:30 pm
DINNER HOURS: 17:30 pm-22:30 pm
LAST ORDER DINNER: 22:20 pm
WEBSITE: www.downing8.com

VEGETARIAN DISHES: 5-10
NO SMOKING SECTION: Yes
CAR VALET: Yes
CREDIT CARDS: AE, D, J, MC, V
YEAR ESTABLISHED: 2010
PRICE: RMB 500/Person

QIAN FU HUI

♨ 8   🍴 8   🍷 9   🎀 8

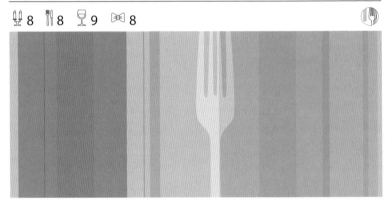

SETTING: The beauty of Hangzhou lies in the landscape. The restaurant, meticulously designed by famous architects from Hong Kong, uses soft sheer curtains with the charming lights, crystals hanging from the ceiling that pleasantly jiggle and hidden fragrances floating in the air.

SIGNATURE DISHES
> Curry Prawn
> Chef's salad
> Stone pot tofu

FOOD: River food is the specialty of the restaurant. You simply must have two of the dishes on offer in Qian Fu Hui. One is Stewed Wild Duck with Herbs: the wild duck raised in the Qiantang River is stewed slowly over water with excellent ham shank, high-grade Shaoxing wine and Chinese caterpillar fungus. The soup is light and savory and the aftertaste is wonderfully strong. Another must try is the Traditional Style Steamed Shad Fish, this excellent dish, from the local river, is elegant in appearance and has delicate taste. Being comprehensive in its theme for healthy food, , Qian Fu Hui also attaches much importance to the nutrition and balance of its cuisine. The top-grade abalone, shark's fin and bird's nest are also signature dishes of Qian Fu Hui. The cook, from Hong Kong, is said to have prepared bird's nest soup for presidents on many occasions and is able to cook the Full Mancu-Han Banquet. It costs just about RMB 100 Yuan for young couples to enjoy a romantic dinner alongside the river.

WINE: There are rich vintage wines, beers, grape wines and various white spirits and yellow wines.

SERVICE: The service here is meticulous with considerate and done with a modest attitude. Whether clearing away dishes or answering questions, the waiters use a soft voice and arrange everything for the guests efficiently.

908 ZHIJIANG ROAD, HANGZHOU **TEL:** 0571-87882888/87821777
地址： 杭州市上城区之江路908号（钱江三桥广电大楼旁）

RESERVATIONS: Recommended
DRESS CODE: Smart casual
LUNCH HOURS: 11:30 am-14:30 pm
DINNER HOURS: 17:30 pm-22:30 pm
LAST ORDER DINNER: 22:20 pm
WEBSITE: No

VEGETARIAN DISHES: 5-10
NO SMOKING SECTION: Yes
CAR VALET: Yes
CREDIT CARDS: AE, D, J, MC, V
YEAR ESTABLISHED: 2009
PRICE: RMB 200/Person

VERANDA

🍴 8   🍴 9   🍷 9   🎀 9

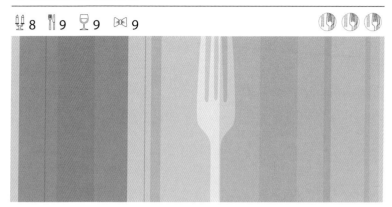

SETTING: The Veranda Restaurant is a fashionable venue replete with elegance and exquisite design. Its open kitchen, simple log tables and paintings of famous modern artists are suffused with a hint of Italian romanticism.

FOOD: Veranda Italian Restaurant is committed to using first-class authentic Italian ingredients, which include the top highest grade olive oil and chateau wines, the scented Parmesan Cheese and various fresh vegetables, all of which preserve the original tastes. The delicious pre-prandial bread is golden yellow and toasted to perfection. There are crackers and grissini served with various sauces and condiments. Be careful not to fill yourself up on them though. Spinach Linguine with Salmon is a nutritious dish with an enticing color. The green linguine is handmade with fresh spinach juice. The sliced salmon tasted smooth and was shaped into beautiful pink rose petals. Mixed with capers, the flavor becomes a little spicy and has a wonderful fragrance. Beyond any expectation is the size of Fragrant King Prawns, even one can make you almost full. There are, of course, various pastas for you to choose from. Mushroom pasta, the freshness of which was absorbed by the fine king prawns, is sweet and succulent.

SIGNATURE DISHES
> Antipasto veranda
> Forever "caprese"
> Ossobuco alla Milanese
> Fettine di vitello al vino marsala
> Pizza mascarpone e prosciutto

WINE: A wide range is provided on the wine list including champagne, red wine and white wine from both the New World and the Old World, and even remarkable vintages from well-known Chateaus can be found.

SERVICE: Guests feel comfortable with considerate service.

1F, 120 SHUGUANG ROAD, HANGZHOU **TEL:** 0571-87998833-6708
地址： 杭州市西湖区曙光路120号黄龙饭店1楼

RESERVATIONS: Recommended
DRESS CODE: Smart casual
LUNCH HOURS: 11:30 am-14:30 pm
DINNER HOURS: 17:30 pm-22:30 pm
LAST ORDER DINNER: 22:20 pm
WEBSITE: www.dragon-hotel.com

VEGETARIAN DISHES: 5-10
NO SMOKING SECTION: Yes
CAR VALET: Yes
CREDIT CARDS: AE, D, J, MC, V
YEAR ESTABLISHED: 2009
PRICE: RMB 300/Person

WANG STEAK

♨ 8   🍴 8   🍷 8   🎀 9

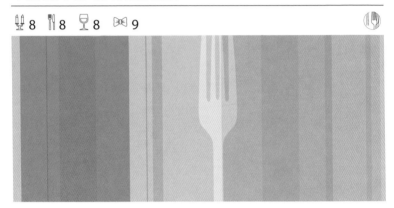

SETTING: Beautiful Greek murals adorn stylish glasses, making up a grand and magnificent wall. The hanging ceilings of yellow glasses reflect sculptured sofas with red velvets, together with the new classical floor lamps, contrast exquisitely with each other; the faintly seen Hepburn in the magnificent carved picture frame in the private room smiles at you elegantly, and together with the crystal droplights and mulberry carved sofas, a perfect combination with fashion and luxury is created.

FOOD: The main courses here include 9 dishes such as Wang Pin Steak, Royal Steak, French-style Mutton Chop with Red Wine, Braised Achyranthes in Red Wine, and Surf and Turf Combos, as well as aperitif bread, salad, and soup and so on. Each dish is exquisite beyond description. After ordering, the soft and warm bread will be served with 4 dips: diced tomato, curry yoghurt, goose liver and butter. The varying tastes are delightful. Just when the bread is running low, the main course, Wang Pin Steak, will appear. Each tender mouthful is rich in flavor and fragrance. After dinner, you can enjoy a plate of hot and dense chocolate Lava cake. When the rich and syrupy hot chocolate runs out from the Lava cake you feel and indulgent joy. The Fragrant Rose Dew with Rose Petals is a less extravagant choice.

SIGNATURE DISHES
> Wang Steak
> Seafood salad
> Cheese Cake

WINE: There are rich varieties for the customers to choose from.

SERVICE: The waiters here are polite and professional. There are numerous special services in Wang Pin. On your birthday, they will send you a birthday cake; on a wedding anniversary, they will give you a meticulously selected Love present that you'll never forget.

7F, BUILDING C, 230 HUANCHENG ROAD N., HANGZHOU **TEL:** 0571-85270475
地址：杭州市环城北路230号杭州大厦C座裙楼7层

RESERVATIONS: Recommended
DRESS CODE: Smart casual
LUNCH HOURS: 11:30 am-14:00 pm
DINNER HOURS: 17:30 pm-21:00 pm
LAST ORDER DINNER: 21:00 pm
WEBSITE: No

VEGETARIAN DISHES: 5-10
NO SMOKING SECTION: Yes
CAR VALET: Yes
CREDIT CARDS: AE, D, J, MC, V
YEAR ESTABLISHED: 2010
PRICE: RMB 238/Person

WEST LAKE INTERNATIONAL TEA FANS VILLAGE

🍴 9 🍴 9 🍷 9 🎀 9

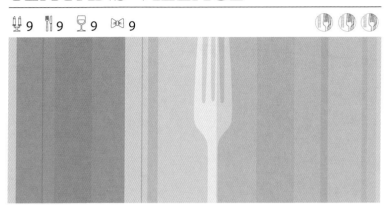

SETTING: A classical garden building with the style common of the area near the Yangtze River, is near the West Lake, and features white walls and black tiles. There are mountains and bamboos shadows reflected in the lake, winding paths and the sounds of nature. Dining areas are set in the private rooms whose decoration show the elegant style particular peculiar to the area in the south of Yangtze River.

FOOD: West lake International Tea Fans Village established its fame of "unforgettable" food and "wonderful" tea as soon as it opened. Gourmands and tea lovers from Hangzhou came in a throng. Cantonese cuisine here specializes in Abalone, Shark's Fin and Bird's Nest, which uses authentic, natural ingredients and cooking skills. The special appetizer Beef Shank and Stewed Duck Tongue in Soy Sauce has a delicious taste and strong fragrance, and is a perfect starter. Double Boiled Fish Maw Soup with Chinese Herb is a clear and aromatic soup. The main course Braised Sea Cucumber in Abalone Sauce is also an exceptional. Steamed Merlion and Stir-Fried Chinese Flowering Cabbage are well worth recommending. Dim sum Crispy Durian Cake should not be missed for its crispy and delicious taste.

SIGNATURE DISHES
> Marinated duck tongue
> Daily house soup
> Braised sea cucmber & yoshihama abalone 32
> Double-boiled beef rib in wine
> Stewed rice with sea cucumber

WINE: The wine here is abundant with vintage wines from the New and Old World. In addition, there are many choices of high-grade Chinese spirits and yellow wine.

SERVICE: The club-style service is very good.

87-1 NANSHAN ROAD, HANGZHOU **TEL:** 0571-87080943
地址： 杭州南山路87-1号

RESERVATIONS: Necessary
DRESS CODE: Smart casual
LUNCH HOURS: 11:00 am-13:00 pm
DINNER HOURS: 17:30 pm-21:00 pm
LAST ORDER DINNER: 20:30 pm
WEBSITE: www.guilingarden.com

VEGETARIAN DISHES: 10+
NO SMOKING SECTION: Yes
CAR VALET: Yes
CREDIT CARDS: AE, D, J, MC, UP, V
YEAR ESTABLISHED: 1995
PRICE: RMB 400/Person

KING LION PLAZA BRANCH

🕯9 🍴9 🍷8 🎀8   ✋ ✋

SETTING: The restaurant is elegant, magnificent and dreamlike with all its elements such as arches, white walls, black balcony bars, white grand piano in the lobby and stunning visual impact created by the scattered lights.

FOOD: The excellence of the "classical Huaiyang cuisine", such as Stuffed Chicken with Shark's Fin Soup in Royal Court, Boiled Salted King Pigeon and Stewed Pork Ball, is spread by word of mouth among the customers in Nanjiang. Stuffed Chicken with Shark's Fin Soup in Royal Court, which has been on the news because of its sales topping one RMB a million Yuan, is naturally the specialty of King Lion Mansion Restaurant. The expensive price, near RMB 1,000 Yuan per dish, doesn't deter customers. The 30 dishes sold daily of Stuffed Chicken with Shark's Fin Soup in Royal Court are prepared each day. After the whole year old deboned hen is stuffed with Shark's Fin, they were stewed on a low heat in broth for a long time to create the authentic, flavorful soup. The delicious taste of seafood and meat combines beautifully with the fragrant soup. The dish requires exception skill and so each perfect dish is worth of great praise. The Boiled Salted King Pigeon, of which several hundred are sold each day, resembles the Nanjing style Boiled Salted Duck.

SIGNATURE DISHES
> Shark's Fin Soup
> Saulted Pigeon

WINE: The wine list is abundant, including all kinds of middle and high-grade wines.

SERVICE: The service here is satisfactory.

2 LION BRIDGE, HUNAN ROAD, NANJING **TEL:** 025-83300781
地址：南京市鼓楼区湖南路狮子桥2号，近湖北路

RESERVATIONS: Necessary
DRESS CODE: Smart casual
LUNCH HOURS: 11:00 am-14:00 pm
DINNER HOURS: 17:30 pm-21:00 pm
LAST ORDER DINNER: 21:00 pm
WEBSITE: www.njshiwangfu.com

VEGETARIAN DISHES: 3-5
NO SMOKING SECTION: No
CAR VALET: No
CREDIT CARDS: AE, D, J, MC, UP, V
YEAR ESTABLISHED: 2000
PRICE: RMB 500/Person

LOTUS RESTAURANT

9 8 8 9

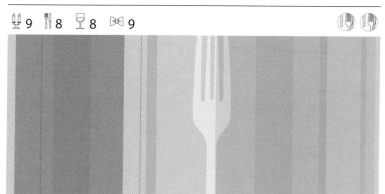

SETTING: Guests can sometimes enjoy performance over their meal. At the same time, the Southeast Asian decorations in the restaurant make guests feel as if they are on an exotic vacation.

FOOD: Lotus Restaurant serves South-East Asia and Western style delicacies. Excellent design and a cozy atmosphere give prominence to its features. The tailored Thai dishes by the renowned chef are excellent whether for business banquets or family and friend. The appetizer Papaya Salad, in true Thai style, integrates tastes of sourness, sweetness, saltiness and spiciness into one. The appetizer is made by mashing papaya, peanuts, dried shrimps with fish sauce, sugar and lemon juice, so it is both healthy and refreshing. Highly recommended are the Chili Crabs and Yellow Chicken Curry, the highlight in the Curry series, which are cooked with yellow curry imported from Thailand. The dishes have a strong fragrance, a sweet creamy taste, endless aftertastes of coconut and other spices and the extremely delicious crabmeat. Another specialty is Thai Shrimp Cake with Plum Sauce, which has a wonderful bouquet; bite it, the filling is still steaming and tastes sour, sweet and crisp all at once.

SIGNATURE DISHES

> Seafood salad
> Papaya salad
> Caesar Salad
> Crab in curry sauce
> Fried beef fillet
> Pan-fring goose liver

WINE: The beverages are very numerous. There are many choices in the wine list. All levels of the Chinese wines are served here.

SERVICE: The service here is intimate, friendly and efficient.

E5, 388 YINGTIAN STREET, NANJING **TEL:** 025-51885688
地址：南京市秦淮区应天大街388号第E5幢

RESERVATIONS: Recommended
DRESS CODE: Smart casual
LUNCH HOURS: 11:00 am-14:00 pm
DINNER HOURS: 17:00 pm-22:00 pm
LAST ORDER DINNER: 22:00 pm
WEBSITE: www.regalia.com.cn

VEGETARIAN DISHES: 5-10
NO SMOKING SECTION: Yes
CAR VALET: No
CREDIT CARDS: AE, D, J, MC, V
YEAR ESTABLISHED: 2010
PRICE: RMB 200/Person

MA XIANG XING

🕯7 🍴8 🍷7 🎀8

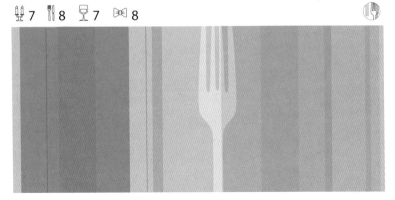

SETTING: Ma Xiang Xing, founded during the Daoguang period of the Qing Dynasty, has a history of over 160 years. Time flies and Ma Xiang Xing, nowadays, has become the representative of Muslim flavors in Nanjing.

FOOD: The specialty of Duck Liver, cooked with sliced celery, with an attractive color and flavor and creamy white appearance, tastes very fresh and tender. The texture isn't grainy like most liver. As it is sliced thinly and fried with lee after being quickly fried with duck fat, the flavor is strong; in addition, there is a slightly sweet aftertaste. Actually, the key to the dish lies in the cooking time and controlling the heat. In particular, the quick boiling in hot water, soaking in cool water and quick frying and boiling water are essential. Ma Xiang Xing has four famous specialties, namely "Braised Mandarin Fish in Shape of Squirrel", "Fried eggs" and "phoenix-tailed prawns" besides the foresaid Duck Liver. When the Fried egg is served, it has a surprising appearance. It is common for the filling to be wrapped with egg cream; the egg skin is slippery and plump, and is more plentiful than ordinary egg dumplings. The filling is diced shrimps. The shrimps are cut into the shape of rice grains so the taste is tender and succulent. The egg and shrimp are seasoned with green onion and wine in advance for added flavor.

SIGNATURE DISHES
> Duck liver
> Braised Mandarin Fish
> Egg Dumpling
> Phoenix-tailed prawns

WINE: In the Muslim restaurant, a variety of soft drinks are served.

SERVICE: Humble service makes people comfortable.

32 YUNNAN ROAD N., NANJING **TEL:** 025-83286388
地址: 南京市鼓楼区云南北路32号，近湖北路

RESERVATIONS: Recommended, Necessary for Rooms
DRESS CODE: Smart casual
LUNCH HOURS: 11:00 am-13:30 pm
DINNER HOURS: 17:00 pm-20:30 pm
LAST ORDER DINNER: 20:30 pm
WEBSITE: No

VEGETARIAN DISHES: 1-2
NO SMOKING SECTION: No
CAR VALET: No
CREDIT CARDS: AE, D, J, MC, UP, V
YEAR ESTABLISHED: 2006
PRICE: RMB 100/Person

MANDARIN GARDEN HOTEL

♨8 🍴8 🍷8 🎀8

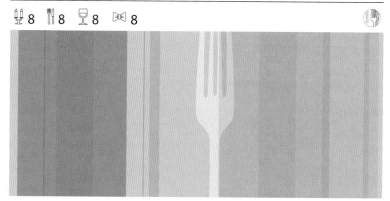

SETTING: Even as an old and famous hotel, the restaurant never falls behind the times. Besides bar Firenze, cafeteria Venice, it is equipped with many functional theme halls. The halls such as Huicui Hall, Jinli Hall, Shilin Hall, Yushan Hall, Gonghua Hall, Qionglin Hall and others are all names that are carefully chosen. The rich cultural ambience seems to invite you into an old palace.

1FOOD: The restaurant offers authentic Nanjing snacks, fine Huaiyang cuisine, high-grade Cantonese cuisine such as Braised Abalone, Shark's Fin and Bird's Nest and fusion food that combines Chinese and Western styles, so the restaurant is a veritable garden of rich delicacies. What must be eaten in Mandarin Garden Restaurant is Boiled Salted Duck, which is cooked with secret ingredients. It boasts a fragrant, supple skin and tender meat. The meatballs are expertly prepared, thus the dish is soft and thick. In addition, the specialties of the restaurant such as Buddha Skipping Wall, Sweet memories and Crispy Deep-fried Goose Liver are all worth trying.

SIGNATURE DISHES
> Salted Duck
> Fo Tiao Qiang
> Fried Goose Liver

WINE: The wine list is relatively abundant, and there are all kinds of middle and high-end wines to choose from.

SERVICE: The service here is high quality; the waitress are well-trained and helpful.

9 ZHUANGYUANJING, NANJING **TEL:** 025-52202555
地址： 南京市秦淮区夫子庙状元境9号状元楼酒店

RESERVATIONS: Recommended
DRESS CODE: Smart casual
LUNCH HOURS: 11:30 am-14:00 pm
DINNER HOURS: 17:30 pm-20:00 pm
LAST ORDER DINNER: 20:00 pm
WEBSITE: www.mandaringardenhotel.com

VEGETARIAN DISHES: 5-10
NO SMOKING SECTION: Yes
CAR VALET: No
CREDIT CARDS: AE, D, J, MC, UP, V
YEAR ESTABLISHED: 1991
PRICE: RMB 200/Person

MEZZEH

🕯8 🍴8 🍷8 🎀8

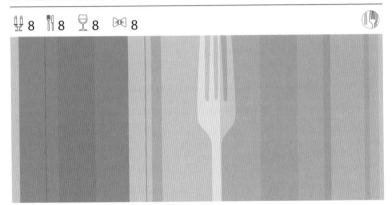

SETTING: MEZZEH is not a large restaurant and seats less than 30. However, the creation of the dining atmosphere and the arrangement of tables are clearly organized by the owner, together with the soft Middle East style music that lingers in the air and waiters in exotic costumes to create an enchanting dining ambience.

SIGNATURE DISHES
> Mezzeh Cold Dish
> Lebanon Bean Soup
> Peanut Dim Sum with Strawberry Gel

FOOD: Lebanon has four distinct seasons that offer different scenery. The majority of Lebanon's population, over 400 million, are Arabs, so the food and drink there displays the flavor of Arabia and the Mediterranean. The dishes, though taking a while to arrive, are beautifully decorated. Like Western-style food, Lebanon dishes are characterized into cold dishes, soup, main course, dessert and so on. But the content differs greatly. The cold dish Meizi, made with fresh ingredients such as sauce, roast eggplant, onions and tomatoes, has a distinctive taste. Lebanon lentil soup, or "Xiaolabate Adasi" in Lebanese, is very popular. The waiters ask you to take care with the soup or you might burn your tongue as it is very spicy. It has a rich curry color and gives off a strong aroma of cumin that smells delicious. The lentils, cumin and curry flavor go very well together and warm the stomach nicely.

WINE: Arabs' interest in spices is not only reflected in their dishes but also in coffee. They even add seasoning into their coffee. If you are interested, and have the courage, you can order a small cup of Lebanon coffee.

SERVICE: The service here is thoughtful and full of enthusiasm.

9 HUANLING ROAD, NANJING **TEL:** 025-85408888
地址： 南京市玄武区环陵路9号

RESERVATIONS: Recommended
DRESS CODE: Smart casual
LUNCH HOURS: No
DINNER HOURS: 17:00 pm-22:00 pm (Except Monday)
LAST ORDER DINNER: 21:30 pm
WEBSITE: www.sofitle.com

VEGETARIAN DISHES: 3-5
NO SMOKING SECTION: Yes
CAR VALET: No
CREDIT CARDS: AE, D, J, MC, UP, V
YEAR ESTABLISHED: 2006
PRICE: RMB 200-250/Person

PLUM GARDEN

🍽 9 🍴 9 🍷 8 🎀 9

SETTING: In the past decade, it has received numerous dignitaries and heads of state. Just from the gate, you can sense the grand atmosphere and its extraordinary style.

FOOD: According to historical records, "cuisine in Nanjing, Jiangsu" appeared in Nanjing during the Qing Dynasty. Yuan Mei, a gifted scholar in the Qing Dynasty, wrote many poems and articles. He once wrote a cooking masterpiece "Suiyuan Menu" on Cangshan Hill in Nanjing; moreover, the records of famous dishes in A Dream of Red Mansions by Cao Xueqin provide abundant evidence for the high standing of the "cuisine in Nanjing, Jiangsu". Nowadays, the most authentic dishes of "cuisine in Nanjing, Jiangsu" come from Meiyuan Chinese Restaurant in Jinling Hotel. Soft Pocket, the top ten of famous dishes in Jiangsu, is the specialty of the restaurant. It is ordered by almost every table like, as is the Boiled Salted Duck. Soft Pocket is cooked with eels which are plentiful in the regions around Yangtze River and Huai River, and the people in Huai'an are expert in cooking eel. Also, the centuries-old recipe of Boiled Salted Duck in old brine at the restaurant is widely recognized as the best in Nanjing. Millennium Shrimps in Ginkgo soup boasts a strong flavor and is a very special dish ginkgo are picked from1000- year old ginkgo tree.

SIGNATURE DISHES
> Jinling Boiled Salted Duck
> Soft Pocket
> Minced Crab meat & Bean
> Curd and Stir-fried Shelled Shrimps

WINE: The wine list at the five-star hotel is naturally wonderful.

SERVICE: The restaurant managers and the waiters have worked here for decades. They are familiar with the habits of guests, so everyone can feel comfortable and at ease. The service is intimate but not excessive.

2F, 2 HANZHONG ROAD, NANJING **TEL:** 025-84711888
地址： 南京市白下区汉中路2号金陵饭店2楼

RESERVATIONS: Necessary
DRESS CODE: Smart casual
LUNCH HOURS: 11:30 am-14:00 pm
DINNER HOURS: 17:30 pm-21:30 pm
LAST ORDER DINNER: 21:30 pm
WEBSITE: www.nanjing.jinlinghotel.com

VEGETARIAN DISHES: 10+
NO SMOKING SECTION: Yes
CAR VALET: Yes
CREDIT CARDS: AE, D, J, MC, UP, V
YEAR ESTABLISHED: 1983
PRICE: RMB 250/Person

THAI SPICES

8 8 8 8

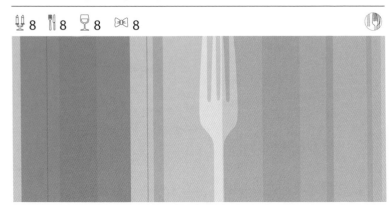

SETTING: The location of the restaurant is quite ingenious as when you exit the elevator of Deji Plaza, where is considered a high-end shopping mall in Nanjing, you will only see shops; however, when you came back to the elevator, you will find that Thai Spices has appeared just opposite, as if by magic. The expensive flowers are the same color as the decorations. The white tablecloths and black chairs are exactly the same as in Branch 1912. Swaying curtains separate dining areas from corridors, so the surroundings appear comfortable and luxurious. The cartoon oil paintings of famous paintings such as the Mona Lisa are very interesting.

FOOD: The reason why Thai the cuisine here is so popular is that the dishes use only the ingredients and are very authentic. Crab in Balinese Sauce, a specialty of the restaurant, is probably the most delicious in all of Nanjing. The crab is very sweet, tender and the sauce delicious. Its natural flavor matches the curry sauce beautifully. You must also try the Tom Yum Kung soup, a Thai delicacy. It is full of wonderful flavors and not to be missed. It is recommended that you drink a cup of lemongrass tea before having Thai food as the tea clears the palate and also soothes the stomach before the spicy Thai food.

SIGNATURE DISHES
> Curry Crab
> Tom Yum Teley

WINE: The wine list is relatively simple, but special lemongrass tea is worth trying.

SERVICE: The service here is warm and considerate.

301 DEJI PLAZA, 18 ZHONGSHAN ROAD, NANJING **TEL:** 025-84712608
地址： 南京市白下区中山路18号德基广场301号

RESERVATIONS: Recommended
DRESS CODE: Smart casual
LUNCH HOURS: 11:00 am-17:00 pm
DINNER HOURS: 17:00 pm-22:00 pm
LAST ORDER DINNER: 21:00 pm
WEBSITE: www.lemeridien.com/royalshanghai

VEGETARIAN DISHES: 10+
NO SMOKING SECTION: No
CAR VALET: Yes
CREDIT CARDS: AE, D, J, MC, UP, V
YEAR ESTABLISHED: 2006
PRICE: RMB 150-200/Person

THE PURPLE PALACE

 9 9 8 9

SETTING: Through the clear glass windows, a beautiful and verdant forested mountain vista can be seen; birds sing all around and the scent of fragrant flowers fills the air.

FOOD: In each season, the restaurant offers dishes cooked with vegetables, game and seafood. All the dishes are exquisitely presented, and have a delicate but delicious taste. In addition, the restaurant also offers Shanghai cuisine and upscale Cantonese cuisine. However, while the dishes are excellent, it is the magnificent scenery that is the greatest draw. As the saying goes "Beautiful view can build up an appetite for dishes". The emergence of numerous scenic restaurants is not a coincidence. The beautiful scenery outside the glass windows is excellent sauce. The Purple Palace, surrounded by mountains, is hidden among multiple ranges of hills and green woods. Graceful buildings, with white walls and gray tiles, exist in perfect harmony with the bluish waves and green wooded mountains. 20 banquet rooms are scattered among them. Each private banquet room by the lake has bird's-eye view. Open the windows and you can enjoy the picturesque lake, green mountains, sun-washed waves at sunrise and sunset and the birds' twittering in the woods.

SIGNATURE DISHES
> Shark's Fin
> Bird Nest
> Abalone

WINE: There are many choices on the wine list.

SERVICE: Club-style service here is intimate and comfortable.

18 HUANLING ROAD, NANJING **TEL:** 025-84858888
地址： 南京市玄武区环陵路18号

RESERVATIONS: Necessary	**VEGETARIAN DISHES:** 10+
DRESS CODE: Smart casual	**NO SMOKING SECTION:** Yes
LUNCH HOURS: 11:30 am-14:00 pm	**CAR VALET:** Yes (07:00-19:00)
DINNER HOURS: 18:00 pm-22:00 pm	**CREDIT CARDS:** AE, D, J, MC, UP, V
LAST ORDER DINNER: 22:00 pm	**YEAR ESTABLISHED:** 2006
WEBSITE: www.jinlinghotel.com	**PRICE:** RMB 400/Person

YI PALACE

⚑ 9 🍴 9 🍷 9 ✉ 8   (( )) (( )) (( ))

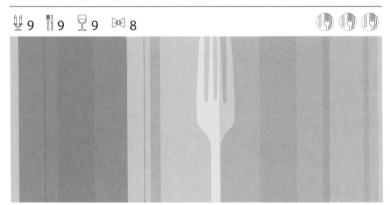

SETTING: The restaurant is equipped with 7 private rooms of various sizes, one of which boasts the largest private dining area in Nanjing. The decoration of the largest private room is both comfortable and luxurious, for there are two areas: one for rest and the other for dining, so it is an ideal place for high-end business banquets.

FOOD: Yi Palace serves many kinds of Chinese cuisine, and you can enjoy authentic Cantonese and Huaiyang cuisine. It has a number of private rooms available. Its excellent cuisine and beautiful landscape make this a great venue. The cold dishes, Qingyuan Chicken and Boiled Salted Duck, are both wonderful and are characterized by fragrant skin, tender meat and pleasant taste. Grouper is the signature dish of the restaurant. The whole fish, soaked in authentic shark's fin soup, is fresh and supple, and the strong soup has a delicious taste. Another specialty is Roast Spring Pigeon. The skin of the pigeon is a crisp golden yellow and its meat is smooth and tender. The Crab Powder Balls are also a highly recommended dish. The large meatballs are very juicy and melt in the mouth.

SIGNATURE DISHES
> Crispy preserved radish
> Chrysanthemun beab curd
> Aloe with coconutmilk
> Stew sea cucumber
> Fried veal rib
> Griddle Cooked beef and wild mushrooms

WINE: The wine list here is abundant.

SERVICE: The service here is friendly, considerate and efficient.

E5, 388 YINGTIAN STREET, NANJING **TEL:** 025-51885688
地址： 南京市秦淮区应天大街388号第E5幢

RESERVATIONS: Recommended
DRESS CODE: Smart casual
LUNCH HOURS: 11:00 am-14:00 pm
DINNER HOURS: 17:00 pm-22:00 pm
LAST ORDER DINNER: 22:00 pm
WEBSITE: www.regalia.com.cn

VEGETARIAN DISHES: 5-10
NO SMOKING SECTION: Yes
CAR VALET: No
CREDIT CARDS: AE, D, J, MC, V
YEAR ESTABLISHED: 2010
PRICE: RMB 200/Person

YUE HONG HE 1912

🕯8   🍴8   🍷8   🎀8

SETTING: Taking black as its main theme, magnificent crystal lamps and the warm "Welcome" from waiters wearing gorgeous costumes instantly make guests feel that this will be an enjoyable experience. Inside the restaurant, black velvet sofas, black crystal and wall paintings with a black and white theme create a great ambience and wonderful, quite beautiful symmetry.

FOOD: Roast Spring Pigeon is highly praised by locals. It is cooked in a unique way in the restaurant, a combination of Nanjing roast duck and Cantonese Siu mei. The little, crisp and tender Roast Spring Pigeon is golden yellow and is wonderfully juicy. The flavor is just perfect. The ingredients of Stewed Black-Bone Chicken with Ordycep are fresh and locally sourced. After being stewed, its soup becomes snow-white and is very attractive. Cantonese Cuisine features many dishes that are based dishes originating from Western cuisine but cooked in a Chinese style. That is to say, the Western dishes are cooked with Chinese seasoning and style. Pan-fried tenderloin with caviar is the best example. The flash fried tenderloin with caviar not only looks sumptuous but has particularly splendid flavor.

SIGNATURE DISHES
> Crispy Pigeon
> Abanlone

WINE: The wine list here is abundant, and guests can choose their wine according to their budget.

SERVICE: The service is warmhearted from beginning to end.

A10, 52 TAIPING ROAD N., NANJING **TEL:** 025-84458766
地址： 南京市玄武区太平北路52号南京1912商业区A10

RESERVATIONS: Necessary
DRESS CODE: Smart casual
LUNCH HOURS: 9:30 am-13:30 pm
DINNER HOURS: 13:30 pm-23:30 pm
LAST ORDER DINNER: 23:30 pm
WEBSITE: www.njyhh.com

VEGETARIAN DISHES: 10+
NO SMOKING SECTION: No
CAR VALET: Yes
CREDIT CARDS: AE, D, J, MC, UP, V
YEAR ESTABLISHED: 2006
PRICE: RMB 150/Person

CHAO YONG XUAN RESTAURANT

🍴 8   🍴 9   🍷 8   🎀 9

SETTING: Chaoyongxuan Restaurant takes full advantage of its excellent location, where the beautiful riverside views are balanced with the interior decorations.

FOOD: As the top-rated Cantonese restaurant in Ningbo, Chaoyongxuan Restaurant offers Bird's Nest, Abalone and Shark's Fin, which are all very popular. By using only high-quality ingredients, the experienced Cantonese chiefs create superb dishes. The Abalone is elastic and tangy, the Shark's Fin is delicious, and the Bird's Nest comes in many varieties, such as ginseng juice, royal jelly, pollen juice, truffle juice, red date juice and Chinese caterpillar fungus juice. Even those who dislike the Bird's Nest can't help but try, so inviting is are its fragrance and appearance. The most popular dish is the Caviar Steak, with a sour yet sweet taste, and a rich fragrance of garlic. It is tender, fresh and delicious. The Sautéed Fish Head is a very special dish unique to the restaurant. The fish jaw is wrapped in paste and slightly fried in oil, and tastes delicate. The hot Crispy Durian Cake and Wood Frog Egg Tart are other specialties, which should not be missed. The Crispy Durian Cake boasts a rich taste of Durian, and those who love Durians won't be able to get enough.

SIGNATURE DISHES

> Ginseng panax sauce
> Braised beef steak with caviar
> Fried fish head

WINE: The restaurant has a rich collection of wines, most of which are Chinese wines and white spirits. The foreign red wines are of small quantity.

SERVICE: As a top restaurant, the service is very considerate. One private room is provided with three waiters, who work hard and offer good service.

121 HUAISHU ROAD, NINGBO **TEL:** 0574-87662688
地址： 宁波市江北区槐树路121号

RESERVATIONS: Recommended
DRESS CODE: Smart casual
LUNCH HOURS: 9:00 am-14:00 pm
DINNER HOURS: 12:00 pm-22:00 pm
LAST ORDER DINNER: 21:30 pm
WEBSITE: No

VEGETARIAN DISHES: 10+
NO SMOKING SECTION: Yes
CAR VALET: Yes
CREDIT CARDS: AE, D, J, MC, UP, V
YEAR ESTABLISHED: 2003
PRICE: RMB 300-500/Person

CHINESE RESTAURANT OF NANYUAN HOTEL

♨ 9 🍴 8 🍷 9 🎀 8

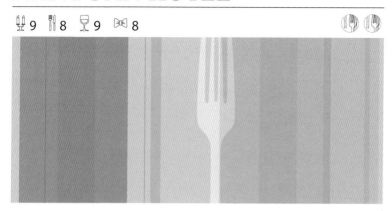

SETTING: Sitting in the private room of the Honored Guests' Hall, accompanied by melodious music played on the traditional stringed and woodwind instruments of the Jiangnan area, you are surrounded by wonderful decoration, cream-colored seats and sofas and exquisite tableware.

FOOD: The Large Yellow Croaker with Pickled Cabbages and Shredded Bamboo shoots comes in a surprisingly large portion. A large yellow croaker is mixed with the pickled cabbages and shredded bamboo shoots, and is so delicious that everyone will want more. Mr. Lin, the Executive Chef of Nanyuan Restaurant, said that this dish uses large, wild yellow croakers, which are worth over one thousand Yuan, and far more delicious than the cultured ones. The salty flavor of the pickled cabbages goes well with the freshness of the shredded bamboo shoots and the delicious and tender yellow croaker meat. The dish perfectly illustrates the basis of Ningbo cuisine for 'the integration of freshness and salty flavor". Other favorites are Tasty Hairy Crab, Boiled White Shrimps with Salt and Assorted Four Cured Meats. The Tasty Hairy Crab is highly praised. The dish is very creative. The steamed crabs taste more delicious and sweeter after being dipped in sauce.

SIGNATURE DISHES
> Steamed Dazha Crabs
> Poached Salted White Shrimp
> Four Ingredient Hors D'oeuvres

WINE: The five-star wine collections are always well received.

SERVICE: The restaurant offers the cozy family-style service, which is no different between the private rooms and the individual tables, and the waiters' familiarity with the dinnerware and wine set is also good.

2F, 2 LINGQIAO ROAD, NINGBO **TEL:** 0574-87095777
地址： 宁波市海曙区灵桥路2号主楼2楼

RESERVATIONS: Recommended
DRESS CODE: Smart casual
LUNCH HOURS: 11:30 am-14:00 pm
DINNER HOURS: 17:30 pm-21:30 pm
LAST ORDER DINNER: 20:30 pm
WEBSITE: No

VEGETARIAN DISHES: 10+
NO SMOKING SECTION: Yes
CAR VALET: Yes
CREDIT CARDS: AE, D, J, MC, UP, V
YEAR ESTABLISHED: 1999
PRICE: RMB 200-300/Person

FEAST MODERN RESTAURANT

♼ 9 ⫿ 8 ♈ 8 ⋈ 8   🖐 🖐

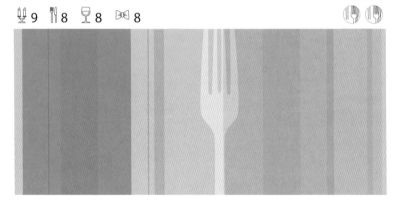

SETTING: Black bricks, winding corridors, glazed lamps, panes with carved designs, carmine floral decorations, all of these give an expression of the authentic, old Shanghai.

FOOD: Specializing in Ningbo cuisine, this restaurant offers other dishes. Guests can try Beef Steak with Black Pepper, Japanese Sashimi and Crispy Durian Cake. It's said that the beef steak dish is a must-order. The beef is very tender and melts in the mouth. Being a typical Ningbo restaurant, the seafood is excellent and highly recommended. The assorted cold dishes made up of river white shrimp, live mud snails and crab meat are fantastic, boasting fresh ingredients and rich tastes. The Baked Prawns with Salt are plump and delicate while the Yellow Croaker Spring Rolls, in which the yellow croakers are wrapped in bean curd sheets, have a pleasant salty and fresh taste. The Steamed Reeves Shad in Clear Soup is split down the middle into two halves, with each half served in one plate, and has a very delicate flavor as no seasoning added during cooking.

SIGNATURE DISHES
> Pan-fried beef steak with black pepper
> Sashimi with Japanese style
> Crispy durian cake

WINE: The restaurant is famous for its rich collection of wines from Ningbo, and some luxurious wines are also offered to match the dishes.

SERVICE: With considerate and polite service, the waiters always wait at your service but maintain a certain distance, and refill your glass immediately.

87 HUAISHU ROAD, NINGBO **TEL:** 0574-87351111
地址： 宁波市江北区槐树路87号

RESERVATIONS: Recommended
DRESS CODE: Smart casual
LUNCH HOURS: 10:30 am-14:00 pm
DINNER HOURS: 17:00 pm-21:30 pm
LAST ORDER DINNER: 20:30 pm
WEBSITE: No

VEGETARIAN DISHES: 10+
NO SMOKING SECTION: Yes
CAR VALET: Yes
CREDIT CARDS: AE, D, J, MC, UP, V
YEAR ESTABLISHED: 2005
PRICE: RMB 250-350/Person

HAN TONG SEAFOOD RESTAURANT

 8　 8　🍷 8　🎀 9　

SETTING: When entering the Hantong Hotel, you are immediately struck by its luxurious, grand hotel style, and the golden Maitreya Buddha in the lobby smiles, extending a warm welcome to every guest.

FOOD: As a typical Ningbo seafood restaurant with new and old dishes, Hantong Restaurant branches have been opened all over China. The baby soles are beautifully presented in the black juice and unique to the restaurant. The baby soles appear more delicate than those available from the open-to-order area. The black sauce is made from cuttlefish mixed with the pickle brine, and becomes black. It might look strange, but it is delicious. The baby soles are roasted in the black juice with a skill unique to Ningbo chefs, which makes the baby soles a must try. The Roasted Seashells on Iron Plate and Seaweed Delicacies Soup are also recommended and characterized by the freshness. It's easy to see the Seashells with Spring Onion, but hard to see the Roasted Seashells on Iron Plate. In this dish, oversized seashells are used. First, the sauce with secret ingredients is poured onto the preheated iron plate, and then the seashells are put in the sauce. All the seashells open their shells under the heat, releasing an intoxicating fragrance, and causing a rush to sample them.

SIGNATURE DISHES

> Peeled prawns and fried codfish

> Braised Australian fresh whole abalone in oyster sauce

> Steamed shrimp balls stuffed with goose liver

WINE: The restaurant offers a wide variety of wines, most of which are Chinese red wines and white spirits. The selection of foreign red wines is limited.

SERVICE: As a top restaurant, the service is excellent. One private room is provided with three waiters, who work hard and offer good service.

BUILDING 3, HARBORLAND THEME PARK, NING BO **TEL:** 0574-26857777
地址： 宁波北仑区凤凰山主题公园北区3号楼

RESERVATIONS: Recommended
DRESS CODE: Smart casual
LUNCH HOURS: 9:00 am-14:00 pm
DINNER HOURS: 12:00 pm-22:00 pm
LAST ORDER DINNER: 21:30 pm
WEBSITE: No

VEGETARIAN DISHES: 10+
NO SMOKING SECTION: Yes
CAR VALET: Yes
CREDIT CARDS: AE, D, J, MC, UP, V
YEAR ESTABLISHED: 2003
PRICE: RMB 300-500/Person

LOBSTER BAR AND GRILL

♨ 8   🍴 8   🍷 9   ✉ 8

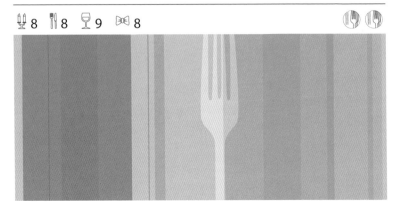

SETTING: With a romantic and elegant atmosphere, Lobster Bar and Grill is equipped with chairs decorated with leather and gorgeous fabrics, and long counters made of marble and rosewood.

FOOD: The guests will savor fresh ingredients, prepared with traditional and classic European-style cooking techniques. The dishes include fresh seafood, grills and so on. The delicacies in the restaurant include: VSOP Brandy Lobster Soup (cooked at the dining table), Pumpkin Paste and Tomato Sauce with Pan-Fried Goose Liver, Boston Lobster and Toadstool with Risotto, First-Class Angus Beef Fillet with Spinach, Onion Paste with Miller Red Wine, White Beef Fillet with Chinese-Style Fried Noodles, Roasted Mongolian Mutton Chop with Rosemary Sauce and Eggplants, Oil-Seal Duck with Potato Paste and Oranges, Lobster Mousse with Steamed Chicken Breast, Boston Lobster (cooked with Brandy on site), Big Crawfish and Truffle Champagne Sauce, Vegetable Stews and Brazilian Tomato Sauce with Pan-Fried Spotted Garoupa and Chilled Boston Lobster Soup with Assorted Sea Foods (including Alaska king crabs, abalones, shrimps, prawns, scallops, clams, smoked salmon, oysters and sauce).

SIGNATURE DISHES
> Lobster tartar
> Mushroon and foie gras cappuccino
> Prime black angus beef fillet
> Mongolian Lamb rack
> Steamed breast of chicken
> Boston lobster

WINE: The wine connoisseurs can sample a wide variety of high-quality wines in the restaurant, including "Bordeaux Chateau Lafite Rothschild First Cru 2004", "Bordeaux Chateau Margaux First Cru 1998", and "Bordeaux Chateau Latour First Cru 1994".

SERVICE: The service is generally excellent.

88 YUYUAN ROAD, NINGBO **TEL:** 0574-87997888
地址： 宁波市江东区豫源街88号宁波香格里拉大酒店

RESERVATIONS: Recommended
DRESS CODE: Smart casual
LUNCH HOURS: No
DINNER HOURS: 17:30 pm-22:00 pm
LAST ORDER DINNER: 22:00 pm
WEBSITE: www.shangri-la.com

VEGETARIAN DISHES: 3-5
NO SMOKING SECTION: Yes
CAR VALET: No
CREDIT CARDS: AE, D, J, MC, UP, V
YEAR ESTABLISHED: 2009
PRICE: RMB 500/Person

SUNWARD FISHERY RESTAURANT

🍴 8   🍴 8   🍷 8   🎀 9

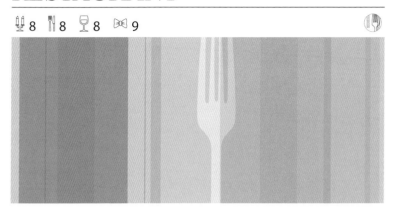

SETTING: Sunward Fishery Restaurant has numerous branches in Ningbo. The Caihong branch is located at the intersection of Hecheng Road of Guangdong District and Caihong Road (S). Although it is not the busiest restaurant in Ningbo, the graceful decoration makes this hotel still quite popular. There are five storeys with many private rooms of varying sizes. Strolling beside the large seafood aquarium, you can select the one that you like and wait for the dish while drinking tea.

FOOD: The unexpected thing in Ningbo Restaurant is that the dishes are served quickly. The cold and hot dishes are jammed together on the table. The portions are surprisingly large and somewhat daunting. The red salty grease crab is most enticing for its vivid color. Ningbo chefs are of the highest skill in preparing both cold and live cold dish. Although the taste is a little rich, the salty grease crab well deserves trying. The steamed baby croaker is also recommended. The baby croaker is also known as big head baby croaker. The steamed baby croaker is similar to a small yellow croaker, but its head is bigger and the color is more golden. The meal is brought to a perfect end by a bowl of Ningbo dumplings.

SIGNATURE DISHES
> Red salted cream crabs
> Steamed culter
> Ningbo glutinous rice dumpling

WINE: It offers a rich variety of wines, especially Chinese wines and distilled spirits.

SERVICE: The first feeling for Sunward Fishery Restaurant is kindness. The service staff will lead you to the elevator and the private room. They always answer questions with a smile. During dining, they provide high quality service.

236 CAIHONG ROAD S., NINGBO **TEL:** 0574-87871111
地址：宁波市江东区彩虹南路236号

RESERVATIONS: Recommended
DRESS CODE: Smart casual
LUNCH HOURS: 10:30 am-14:00 pm
DINNER HOURS: 17:00 pm-21:00 pm
LAST ORDER DINNER: 20:30 pm
WEBSITE: www.xyyg.com

VEGETARIAN DISHES: 10+
NO SMOKING SECTION: Yes
CAR VALET: Yes
CREDIT CARDS: AE, D, J, MC, UP, V
YEAR ESTABLISHED: 2000
PRICE: RMB 150/Person

TRIPLERIVER

♉ 9 ⏐❙ 8 ♉ 8 ⋈ 8

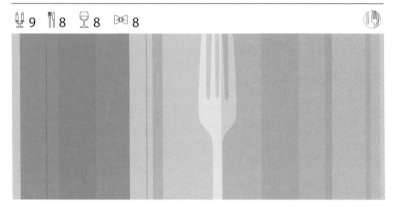

SETTING: Located at Ningbo Grand Theater, the restaurant has a strong sense of art. The Statue of David and unmatched watercolors in the private rooms offer a great sense of style and sophistication. Each of the private rooms features a unique design, in both Chinese and European styles.

FOOD: The restaurant has many tanks for live fish in the lobby, which features many varieties. The staff are able to provide advice for guests on how each fish can be prepared. The restaurant focuses on Ningbo cuisine and Xiangshan cuisine. Grease crab is a dish that must be sampled. Compared to most other dishes, although this dish is somewhat expensive, the dish is delightfully fresh and of excellent quality. Fresh octopus is prepared in the style of Japanese sashimi. The steamed Hunan style fish head with pepper sauce is the special feature of the Hunan dishes.

SIGNATURE DISHES
> Fresh octopus
> Chilli fish head with sauce

WINE: The wine selection is rich.

SERVICE: Upon entering the restaurant, you will be led by the service staff to select the seafood and told which cooking method is best. The service staff will help you with dish selection in accordance with your taste.

BLOCK 7, NINGBO GRAND THEATER, 1 DAZHA ROAD, NINGBO **TEL:** 0574-87669999
地址：宁波市江北区大闸路1号宁波大剧院7区

RESERVATIONS: Recommended
DRESS CODE: Smart casual
LUNCH HOURS: 9:30 am-13:30 pm
DINNER HOURS: 17:00 pm-22:30 pm
LAST ORDER DINNER: 21:30 pm
WEBSITE: No

VEGETARIAN DISHES: 10+
NO SMOKING SECTION: Yes
CAR VALET: Yes
CREDIT CARDS: AE, D, J, MC, UP, V
YEAR ESTABLISHED: 2003
PRICE: RMB 150/Person

Y-TOWN CLUB

♨ 9　🍴 8　🍷 8　🎀 9　　🖐 🖐

SETTING: It is an old-style two-storey building located at the Y-Town of Ningbo. It is a typical high grade restaurant in Ningbo in the most modern part of the city. The decoration in Y-Town Club is very distinctive.

FOOD: The restaurant focuses on Japanese tempenyaki set meals and the price starts at RMB 268 Yuan. Besides the selected dishes of each set meal, it also includes snacks, soup, vegetables before the meal and fruits afterwards. It is very rich. While the number of people sharing the set meal is not asked, the quantity is enough for several people and the staff will separate it into several portions for guests. The Australian lobster, flown in fresh, is highly recommended. It is very fresh and tender, and somewhat sweet. Salmon and goose liver are very popular and the quality of the ingredients and authentic tempenyaki methods employed by the chefs ensure a wonderful meal. Coffee and desserts are offered on the second floor before or after your meal. If you do not like coffee, a nice chrysanthemum tea can be ordered. It is relaxing to enjoy your drink tea and gaze at the scenery of Sanjiang River while resting against the banister.

SIGNATURE DISHES
> Australian lobster
> Marinated salmon and goose liver

WINE: The Japanese wine is excellent and some imported vintage grape wines, red and white wines and some sparkling wine are offered.

SERVICE: As a top club, it offers polite and perfect service.

17 WAIMA ROAD, NINGBO **TEL:** 0574-87351638
地址: 宁波市江北区外马路17号

RESERVATIONS: Recommended
DRESS CODE: Smart casual
LUNCH HOURS: 9:00 am-14:00 pm
DINNER HOURS: 14:00 pm-00:00 pm
LAST ORDER DINNER: 22:30 pm
WEBSITE: No

VEGETARIAN DISHES: 10+
NO SMOKING SECTION: No
CAR VALET: No
CREDIT CARDS: AE, D, J, MC, UP, V
YEAR ESTABLISHED: 2009
PRICE: RMB 200-500/Person

ZHUANG YUAN LOU

♨ 9 🍴 8 🍷 8 🎀 9

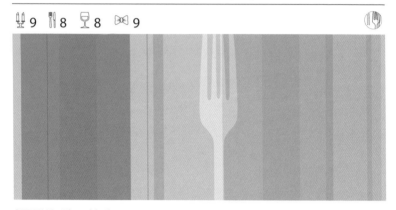

SETTING: The old Zhuang Yuan Lou Restaurant has undergone a cultural and historical restoration. There is a sedan chair, an examinee's food box and Zhuang Yuan basket in the central area. In the lobby hall on the first floor hang many of paintings of traditional stringed and woodwind instrument, worms and birds. On the other side there is a big wine cabinet. Red wine, distilled spirits and rice wine are well stocked. In a sense, the new Zhuang Yuan Lou Hotel not only restores the cuisine of the old Zhuang Yuan Lou restaurant, but also preserves Zhuang Yuan culture.

FOOD: The new Zhuang Yuan Lou restaurant offers exquisite food. Besides the top ten famous dishes such as Steamed Turtle in Crystal Sugar Soup, Stewed Yellow Croaker with Bamboo Shoots and Potherb Mustard, Dry Fried River Eel and Goose Liver Fried with Pork Fat a selection of new dishes have been developed. The wild turtle is now rare and thus the availability of Steamed Turtle in Crystal Sugar Soup is limited. The restaurant has developed a garden for growing fresh vegetables and breeding poultry. The water for cooking dishes and making tea is mineral water from the Siming Mountain.

SIGNATURE DISHES
> Steamed turtle in crystal sugar soup
> Stewed yellow croaker with bamboo shoots and potherb mustard
> Ningbo salty crab

WINE: The selection of red wine, distilled spirits and rice wine is large.

SERVICE: The staff is well trained and very familiar with the top ten dishes.

2-10 HEYI ROAD, NINGBO **TEL:** 0574-27966666
地址：宁波市海曙区和义路2-10号

RESERVATIONS: Recommended
DRESS CODE: Smart casual
LUNCH HOURS: 11:00 am-14:00 pm
DINNER HOURS: 18:00 pm-22:00 pm
LAST ORDER DINNER: 22:00 pm
WEBSITE: No

VEGETARIAN DISHES: 10+
NO SMOKING SECTION: Yes
CAR VALET: Yes
CREDIT CARDS: AE, D, J, MC, UP, V
YEAR ESTABLISHED: 2009
PRICE: RMB 300/Person

ZOU MA LOU

♨ 9   🍴 8   🍷 8   🎀 8

SETTING: . The restaurant is built based on the former residence of famous financer Mr. Ge Shenmu, and most of the original styles have been kept. Meanwhile, a lot of fresh elements have been injected into the restaurant.

FOOD: Country dishes are served in Zou Ma Lou Restaurant but its appearance is stunning. Several signature dishes are unique to the restaurant and not to be found elsewhere. The bean products here are very famous. Heron is prepared with tofu in a country style and is fairly limited. It tastes great when dipped in the light yellow lobster sauce. The soybean milk is sweet. The shrimps with dried vegetable are stirred to a delicate crispness. The preserved vegetables are also delicious. The chicken soup with ginger and yellow wine is savory and delicious. Although steamed herring with wine sauce is very popular, it is a seasonal dish so not always available. The herring is very fresh. The walnut soup with wine is also very popular among guests. Some can drink several bowls. The Wine Kuchen made of red and white rice with crisp walnut kernel is sweet and tasty. If you like desserts or civet durian, do try the civet durian sweet cake. The taste is subtle and the skin is baked well.

SIGNATURE DISHES

> Durian cake
> Chicken soup
> Sweet fermented rice

WINE: The choice of wine is comprehensive.

SERVICE: The restaurant in offers homelike service and the waiters provide considerate service like that of an executive housekeeper of a rich, long standing family.

---

117 MINQUAN ROAD, NINGBO **TEL:** 0574-87570777
地址: 宁波市江北区慈城民权路117号

RESERVATIONS: Recommended
DRESS CODE: Smart casual
LUNCH HOURS: 10:30 am-12:00 pm
DINNER HOURS: 17:00 pm-20:00 pm
LAST ORDER DINNER: 19:30 pm
WEBSITE: No

VEGETARIAN DISHES: 10+
NO SMOKING SECTION: Yes
CAR VALET: Yes
CREDIT CARDS: AE, D, J, MC, UP, V
YEAR ESTABLISHED: 2005
PRICE: RMB 80-150/Person

ESSENCE

🍴 8   🍴 8   🍷 8   🎀 9

SETTING: The open kitchen makes guest appreciate the chef's expert cooking skills as they savor delicious cuisine. There are 2 luxurious VIP rooms in Jingcheng Restaurant that have a wonderful view of the beautiful scenery of Yangcheng Lake.

FOOD: All-day-dining at the western restaurant ESSENCE has a diversified international menu. The buffet dinner is very rich, and includes Japanese cuisine, western style snacks and some Southeast Asian cuisine. Appetizers are in the western style. Do not miss the steamed vegetables, for they are organic and very fresh. All organic vegetables come from the ecological farm that belongs to the hotel. The cauliflower is soft and fragrant and the lotus root tastes crisp. The potato absorbs the beef broth and is exquisite. The curry is a little peppery, while main courses focus on stewed dishes. The stewed mutton with cauliflower, braised beef and fried lung are all delicious. Personnel are assigned specially for cutting roast beef and turkey and each is cut into two slices. The succulent beef is medium stewed, and it is neither fatty nor overly lean. Various sea foods including sea crab and shellfish look beautiful and are delicious. At the sushi area the chef makes sushi on the spot, which taste fresh and succulent.

SIGNATURE DISHES
> Si-Sa-Hai
> Vegetable Samosa
> Ginger Beef "PS"
> Shandong-Beef Tenderloin

WINE: There are 4 kinds of fruit juice in the buffet dinner. Various wines are available, but at extra cost.

SERVICE: Because it is a buffet dinner waiters, in general, do not disturb quests except for changing tableware.

3668 MA'ANSHAN ROAD W., SUZHOU **TEL:** 0512-57800888-25
地址：昆山市马鞍山西路3668号

RESERVATIONS: Recommended
DRESS CODE: Smart casual
LUNCH HOURS: 11:30 am-14:30 pm
DINNER HOURS: 17:30 pm-21:30 pm
LAST ORDER DINNER: 21:00 pm
WEBSITE: www.fairmont.com

VEGETARIAN DISHES: 10+
NO SMOKING SECTION: Yes
CAR VALET: No
CREDIT CARDS: AE, D, J, MC, UP, V
YEAR ESTABLISHED: 2009
PRICE: RMB 158 or 178/Person

JIN XIU TIAN TANG

 8   8   8   8

SETTING: The interior architectural decoration of the restaurant's lobby is bright and clean. The deep color stresses the elegance of the private rooms: tassel drapes, paintings and calligraphy on the lacquer walls, together with the tastefully furnished restaurant creates a classic, unique style that is quiet and comfortable.

SIGNATURE DISHES
> Rice Cake
> Old Duck Stewed With Bamboo Root & Ham

FOOD: Elaborately-handcrafted dishes that originate south of the Yangtze River strive for the purity and strong flavors of rural life. Baked Chicken in Salt features light yellow, smooth and tender meat and slightly crispy chicken skin. How it's made: the fresh and fat hen is diced after quick-boiling, and then the chicken is pieced together and plated. Walnut Soup with rice is made with red and white sweet ferment rice and walnuts. The dish is characterized by a hearty bouquet, tasty walnuts and a sweet yet not greasy soup. It makes a great appetizer. Sautéed Three White Slices with Rice Wine Sauce is made with pickled chicken feet, soybean and pig stomach. The brine reflects the freshness and succulence of the ingredients perfectly. Homemade bean curd can be supplemented with many seasonings such as chilli sauce, meat paste, peanut powder, chopped tuber mustard, soy sauce and sesame oil, which add freshness and spiciness to the bean curd.

WINE: There are many varieties of wine on the winelist for people to choose. The different yellow wines, nicely matured, agree very well with the pickled vegetables with Zhejiang and Jiangsu style.

SERVICE: The service here is excellent, satisfying the needs of different customers.

---

109 BAIHUA ROAD, SUZHOU **TEL:** 0512-65188777
地址： 苏州市百花路109号

RESERVATIONS: Recommended
DRESS CODE: Smart casual
LUNCH HOURS: 11:30 am-13:30 pm
DINNER HOURS: 17:00 pm-22:00 pm
LAST ORDER DINNER: 20:30 pm
WEBSITE: No

VEGETARIAN DISHES: 10+
NO SMOKING SECTION: Yes
CAR VALET: Yes (11:00-20:00)
CREDIT CARDS: AE, MC, UP, V
YEAR ESTABLISHED: 2003
PRICE: RMB 100-150/Person

LOTUS PAVILION

🍴 9 🍴 9 🍷 9 🎀 9   🖐 🖐 🖐

SETTING: Combining the concepts of a flower garden and the home, this restaurant and the guestrooms are built resembling the villa of a Suzhou style garden with spacious a lotus pond outside the French window and a waterside pavilion and pavement, which forms the most natural and beautiful man-made landscape in the restaurant.

FOOD: In the traditional, simple style, the perfect Su cuisine is warm and gracious. The appetizer of Steamed Pork Meat with Glutinous Rice on Leaves is full of sweetness and fragrance, with leaves covering the small red sauce pork cubes. Boiled Ribbonfish with Glutinous Rice will bring back childhood memories with the fresh ribbonfish accompanying the fragrant smell of rice wine. Care must be taken with the ribbonfish as it has a lot of fishbones. The Balloonfish from Yangtze River is the signature dish of the restaurant and must be tried. The Balloonfish is boiled in red sauce, the skin covering the fish, and the succulent fish lung as decoration around the fish. It is served with seasonal vegetables and rice. The dish is wonderfully moreish. The Chinese Beef Stew is a popular choice, and is cooked in the traditional style, so that the beef is exceptionally tender. The taste can be enhanced by a dash of pepper.

SIGNATURE DISHES

> Meat with glutinous rice
> Belt fish in rice wine sauce
> Stew shark's fins with chicken
> Garden hotel fresh fish braised in brown juice
> Chinese-style stew beef

WINE: All kinds of drinks served, including various foreign and domestic vintage wines.

SERVICE: The service is considered and professional. Familiar with the dishes, waiters may provide on the spot recommendations.

99 DAICHENGQIAO ROAD, SUZHOU **TEL:** 0512-67786778-6730
地址：苏州市带城桥路99号

RESERVATIONS: Recommended
DRESS CODE: Smart casual
LUNCH HOURS: 11:30 am-13:30 pm
DINNER HOURS: 17:30 pm-21:00 pm
LAST ORDER DINNER: 21:00 pm
WEBSITE: www.gardenhotelsz.com

VEGETARIAN DISHES: 10+
NO SMOKING SECTION: Yes
CAR VALET: No
CREDIT CARDS: AE, D, J, MC, UP, V
YEAR ESTABLISHED: 2006
PRICE: RMB 150/Person

LOTUS RESTAURANT

 9 8 8 8

SETTING: A featured restaurant of Regalia, embraces a decorative style of Chinese and Southeast Asian. The swimming pool of Lotus Restaurant extends to the veranda beside the lake and faces its most beautiful scene, creating a tranquil retreat in which customers can enjoy the delicious food served by the restaurant.

FOOD: It serves meticulously cooked Thai dishes and the traditional or improved Jiangnan dishes. A fine appetizer is Thai chutney on fried shrimp crackers, which are tender and delicious with plenty of shrimp meat, though the shrimp crackers seemed somewhat old. We ordered the Western style Mushroom Soup and the classical Thai Hot and Sour Shrimp Soup that is very authentic and has a perfect balance of hot and sour seasoning, and the appropriate proportion of citronella making the soup refreshing and fragrant. Also, we ordered Thai Shrimp Cake which has a golden coating and pink body and is tastes light and refreshing. We also sampled the Fried Curry Crab and Curry Beef in the outstanding Curry Series, the Thai crabs being a classic and are very fresh and authentic. The Curry Beef is tender and slightly sweet. A perfect ending to your evening would be a walk along the veranda, gazing at thte bright moon reflected by the crystal clear water of Jinji Lake.

SIGNATURE DISHES

> Thai chicken salad
> Papaya salad
> Thai shrimp chips
> Thai Prawn Cake
> Crab in curry sauce
> Beef masaman

WINE: The restaurant serves many kinds of drinks, including western and Chinese wines and soft drinks.

SERVICE: The service here is warm, friendly and capable.

2 LIGONGDI,SUZHOU **TEL:** 0512-62950888
地址：苏州工业园区李公堤2号

RESERVATIONS: Recommended
DRESS CODE: Smart casual
LUNCH HOURS: 11:00 am-14:00 pm
DINNER HOURS: 17:00 pm-22:00 pm
LAST ORDER DINNER: 22:00 pm
WEBSITE: www.regalia.com.cn

VEGETARIAN DISHES: 5-10
NO SMOKING SECTION: Yes
CAR VALET: No
CREDIT CARDS: AE, D, J, MC, UP, V
YEAR ESTABLISHED: 2007
PRICE: RMB 200/Person

PAULAMER BRAUHAUS

🕯 8 🍴 9 🍷 8 🍽 9

SETTING: Kempinski Hotel Suzhou is located near Dushu Lake in the Suzhou Industry Park and borders the golf course of Jinji Lake. The hotel is luxuriously decorated. Paulamer Restaurant on the first floor of the hotel is an authentic German restaurant. In true German style, the restaurant also has the equipment needed to brew its own beers.

FOOD: The authentic Germany feel is evident from decoration as well as the drinks. All the ingredients are imported from Germany. The starter dishes include are fried eggs and ham with bread. It goes well with the homemade ham salad. The various cheeses are tasty. The signature dish, roast pork hock, is matched with Chinese cabbage and bread rolls. The pork hock is roasted well and it is crisp on the outside and tender inside. The skin has much fragrance after roasting is crisp but not fatty. The meat quality is excellent. Goes best with a freshly brewed beer. In addition, another signature dish is assorted meats with German style mashed potatoes, recommended by the restaurant, which focuses on various sausages and ham salad. The sausages are bratwurst style, Bavarian white sausage and Frankfurters, among others. Each of them are unique, plentiful and wonderful.

SIGNATURE DISHES
> S trammer max
> Selection of cold ham&cheese
> Home made sausage salad
> Paulaner sausages and meat platter
> Crispy pork knuckle

WINE: The restaurant has a variety of homemade beers such as black beer, wheat beer and golden beer. Various middle and high grade wines are also included as well as soft drinks.

SERVICE: It offers the five-star hotel service, which is always polite. The German restaurant manager makes guests feel at home.

1 GUOBIN ROAD, SUZHOU **TEL:** 0512-62897888
地址： 苏州工业园区国宾路1号

RESERVATIONS: Recommended
DRESS CODE: Smart casual
LUNCH HOURS: 11:00 am-14:30 pm (Only Sat and Sun)
DINNER HOURS: 16:30 pm-24:00 pm
LAST ORDER DINNER: 23:00 pm
WEBSITE: www.kempinski.com/suzhou

VEGETARIAN DISHES: 10+
NO SMOKING SECTION: Yes
CAR VALET: No
CREDIT CARDS: AE, D, J, MC, V
YEAR ESTABLISHED: 2009
PRICE: RMB 120/Person

PEONY PAVILION

🍴 9   🍴 8   🍷 8   🎀 9   🖐 🖐 🖐

SETTING: Fashion Creative Restaurant of the Peony Pavilion of Suzhou is located at Ligongti Dongyu by the beautiful Jinji Lake. The layout of the restaurant is designed so that a winding path leads to the quite area. The furnishings belong to the luxurious Shanghai Style of the Republic of China.

FOOD: The restaurant mainly serves Jiangsu cuisine, Guangdong cuisine and Western-style set meals. The goose liver with Dalian abalone and salty green soy bean is the signature appetizer. The taste is light and it retains the sweetness of the soy bean. The goose liver is fatty but not oily, The kidney bean with preserved arbutus in Soviet Union style uses cream preserved arbutus. It is the taste of old Suzhou. Afterwards, the waiter brings an elaborate tea set, which they explain contains a soup and is to refresh the palate. Another dish, Pork with Mushroom, is shaped like a butterfly and is truly wonderful. Make sure you sample the fresh water fish and shrimp. The signature dish of braised barb and river shrimp with XO sauce, made using fresh ingredients, has a perfect flavor. It is a little sweet and the color is distinctive. The taste of the river shrimp is fresh and sweet. It is worthy of recommendation due to its exquisite taste and is truly a signature dish.

SIGNATURE DISHES
> Dalian abalone
> Soviet-style plum kidney beans
> Soviet Duck
> Purple East to cultural soup
> Private wine abalone
> XO sauce with River Shrimp

WINE: It serves various middle and high grade grape wines and foreign wines; High quality Chinese spirits and rice wine and soft drinks are available.

SERVICE: The waiters wear the clothes of 1930s Shanghai. They provide active and considerate services.

E7-9-11 LIGONGDI, SUZHOU **TEL:** 0512-62998777
地址：苏州工业园区李公堤E7-9-11座

RESERVATIONS: Necessary for Dinner
DRESS CODE: Smart casual
LUNCH HOURS: 11:30 am-14:00 pm
DINNER HOURS: 17:30 pm-21:00 pm
LAST ORDER DINNER: 20:00 pm
EMAIL: hwj65518@163.com

VEGETARIAN DISHES: 10+
NO SMOKING SECTION: No
CAR VALET: Yes
CREDIT CARDS: J, MC, UP, V
YEAR ESTABLISHED: 2008
PRICE: RMB 200/Person

WANG HU GE

♨ 8 🍴 9 🍷 8 🎀 8

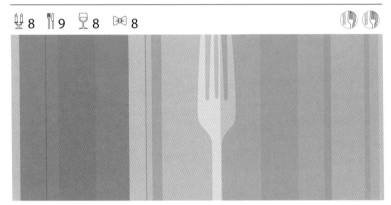

SETTING: Lying on the third floor of the hotel, Wanghuge Chinese restaurant provides elegant private boxes and compartments that are peaceful and comfortable and suitable for both business banquets and private parties.

FOOD: The Restaurant mainly serves Huaiyang cuisine and Cantonese seafood. One of the specialty appetizers is called Refreshing Crown Daisy in Sauce, a dish that tastes fresh and delicious with simple ingredients but made with great skill. The Taihu Fragrant Lotus Root tastes sweet and sticky but not greasy. A highly recommended dish is the Taizhou Shredded Dried Bean Curd. The shredded dried bean curd is rinsed in boiled water until well done, so this dish only uses high-quality bean curd. As for main course, the Pagoda Stratiform Pork, Squirrel-shaped Mandarin Fish and Huaiyang Stewed Shredded Dried Bean Curd are all good choices. Among them, the Dished Pagoda Meat is very special: the sauce-braised pork is sliced into pieces and piled up into a pagoda shape while some sauce-braised dried bamboo shoots are placed under the pagoda; it is then embellished with green vegetables. Served in steamed buns made of coarse wheat grains, this dish tastes oily but not greasy, which is a sign of its excellence.

SIGNATURE DISHES
> Lotus root stuffed with glutinous rice
> Garden chiysanthemum in sesame oil
> Traditional Braised "Dong po"Pork served with chestnut pancakes

WINE: The restaurant offers a rich collection of grape wines and imported wines of low, intermediate and high grades, as well as high-grade Chinese white spirits and yellow rice wines. In addition, there're also a great variety of soft drinks.

SERVICE: With five-star service, the waiters are considerate and polite.

1 GUOBIN ROAD, SUZHOU **TEL:** 0512-62897888

地址： 苏州工业园区国宾路1号

RESERVATIONS: Recommended
DRESS CODE: Smart casual
LUNCH HOURS: 11:30 am-14:00 pm
DINNER HOURS: 17:30 pm-21:30 pm
LAST ORDER DINNER: 21:30 pm
WEBSITE: www.kempinski.com/suzhou

VEGETARIAN DISHES: 10+
NO SMOKING SECTION: Yes
CAR VALET: No
CREDIT CARDS: AE, D, J, MC, V
YEAR ESTABLISHED: 2008
PRICE: RMB 150/Person

WU MEN REN JIA

♨ 8   🍴 9   🍷 8   🎀 9

SETTING: Along with the rich interior design in the old Yamen style and the ornate family dining room, the restaurant is filled with antique flavor; tables and chairs and porcelain jars containing oils and sauces.

FOOD: The cold dishes include egg floss, fish floss, dried scallop floss, celery floss, and ginger floss, which are light and cooked without oil and therefore not greasy, retaining only the original flavor of the ingredients. The celery floss and ginger floss are unique to this restaurant. There is also Sautéed Shrimps. The taste is sweet and salty, and they are very fresh and succulent. Chicken and Bamboo Yarn, made with flat bamboo and chicken breast, boasts a delicate flavor. The Chopped vegetables with Tofu and coriander has a very authentic flavor. Hot dishes: The peeled shrimps, Qingfeng Biyu, are fried with shrimp sauce, so that they retain a strong shrimp flavor. Lotus Duck, Roast duck and lotus pieced into a big "lotus seed", is a signature dish of the restaurant. The bright moon Sea cucumber is crisp, and very tasty with a pigeon egg placed in the moon shape on the dish. Four gods of lotus pond, with cockscomb rice, red caltrop, hoof, and lotus root, looks very attractive.

SIGNATURE DISHES
> Marinated peanuts
> Spicy brined duck
> Chopped vegetables with ToFu and coriander
> Wumen sautéed freshwater shrimps
> Sweet and sour mandarin fish

WINE: White spirits, rice wine, and grape wines are all available.

SERVICE: The waiters are considerate, careful, and provide good advice.

---

31 PANRU LANE, SUZHOU **TEL:** 0512-67288041
地址：苏州民俗博物馆后门潘儒巷31号

RESERVATIONS: Necessary
DRESS CODE: Smart casual
LUNCH HOURS: 11:00 am-17:00 pm
DINNER HOURS: 17:00 pm-22:00 pm
LAST ORDER DINNER: 22:00 pm
WEBSITE: No

VEGETARIAN DISHES: 10+
NO SMOKING SECTION: Yes
CAR VALET: No
CREDIT CARDS: UP
YEAR ESTABLISHED: 1986
PRICE: RMB 300-600/Person

YI FENG COURT

🕯9 🍴9 🍷9 🎀9   🖐 🖐 🖐

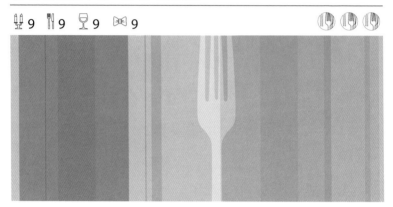

SETTING: Yi Feng Court is located at one corner of the Fairmont Hotel along the bank of Yangcheng Lake. The fascinating scenery can be appreciated through the common seats in the lobby or the VIP rooms. As well as the picturesque Yangcheng Lake, guests can also view the exquisite green yard from the French windows.

FOOD: Mainly a Cantonese cuisine restaurant, the ingredients are all sourced locally. The local produced free range chicken, with the fragrance of garlic, is roasted until yellow and bright and is crisp outside and tender inside. The fresh taste is distinctly linked with the Yangcheng Lake. The gluten in chicken soup also uses local free-range chicken. The simple cooking dining method uses local ingredients cooked by slow, low heat. It looks simple but tastes delicious. The method for cooking crab is very simple. It is marinated with Hua diao wine and steamed for 10 minutes.. The huge crabs from Yangcheng Lake are divided into various sections. The crab is selected carefully and it is very delicious. Eat the crab legs first, leave the body to last, and then dip it in the ginger and vinegar sauce. Aozao noodle has the special flavor of Kunshan. Order a lump of smoked fish and cabbage mustard. The thin noodles are soaked in red oil soup and it tastes wonderful.

SIGNATURE DISHES
> Wood mushroom salad
> Lotus root with Osmanthus flower
> Braised 5 treasures and shark's fin soup
> Stir frid lobster
> Clay pot fish head

WINE: The drinks range from wines, champagnes, and various whiskies, cocktails, coffee, tea and various other drinks are offered.

SERVICE: The service is excellent and attentive.

3668 MA'ANSHAN ROAD W., SUZHOU **TEL:** 0512-57800888-25
地址：昆山市马鞍山西路3668号

RESERVATIONS: Recommended
DRESS CODE: Smart casual
LUNCH HOURS: 11:00 am-15:00 pm
DINNER HOURS: 17:00 pm-22:00 pm
LAST ORDER DINNER: 21:00 pm
WEBSITE: www.fairmont.com

VEGETARIAN DISHES: 10+
NO SMOKING SECTION: Yes
CAR VALET: Yes
CREDIT CARDS: AE, D, J, MC, UP, V
YEAR ESTABLISHED: 2009
PRICE: RMB 200-400/Person

YI JIANG NAN

盤 8   🍴 9   🍷 8   🎀 9

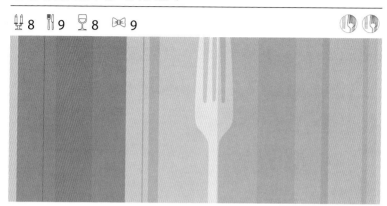

SETTING: The sheer opulence of this restaurant, from the huge ceilings to all encompassing polished surroundings, say this is a high profile and a very high-end space. French cuisine is expressed in very vibrant.

FOOD: The artsy presentation continues with the mains; pan-seared lamb on a potato fondant with micro greens on top is inserted into a 'tunnel' of potato (hair strand-thin potatoes presented in cylinder form, then deep fried to a crisp) that also addsthat playful and visual dishes that often employ modern cooking styles as well as some of the best (and most expensive) ingredients. Beef carpaccio rossigny has thin slices of excellent US Angus tenderloin layered with thin slices of foie gras, the latter adding a lovely creamy dimension, as well as a great colour contrast with the red meat. Another surprise is the avocado and shrimp, a classic French dish that's given a modern twist.

SIGNATURE DISHES
> preserved pig head

WINE: The sheer opulence of this restaurant.

SERVICE: Nice service, the staff is well trained.

99 DAICHENGQIAO ROAD, SUZHOU **TEL:** 0512-67786778-6707
地址： 苏州市带城桥路99号

RESERVATIONS: Recommended
DRESS CODE: Smart casual
LUNCH HOURS: 11:30 am-13:30 pm
DINNER HOURS: 17:30 pm-21:00 pm
LAST ORDER DINNER: 21:00 pm
WEBSITE: www.gardenhotelsz.com

VEGETARIAN DISHES: 3-5
NO SMOKING SECTION: Yes
CAR VALET: No
CREDIT CARDS: AE, D, J, MC, UP, V
YEAR ESTABLISHED: 2010
PRICE: RMB 300/Person

THE RIGHT CHOICE

ONE YEAR AGO, WE WERE ALL LOOKING FORWARD TO WORLD EXPO. AND NOW, JIANG LI YANG TAKES A CLOSE LOOK AT POST-EXPO CATERING IN SHANGHAI

When Jiang Liyang wrote this article for Shanghai Best Restaurant Guide, World Expo Shanghai 2010 had been opened for several months. With the theme of "Better City, Better Life", it brings a safe, convenient and harmonious international expo, reflecting the subject of green, environment-friendly and low-carbon.

The catering service certainly is essential to this World Expo, as it is held in Shanghai, a city that is famous for its cooking style and known as the Oriental Gourmet Metropolis. Many well-known restaurants opened up space here to serve various foods. There is a question comes up: what the catering industry in Shanghai will be like after the World Expo 2010?

The Expo Park provides foods in different styles for covering the demands of all visitors. Convenient, cheap and delicious fast food and snacks are quite popular, such as the traditional Chinese rice dumplings

The Expo Park provides foods in different styles for covering all demands

(zongzi), local cakes and noodles etc. In addition, bean curd sheet roll from Huzhou, Zhejiang and other traditional snacks are very popular. Authentic exotic cuisine also enjoy high favour. Even the Japanese Kaiseki Cuisine averaged at 3000 Yuan per person has no shortage of customers.

Any delicacies, as long as they are safe, healthy and delicious will always find their fans in Shanghai, the big market for catering services. Once, an American reporter asked me if I was afraid of the prevailing western food and lifestyle in an American restaurant. I replied that if I were scared,

he would not see me there. However, I just gave it a try to different food style, I would rather spending most of the time in Shanghai restaurants. This is called parallel running, the meaning of which is like when you go out with a backpack, you could change to any of the hundreds of bus lines every day according to your travel demand, sometimes you can take the metro, taxi or rent a car to drive by yourself.

No matter the guy understood it or not, for me, the most outstanding feature of Shanghai culture is compatibility and plasticity. Shanghai welcomes all kinds of delicacies at different levels from all over the world and gourmets from other places around China as well, all of which are adapted according to Shanghai cuisine.

Do not be pessimistic about the Shanghai cuisine. Since Shanghai opened its port more than 160 years ago, Shanghai cuisine has achieved significant development in the modern times. Although not one of the eight major cooking styles in China, Shanghai cuisine has become a mature cooking style due to the change of its political, economic and cultural status. As seen from popularity of Shanghai cuisine among visitors to the World Expo from different countries and regions therefore, there is no sign of decline and requirement for revitalization. One night at the beginning of June, I was in a restaurant near the Expo Park with a lot of people coming in, who seemed to be foreigners visiting the World Expo. The restaurant owner said their business was booming since the opening of the World Expo. There are too much people came in that sometimes they found it very difficult to handle with. He had a feeling that the best winner in the World Expo seemed to be himself.

Low carbon is one of the significant features of World Expo

Low Carbon Food is the Trend

One of the significant features in this World Expo is low carbon. There was even London zero carbon pavilion. Low carbon is definitely the major trend in Shanghai's catering industry after the World Expo. Shen Siming, Chairman of Shanghai Cuisine Association delivered a keynote speech on low carbon food at the World Expo Food Summit Forum hosted by his organization.

It seems that low carbon food is a distance away, but it's not true. The swill-cooked dirty oil was used by more shopkeepers. Some shopkeepers tried to cut prices and costs, meanwhile many diners wasting food. However, the ultimate reason is related with ourselves. Diners prefer eating fish and meat as fresh as possible because they were afraid that animals were killed by epidemics or other disease. This issue was connected with our system and process of food inspection and quarantine. It is also linked to the integrity of producers and transporters. Some diners ordered too many dishes to show off their wealth. They would rather order more food than they could eat. Of course, they will not take the leftovers away. The Japanese food may be laughed because they are put in small dishes, but as long as you get enough food and enough nutrition, you know when to stop and no need to waste too much. Recently, I met an old colleague who gave me a vivid lesson on nutrition.

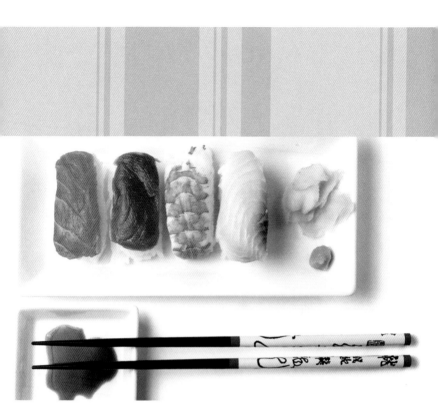

Low Carbon Food Will Not Happen Overnight

On that summit forum I met Susan, the Chairman of a bio-tech group in Singapore. She has an organic agricultural products development company in Shanghai and an organic vegetarian restaurant named Buddha Hut where all dishes are vegetarians. Several days later, I tried Japanese style yam roll in seaweed, roast gluten, braised vegetarian steak with black pepper there.

Susan certainly hoped to turn me into a vegetarian. She said that producing 1kg meat will release 36.4kg carbon dioxide, which is equivalent to emission from driving car for 3h; 2/3 of global acid rain came from livestock. 51% of the greenhouse gas was released from livestock raising industry. I knew a lot things from her, and I know as well that among the 32 teeth of human being, 28 teeth are for vegetables, and only four canine teeth can tear meat. I am not an ascetic, I can not cut carbon dioxide emission, but I am more practical.

At a banquet in Xingguo Hotel several days later I had "goose liver in white jade cup", which was made by filling goose liver into soaked and caved turnip and putting it into the oven for baking. This dish is not so oily as fried goose liver and there's a balanced portion of vegetables and meat. I also tasted wagyu beef puff, which was made by boiling a small piece of beef at a low temperature, smearing it with teriyaki sauce, wrapping it in a puff pastry, and baking it. It seems that such exquisite banquets are also starting to pay attention to low carbon.

Low carbon is a global goal that cannot be achieved overnight. Everyone of us should change our lifestyles and eating habits. Shanghai's catering industry definitely will improve our daily life after the World Expo. We look forward to it, and we also make our contributions, to make our life worthwile as a Shanghai citizen!

AGES TO PERFECTION?

DIFFERENT QUALITY AND SURROUNDINGS RESULT TODIFFERENT LIFE CIRCLE OF WINE.
WHICH ONE IS A GOOD CHOICE, YOUNG WINE OR AGED WINE? WU SHU XIAN WRITES

I n China, it is said that most of those who buy Chateau Lafite-Rothschild are regarded as being deceived. This sounds strange. Isn't Chateau Lafite a good wine? It's true that Chateau Lafite is of good quality, but it is also a truth that most people in China drink Chateau Lafite-Rothschild when it was young.

What is the difference between young wine and aged wine? In fact, wines are different from other kinds of alcoholic drinks, for they are like a living thing, which has a life cycle: infancy, childhood, adolescence, youth, middle age and old age. Of course, each crop and variety of grape wine, due to the variations of type, quality and environment (often seasonal), has a different life cycle and matures in a different way, often resulting in varying taste even among the same brand (chateaus) and type of grape (i.e. merlot, shiraz etc). High quality wines

There are also differences between young and aged wine in the New and Old World

thus often suggest a good vintage.

There are certainly obvious differences between young wine and aged wine, and between red wine and white wine. Generally speaking, ordinary white wines are best enjoyed in the wine's youth, while special types shall be enjoyed in old age. White wine can be compared to women: for young women are radiant and are full of life, while an aged white wine is like those women with a rich inner beauty, dignity and wisdom.

Sparkling white wines are also different from other white wines. Though most sparkling wines should be drunk in youth, wine connoisseurs are often attracted to aged sparkling wines of lasting appeal. In particular, champagnes are highly prized.

Sweet white wines usually have longer life cycles than dry white wines, except for ordinary white wines with little sweetness. Generally speaking, those wines with a greater sweetness have longer life cycles than the highly aged red wines. Quality "noble rot" wines from France, Germany, Austria and Hungary can age for hundreds of years without decaying. Last week, an Austrian chateau owner opened a bottle of "noble rot" wine which is of the same age as me and it tasted as young as a 17-18-year-old wine, which made me question whether it would live longer than me.

For red wines, young wines differ greatly from aged wines. I particularly prefer aged ones, for drinking it is like spending joyous time with mature men. Young wine often suffers from sour tannins and brewage flavor or green vegetable and fruit flavor. It is like a vigrous young man who can be easily excited, careless and capricious and takes much time to become mature through life experience.

Aged red wines, however, are like men aged between 35 and 50 and have experienced years of aging, during which the tannin inside the bottle has become ripe and tastes solid and silky. Meanwhile, a perfectly integrated fragrance (also called mellow) begins to emerge and diffuse slowly from the cup. It is a sheer joy to appreciate the fragrance and delicacy.

There are also differences between young and aged wine in the New and Old World. Young wines from the New World are usually nicer than that from the Old World as the tannin is riper. For example, 2008 Chile fruity red wine tastes good in 2008 and better in 2009, while 2008 Bordeaux red wine is not enjoyable for the hard tannin.

It is understandable that people in

China used to add sprite and cola in Bordeaux red wine, for the young wine is not enjoyable. Even the French will not drink this kind of wines. But nowadays, the French invented a new technology for accelerating red wine ripening ,namely micro-oxidation.

The smoothness of red wine largely depends on the climate. Generally speaking, the New World is warm and gets a lot of sun. For example, Cabernet Sauvignon from Australia, America, Chile and Spain has an obvious black berry flavor, while Bordeaux Cabernet Sauvignon has a green pepper flavor, and it is especially true for the ordinary Cabernet Sauvignon. A vegetable flavor usually suggests that the grape is not ripe enough, but some Cabernet Sauvignon also has a ripe berry flavor .

Spanish wine is a good choice among aged wines of the Old World, because It has already been ripened sufficiently aged in the winery and,

The popularity of these fine wines depend on weather those who have bought them treat them well

certainly, some quality wine can still last for many years. According to the regulations on wine in Spain, "Crianza: At least 12 months in oak barrel and at least 2 years in barrel or larger containers (stainless steel barrel or wooden barrel); Reserva: At least 12 months in oak barrel and it should be aged in bottles or oak barrels but not in large containers (stainless steel barrel or large wooden barrels) and will be in winery for at least 3 years, Gran Reserva: It shall be at least 2 years in oak barrel and 3 years in bottles but

not in large containers (stainless steel barrel or large wooden barrel) and should be in winery for at least 5 years." The future and popularity of these fine wines depend on weather those who have bought them treat them well (kept in safe environment of constant temperature and humidity).

Wine tastes best in its own life cycle, proper temperature and wine glass, all of which release the most beautiful fragrance of the wine. Even the most expensive wine will tastes unpleasant if being unkept properly. Just several weeks ago, one of my friends invited me to taste 3 French Bordeaux Chateau wines. I went to his house excitedly with a bottle of 1994 vintage Rioja red wine. I would say this tasting experience was full of regrets. The Latour was a 1982 vintage, but was reaching old age and had passed its best, while the Cheval Blanc vintage was foggy and tasted like separated flesh and blood. The Moutan

was stable, however, the oak and fruit flavors had not integrated completely because it was of year 2004. The bottle of red Rioja became the star of the night owing to its rich velvet color, wonderful aroma of dried fruit and spice and perfect integration of fruit and oak flavors.

Wine connoisseurs from both home and abroad prefer aged wines. Those who can afford quality aged wine are usually of higher social class and, or, wine collectors. According to them, aged wines taste better and help improve health. The aged red wines are also suitable for Chinese food.

Who drinks more wines, who becomes more picky. To drink aged wine in the future, rather than pay a lot of money to collectors or up-market stores, purchase newly aged wine each year so that, as the years slowly drift by, you will have your supply of aged wine to enjoy.

THE BEST WINES OF 2011

Three wine experts share their tips on 2011
premium wines primed for quaffing and investment

WINE EXPERTS

BARRY BURTON
Chairman of the Hong Kong Wine Society since 1982, Barry has
evaluated wine on every continent and since 1986 has been Regent
of the Commanderie de Bordeaux, Hong Kong Chapter.

JEANNIE CHO LEE
Jeannie is a wine critic, columnist, author, judge, and the first Asian
to be awarded the title Master of Wine (MW) in 2008.

ROY MOORFIELD
Over 35 years, Roy has acquired a reputation as an innovative wine
merchant, event organiser, writer and broadcaster in Australia and
around the world. *photo: Natalie Walker*

"Wines basically fall into two categories: those ready to drink now and those that will benefit from long cellaring." says BARRY BURTON

CLOUDY BAY SAUVIGNON BLANC 2009/2010
Fresh, fruity and zingy, Sauvignon Blancs are best drunk as young as possible. Cloudy Bay Sauvignon Blanc put New Zealand on the world wine map. ($240)

MONTGRAS CARMENERE RESERVA 2008
Ready to drink now and exhibiting toasty, vanilla aromas and soft tannins. One of the finest red grape varieties in Chile. ($69)

CLASSED GROWTH MEDOC 1996
Now approaching peak drinking and will maintain a plateau for at least another ten years. Chateau Talbot 1996 is one of many reasonably priced chateaux. ($600)

CRISTOM VINEYARDS PINOT NOIR EILEEN VINEYARD 2006
This rich, complex, dense wine with black cherry flavours from Oregon's Willamette Valley is superb drinking now and will be at its best until 2020. ($350)

ANTINORI SOLAIA 1997
The trio of "Super Tuscans" Solaia, Ornellaia and Sassicaia are now at their best and will remain so for another decade showing great finesse and elegance. ($2,000)

BEST INVESTMENT IN 2011

QUINTA DO CRASTO

The year 2007 was a classic one for vintage ports. Top British shippers include Taylor and Dow whilst excellent Portuguese houses are Niepoort, Quinta do Meao, or Quinta do Crasto. ($300-$500)

"All great wines are cyclical rather than linear. As a result of this ebb and flow there are some notable vintages primed and drinking beautifully now." says JEANNIE CHO LEE, MW

1988 CHATEAU PICHON-LONGUEVILLE BARON, BORDEAUX, FRANCE
A pleasure to drink now. The wine is all about texture, softness and drinking pleasure. An elegant wine versatile enough to pair with a seafood Cantonese meal. ($1,100)

1997 MAISON LOUIS JADOT CORTON CHARLEMAGNE GRAND CRU, BURGUNDY, FRANCE
Supple, balanced and youthful; it is just reaching its peak. Displays an amazing array of flavours supported by firm acidity and a long, minerally finish. An intense, full-bodied white to savour slowly. ($900)

1991 DOMAINE ARMAND ROUSSEAU CHAMBERTIN CLOS DE BEZE GRAND CRU, BURGUNDY, FRANCE
A great vintage now in its prime, this wine is both elegant and intense. Heady aromatics create an ethereal wine. ($9,000)

1989 GAJA BAROLO SPERSS, PIEDMONT, ITALY
Intensely aromatic wine with seductive perfume, firm acidity and tannins; the complex flavours of this wine spreads across the palate, ending in a long finish. ($2,200)

1996 DOMINUS PROPRIETARY RED, NAPA VALLEY, CALIFORNIA, USA
An incredible wine that is both ripe and dense with a Bordeaux-like elegance. The wine is at its peak with great harmony and length. ($1,000)

BEST INVESTMENT IN 2011

This powerful, full-bodied, intense wine has mouth-filling fruit and ripe, voluptuous tannins reminiscent of the wonderful 1989 and 1990 vintages but will age even longer given its density, length and power. ($1,400-$2,000)

"I look at wine as great background music to our lives. My selection reflects on wines now in their prime." says ROY MOORFIELD

2008 PETER SCHWEIGER GRÜNER VELTLINER,
TERRASSEN RESERVE, KAMPTAL, AUSTRIA
This grape variety is the new darling fitting
well between Chardonnay and Sauvignon
Blanc. Fresh and fruity, it is enjoyable as a
glass on its own. ($178)

2008 CHATEAU D'ESCLANS
"WHISPERING ANGEL"
PROVENCE, FRANCE
The combined experience of winemaker
Patrick Leon and owner Sacha Lichine has
produced a stunning dry pale rosé perfect
with food. ($210)

BEST INVESTMENT IN 2011

2004 CHATEAU PONTET-CANET PAUILLAC,
BORDEAUX, FRANCE
The best of the vintage, like this
wine, will be in demand for the
next 15 years or more.
Will increase in value as Chateau
consistently wins praise.($500)

2008 KOOYONG PINOT NOIR, MORNINGTON
PENINSULA, VICTORIA, AUSTRALIA
The distinctive varietal aroma and grain
tannins give the wine structure. Perfect
with goose or duck, roasted, of course.
($261)

2003 CHATEAU SIRAN, MARGAUX,
BORDEAUX, FRANCE
The balance of fruit and acid is now in
tune with the tannins, making it perfect
toenjoy now. ($480)

2007 FRESCOBALDI MORMORETO,
TUSCANY, ITALY
Round tannins and savoury flavours
work well in this varietal combination
wine. The structure with fresh acidity will
respond well with lusty sauces. ($550)

★ All prices quoted per bottle are in Hong Kong dollars and are subject to change based on market rates.

INDEX (BY ALPHABETICAL)

 THE BEST RESTAURANTS

RESTAURANTS NOT ONLY EXTREMELY GOOD AT FOOD AND WINE BUT ALSO EXCEPTIONAL IN SETTING, SERVICE AND VIEWSERVICE AND SERVICE AND

BEST RESTAURANTS
WITH A GOOD WINE LIST

WINE LIST REPRESENT VARIOUS WINE-GROWING AREAS WITH A GOOD MIX OF LABELS WITHIN EACH CATEGORY OF WINE, GOOD SELECTION REGULARLY.CATEGORY

RESTAURANTS	RATING	PAGE
FAVOLA ITALIAN RESTAURANT	33189999-7778	38
FU 1039	52371878	39
FU 1088	52397878	40
GIOVANNI'S ITALIAN RESTAURANT	62758888-4276	41
GUAN YUE TAI	64391000-3011	42
GUI HUA LOU	68828888-220	43
GUILIN GARDEN 1931	64515098	44
HAIYI HARBOUR PLAZA	62701998	45
HANANO JAPANESE RESTAURANT	62758888-4920	46
HANG YUEN HIN	68809778	47
HENG SHAN CAFE & CHINESE CUISINE	62260525	48
HISAGO	52082873	49
HONG RUI XING	64275177	50
ISSIMO	33024997	51
JADE	52539999-6398	52
JADE MANSION	50127728	53
JADE ON 36 RESTAURANT	68828888-280	54
JEAN GEORGES	63217733	55
JIN XUAN	20201888-1768	56
JING'AN RESTAURANT	22166988	57
JING CHI FANG	64457111	58
JW'S CALIFORNIA GRILL	53594969-6455	59
KATHLEEN'S 5 ROOF TOP RESTAURANT	63272221	60
KOI JAPANESE RESTAURNT	52539999-6326	61
KOREAN BARBECUE RESTAURANT	52081579	62
LAKE VIEW	57799999-7766	63
LAO CHENG XING	69195577	64
LAPIS SKY GARDEN	64747979	65
LEONARDO'S	62480000-1850	66
LOST HEAVEN ON THE BUND	63300967	67
MADO IZAKAYA	60800745	68
MAGGIE'S RESTAURANT	62957199	69
MAISON DE L'HUI AT SINAN	400-820-2028	70
MAISON POURCEL	62879777	71
MANCHURIA	64458082	72
MANDARIN PAVILION	62791888-5301	73
MARDI GRAS	62807598	74
MI TIERRA MEXICAN RESTAURANT & TACO BAR	54655837	75
M ON THE BUND	63509988	76
MOON'S STEAK HOUSE	63365683	77
MR. & MRS. BUND-MODERN EATERY BY PAUL PAIRET	63239898	78
NADAMAN	68828888-260	79

RESTAURANTS	RATING	PAGE
NEW HEIGHTS	63210909	80
NINA SPICY CUISINE	63758598	81
NOBLE HOUSE	58793179	82
NOBLE SEAFOOD RESTAURANT	58207777	83
NOBLE SEAFOOD RESTAURANT	62625555	84
PALLADIO ITALIAN RESTAURANT	62797188	85
PARADISE GARDEN	50477773	86
PELHAM'S	63229988	87
PIN CHUAN	62888897	88
PREGO	63351888-7360	89
RESTAURANT MARTIN	64316639	90
ROOSEVELT PRIME STEAKHOUSE	64338240	91
SAM'S RESTAURANT	64047300	92
SAZANKA TEPPANYAKI	64151111-5211	93
SCENA	20201888-1758	94
SCENERY BUILDING	62198855-5379	95
SHENG HUI TANG	38581188-5218	96
SHINTARO	62568888-1290	97
SHINTORI NULL-2	54045252	98
SICHUAN COURT	62480000-1890	99
SIMPLY THAI	400 800 7729	100
SINCERE RESTAURANT	64332882	101
SIR ELLY'S	23272888-6756	102
STEAK HOUSE	62568888-1270	103
SUMMER PAVILION	62798888-4770	104
T8 RESTAURANT & BAR	63558999	105
TABLE NO. 1	60802918	106
T'ANG COURT	60800733	107
THAI GALLERY	62179797	108
THE CHINOISE STORY	64451717	109
THE DOOR RESTAURANT & BAR	62953737	110
THE GRILL	50491234	111
THE HOUSE OF ROOSEVELT	23220800	112
THE MARKET	60958888-7023	113
THE STRIP PRIME STEAKHOUSE SHANGHAI	60919893	114
VA BENE	63112211	115
VILLAGE GUEST HOUSE	64019777	116
VUE RESTAURANT	63931234-6328	117
WAN HAO RESTAURANT	53594969-6436	118
WAN LI RESTAURANT	38714888	119
WHAMPOA CLUB	63213737	120
WINE BAR & GRILL	62791888-5306	121
XINDALU-CHINA KITCHEN	63931234-6318	122
X-SENSATION	50504888-74602	123
YAMAZATO	64151111-5216	124
YÈ SHANGHAI	63112323	125
YI LONG COURT	23276742	126

RESTAURANTS	RATING	PAGE
YIN CHU XUAN	60958888-7086	127
YU SHANGHAI	63283886	128
YU TING CHINESE RESTAURANT	38789888-6350	129
HANGZHOU:		
28 HUBIN ROAD	0571-87791234	130
BAI YUN	0571-85860000-7220	131
D'CAFÉ	0571-87998833	132
GRAND DRAGON	0571-87998833	133
JADE GARDEN	0571-89705570	134
NUMBER EIGHT DOWNING STREET	0571-87290999	135
QIAN FU HUI	0571-87882888	136
VERANDA	0571-87998833	137
WANG STEAK	0571-85270475	138
WEST LAKE INTERNATIONAL TEA FANS VILLAGE	0571-87080943	139
NANJING:		
KING LION PLAZA BRANCH	025-83300781	140
LOTUS RESTAURANT	025-51885688	141
MA XIANG XING	025-83286388	142
MANDARIN GARDEN HOTEL	025-52202555	143
MEZZEH	025-85408888	144
PLUM GARDEN	025-84711888	145
THAI SPICES	025-84712608	146
THE PURPLE PALACE	025-84858888	147
YI PALACE	025-51885688	148
YUE HONG HE1912	025-84458766	149
NINGBO:		
CHAO YONG XUAN RESTAURANT	0574-87662688	150
CHINESE RESTAURANT OF NANYUAN HOTEL	0574-87095777	151
FEAST MODERN RESTAURANT	0574-87351111	152
HAN TONG SEAFOOD RESTAURANT	0574-26857777	153
LOBSTER BAR AND GRILL	0574-87997888	154
SUNWARD FISHERY RESTAURANT	0574-87871111	155
TRIPLERIVER	0574-87669999	156
Y-TOWN CLUB	0574-87351638	157
ZHUANG YUAN LOU	0574-27966666	158
ZOU MA LOU	0574-87570777	159
SUZHOU:		
ESSENCE	0512-57800888	160
JIN XIU TIAN TANG	0512-65188777	161
LOTUS PAVILION	0512-67786778	162
LOTUS RESTAURANT	0512-62950888	163
PAULAMER BRAUHAUS	0512-62897888	164
PEONY PAVILION	0512-62998777	165
WANG HU GE	0512-62897888	166
WU MEN REN JIA	0512-67288041	167
YI FENG COURT	0512-57800888	168
YI JIANG NAN	0512-67786778	169

INDEX (BY CUISINE & RATING)

RESTAURANTS	RATING	PAGE

HUAIYANG/SHANGHAINESE

Restaurant	🍸	🍴	🍷	✉	Page
JADE MANSION	8	9	9	9	53

HUAIYANG/CANTONESE/SHANGHAINESE/SICHUAN

Restaurant	🍸	🍴	🍷	✉	Page
GUI HUA LOU	9	9	9	9	43

AMERICAN

Restaurant	🍸	🍴	🍷	✉	Page
BUTTERFLY	9	8	9	8	21
PELHAM'S	9	9	9	9	87

MEXICAN

Restaurant	🍸	🍴	🍷	✉	Page
MI TIERRA MEXICAN RESTAURANT & TACO BAR	8	8	8	8	75

CONTINENTAL

Restaurant	🍸	🍴	🍷	✉	Page
CATHAY ROOM	9	8	9	8	24
DINING ROOM	9	9	9	8	31
JING'AN RESTAURANT	9	9	9	9	57
KATHLEEN'S 5 ROOF TOP RESTAURANT	8	8	9	8	60
M ON THE BUND	9	9	9	9	76
NEW HEIGHTS	8	8	8	8	80
SIR ELLY'S	9	9	9	9	102
T8 RESTAURANT & BAR	8	9	9	7	105
TABLE NO. 1	7	9	9	8	106
THE HOUSE OF ROOSEVELT	9	9	9	8	112
VUE RESTAURANT	9	9	9	9	117

JAPANESE

Restaurant	🍸	🍴	🍷	✉	Page
HANANO JAPANESE RESTAURANT	8	8	8	9	46
HISAGO	8	9	9	9	49
KOI JAPANESE RESTAURANT	8	8	8	8	61
MADO IZAKAYA	8	8	9	9	68
NADAMAN	8	9	9	8	79
SHINTARO	8	9	9	8	97
YAMAZATO	8	9	8	9	124

FUSION

Restaurant	🍸	🍴	🍷	✉	Page
100 CENTURY AVENUE	8	9	9	8	11
EPICTURE ON 45 REVOLVING RESTAURANT	8	8	8	8	36
SCENERY BUILDING	8	9	8	8	95

SHANGHAINESE

Restaurant	🍸	🍴	🍷	✉	Page
ART SALON RESTAURANT	9	9	8	9	15
CLUB JIN MAO	9	9	9	9	28
FU1039	9	8	8	9	39
FU1088	9	9	9	9	40
HONG RUI XING	8	8	8	9	50
LAO CHENG XING RESTAURANT	8	8	8	8	64
MAISON DE L'HUI AT SINAN	9	8	8	9	70
THE CHINOISE STORY	8	9	8	9	109
WHAMPOA CLUB	9	9	9	9	120
YÈ SHANGHAI	8	8	8	8	125

CANTONESE

Restaurant	🍴	🍴	🍷	✉	Page
AI MEI CHINESE RESTAURANT	8	9	8	7	12
BAI YU LAN	8	9	9	9	16
DYNASTY	8	9	9	9	33
GUILIN GARDEN 1931	9	9	9	9	44
HAIYI HARBOUR PLAZA	8	9	9	9	45
HANG YUEN HIN	9	9	8	9	47
HENG SHAN CAFE & CHINESE CUISINE	7	8	8	9	48
LAKE VIEW	9	8	8	9	63
MANCHURIA	8	8	8	8	72
NOBLE SEAFOOD RESTAURANT	9	9	9	9	83
NOBLE SEAFOOD RESTAURANT	9	9	9	9	84
T'ANG COURT	9	9	8	9	107
WAN LI RESTAURANT	8	8	8	9	119
YI LONG COURT	9	9	9	8	126

CANTONESE/SICHUAN

Restaurant	🍴	🍴	🍷	✉	Page
YIN CHU XUAN	8	8	8	8	127

CANTONESE/SICHUAN/SHANGHAINESE

Restaurant	🍴	🍴	🍷	✉	Page
JADE	8	9	8	9	52
MANDARIN PAVILION	8	8	8	8	73
YU SHANGHAI	8	8	8	8	128

CANTONESE/HUAIYANG/SICHUAN

Restaurant	🍴	🍴	🍷	✉	Page
SUMMER PAVILION	8	9	9	9	104

CANTONESE/SHANGHAINESE

Restaurant	🍴	🍴	🍷	✉	Page
CHINA BISTRO	8	8	8	9	26
GUAN YUE TAI	9	9	8	9	42
JIN XUAN	8	9	9	9	56
SHENG HUI TANG	9	8	8	8	96
WAN HAO RESTAURANT	8	8	9	9	118

CANTONESE/TAIWANESE

Restaurant	🍴	🍴	🍷	✉	Page
JING CHI FANG RESTAURANT	9	9	9	9	58

VIETNAMESE

Restaurant	🍴	🍴	🍷	✉	Page
CLUB VIETNAM	8	8	8	8	29

YUNNAN

Restaurant	🍴	🍴	🍷	✉	Page
LOST HEAVEN ON THE BUND	9	8	9	8	67

BUFFET

Restaurant	🍴	🍴	🍷	✉	Page
BLD CAFE	8	8	8	9	20
CACHET RESTAURANT	8	9	9	9	22
CAFÉ SWISS	8	8	8	8	23
THE MARKET	8	8	7	8	113
X-SENSATION	8	8	8	9	123

HANGZHOU

GRILL
WANG STEAK — ♙ 8 🍴 8 🍷 8 ✉ 9 — 138

PRIVATE HOME-MADE FUSION FOOD
WEST LAKE INTERNATIONAL TEA FANS VILLAGE — ♙ 9 🍴 9 🍷 9 ✉ 9 — 139

HANGZHOU
28 HUBIN ROAD — ♙ 8 🍴 9 🍷 9 ✉ 8 — 130

HANGZHOU/CANTONESE
BAI YUN — ♙ 9 🍴 8 🍷 9 ✉ 9 — 131
GRAND DRAGON — ♙ 9 🍴 9 🍷 9 ✉ 9 — 133
QIAN FU HUI — ♙ 8 🍴 8 🍷 9 ✉ 8 — 136

SHANGHAINESE
JADE GARDEN — ♙ 8 🍴 8 🍷 8 ✉ 9 — 134

ITALIAN
VERANDA — ♙ 8 🍴 9 🍷 9 ✉ 9 — 137

CANTONESE/JIANGNAN/PRIVATE HOME-MADE
NUMBER EIGHT DOWNING STREET — ♙ 9 🍴 9 🍷 9 ✉ 9 — 135

BUFFET
D'CAFÉ — ♙ 8 🍴 9 🍷 9 ✉ 9 — 132

NANJING

HUAIYANG
KING LION PLAZA BRANCH — ♙ 9 🍴 9 🍷 8 ✉ 8 — 140
PLUM GARDEN — ♙ 9 🍴 9 🍷 8 ✉ 9 — 145
THE PURPLE PALACE — ♙ 9 🍴 9 🍷 8 ✉ 9 — 147

HUAIYANG/CANTONESE
MANDARIN GARDEN HOTEL — ♙ 9 🍴 8 🍷 8 ✉ 8 — 143
YI PALACE — ♙ 9 🍴 9 🍷 9 ✉ 8 — 148

LEBANESE
MEZZEH — ♙ 8 🍴 8 🍷 8 ✉ 8 — 144

ISLAMIC
MA XIANG XING — ♙ 7 🍴 8 🍷 7 ✉ 8 — 142

THAI
LOTUS RESTAURANT — ♙ 9 🍴 8 🍷 8 ✉ 9 — 141
THAI SPICES — ♙ 8 🍴 8 🍷 8 ✉ 8 — 146

CANTONESE
1912 YUE HONG HE1912 — ♙ 8 🍴 8 🍷 8 ✉ 8 — 149

NOTES

RESTAURANT	COMMENTS